The Origins of A...

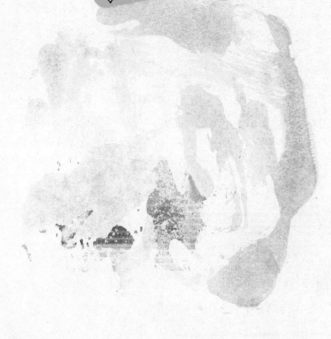

The Origins of America's Civil War

Bruce Collins

Holmes & Meier Publishers, Inc.

New York

©Bruce Collins 1981

First published in the United States of America 1981 by
Holmes & Meier Publishers, Inc.
30 Irving Place, New York, N.Y. 10003

Library of Congress Catalog Card Number: 81-81340

ISBN 0-8419-0714-5
0-8419-0715-3 (pbk)

Printed in Great Britain

Contents

Preface

This book's purpose is mainly pedagogical: to provide a concise, up-to-date, and reasonably wide-ranging *introduction* to a very large subject. The existing literature on the origins of the American Civil War is so voluminous that it would be quite possible to devote the length of this book to a review of the main controversies between scholars and still leave much unsaid. On the whole, however, I have avoided historiographical debates. One consequence of this approach is that I often simplify very complex arguments formulated by historians. I trust that I have committed no gross injustices in my attempt to produce a terse and reasonably straightforward discussion of the most important developments in America's sectional crisis. But the reader should be warned at the outset that virtually every paragraph in this little book concerns a topic that has been extensively written about and debated by other historians.

This book is a by-product of teaching. I therefore owe a considerable debt of gratitude to students at Middlesex Polytechnic in 1974–6 and at Glasgow University since 1977 for questioning my analyses and stimulating my interest in the subject. Colleagues in the British Association for American Studies and in the institutions just mentioned have also provided much stimulation; I should particularly like to thank Mr Donald Ratcliffe and Mr David Scarboro among the former and Mr Bernard Aspinwall and Mr Christopher Black among the latter. Mr Black kindly read an early draft and made valuable suggestions for further work; Mr Geoffrey Finlayson gave timely and important advice; and Miss Patricia Ferguson typed the manuscript with her customary expertise and speed. I owe a great deal to Professor Michael F. Holt for guiding my initial education as an historian of the 1850s and to Professor William Brock for constant support, advice, criticism, and encouragement. My wife – Dr Linda Nash – most generously read, criticized, and improved an earlier draft.

Bruce Collins
University of Glasgow
June 1980

1 Introduction

Perspectives

At first glance the American Civil War seems a straightforward affair. Compared with the other major civil wars that have affected Western man, America's conflict has a pleasing simplicity. Geographical lines fairly clearly divided the two sides; the slave states of the South fought the free states of the North with a handful of border states caught divided in between. The American Civil War did not apparently spawn the complex ideological disputes and bizarre, exotic radical groups that have arisen in some of Europe's revolutionary struggles. Nor did the American Civil War involve the various rises, falls, and subdivisions of aristocratic and middle classes which are the stuff of European domestic upheavals. Yet few Americans at the time believed that their differences were clear-cut or simply defined.

Americans initially disagreed over what to call the events that afflicted them for the four years following 15 April 1861. For many Northerners, they constituted simply the Great Rebellion or the War for the Union; officially they were part of the War of the Rebellion. For leading Northerners, the fighting meant different things. Horace Greeley, a prominent Northern newspaper editor, saw the war as the American Conflict; President Lincoln emphasized that it was 'a people's contest' with republican and democratic government at stake; one of his party colleagues, Senator Henry Wilson, later wrote his account of the years from the 1840s to the 1860s and entitled it *History of the Rise and Fall of the Slave Power in America*. To Southerners, different names seemed appropriate. When the Confederate president Jefferson Davis wrote his memoirs he placed his emphasis on the Confederacy itself, on the attempt to create a new government; when his vice-president, Alexander H. Stephens, did the same he called his book *A Constitutional View of the Late War between the States*; and a modern historian has aptly referred to the War for Southern Independence.[1]

These differences of nomenclature suggest deeper disagreements over the nature of the crisis that confronted Americans in the 1860s. Did Northerners fight Southerners simply to maintain the Union? Did

[1] A useful discussion of contemporaries' and historians' interpretations is Thomas J. Pressly, *Americans Interpret Their Civil War* (New York, 1962 edn); Eugene D. Genovese, *The Political Economy of Slavery* (New York, 1965), esp. pp. 5–10.

Southerners fight as a self-conscious, fully fledged nation for an independence based on constitutional right; or were they led disingenuously into revolution by the so-called Slave Power, the slaveowning élite? Was the war a clash between two peoples, or a sectional rebellion by the Southern states brought about either by class interests or by widely resented Northern infringements of Southerners' rights? At the time, then, the war was variously interpreted; not surprisingly, its origins have been much discussed and disputed ever since.

The Civil War was a great explosion in nineteenth-century America. It was one of the most bloody major wars fought by 'Western man' before the twentieth century; from a population of 31 million in 1861, at least 600,000 people died as a result of the war. It is often regarded as the first 'modern' war: vast conscript armies were used; railways provided previously unattainable military mobility; campaigns of prolonged attrition in Virginia foreshadowed the mauling process that was Europe's Western Front in 1914–18; and, when the Northern breakthrough into the heartland of the Confederacy occurred, the civilian population in parts of the South experienced the novel ugliness of 'total' war.

Nor did conflict end in 1865. Most confederate states were occupied by federal forces for much of the period until 1870–2 and three of them remained subject in part to Northern rule until 1877. The war also left deep psychological wounds. The sectional antagonism existing before 1861 degenerated further into a deep-grained, bitter hatred felt by Southerners towards Yankees and the North after 1865. Southerners, uniquely among Americans until the Vietnam war, bore the stigma of military defeat and moral obloquy.[2] Not until the 1960s did a genuine easing of sectional tensions begin to erase the memory of what white Southerners continued to call the War between the States. Historians have therefore rightly pondered the reasons why a war so long, intense, and bloody, whose psychological effects have been so persistently and keenly felt, came about.

Historians' perspectives on the origins of the war are shaped to an extent impossible to estimate by their assessment of its impact on American development. Many have seen the Civil War as a positive contribution to American progress. For some, it resulted in the triumph of industrialism and modernity over agrarianism and a semi-feudal order. This victory may not be desirable, but it is an inevitable part of Western social progression. For many, the war vindicated American morality and advanced American notions of civil rights; John Stuart Mill, pre-eminent English political economist of the mid nineteenth century, found something to respect in the nation of 'dollar-hunters' when Northerners resisted the Slave Power and destroyed slavery.[3] And for

---

[2] C. Vann Woodward, *The Burden of Southern History* (New York, n.d.), pp. 167–71.
[3] John Stuart Mill, *Principles of Political Economy. With Some of Their Applications to Social Philosophy. Book IV and V*, ed. with an intro. by Donald Winch (London, 1970), pp. 113–14.

many Northerners, it consolidated a great nation and quashed an attempt to fragment that nation. Yet to many contemporaries – including, notably, Abraham Lincoln – the war was an unfortunate, indeed tragic, result of fraternal misunderstanding.

One crucial Northern assumption was that the slave-owning South and the free states of the North were two sections of essentially one nation, not two disparate societies. Yet the extent to which the North and South were *different* clearly lay behind the sectional crisis in 1861 and has caused confusion among historians ever since. Contemporaries also were deeply perturbed at the precise extent and meaning of sectional distinctions. The man who did more than any other politician to promote Southern consciousness, John C. Calhoun, wrote privately in 1838:

> We cannot and ought not to live together as we are at present, exposed to the continual attacks and assaults of the other portion of the Union; but we must act throughout on the defensive, resort to every probable means of arresting the evil, and only act . . . when we shall stand justified before God and man in taking the final step . . . . it is the most difficult process in the world to make two people of one.[4]

Twenty years later, some of his political heirs indeed asserted that two separate countries existed. Lincoln, however, always held that the Union remained a national entity. In his 'house divided' speech of 1858, he declared 'this government cannot endure permanently half slave and half free'; but he added 'it will become all one thing, or all the other'. The vital and massive difference between North and South did not, according to Lincoln, vitiate all the affinities and affiliations that had kept Americans together for nearly three generations; nor would it do so, for America would either uniformly adopt slavery or uniformly abolish it. And when war began, Lincoln claimed that most Southerners remained loyal to the Union: 'It may well be questioned whether there is to-day a majority of the legally qualified voters of any State except perhaps South Carolina in favor of disunion'.[5] Lincoln and the Republican Party explained secession as a political product of the Southern social order, the handiwork of the Slave Power; the mass of ordinary Southerners were loyal to the Union and less wedded to the institution of slavery than was the Southern political élite. Republicans therefore did not regard the South as an alien land. Not all historians have agreed with them.

Some historians have been tempted to see so big an event as the American Civil War as part of the broad pattern of Western social development from medieval agrarianism and feudalism to modern industrialism. The South, it is claimed, possessing a system of forced

---

[4] 'Correspondence of John C. Calhoun', ed. by J. Franklin Jameson, *Annual Report of the American Historical Association for the Year 1899* (Washington, D.C., 1900), II, p. 391.

[5] A convenient source is Henry Steele Commager (ed.), *Documents of American History. Vol. I: to 1898* (New York, 1963 edn), pp. 345, 395.

labour, overwhelmingly agrarian pursuits, and a plantation-owning ruling class, was infused with sufficient elements of feudalism to be pre-modern in the mid nineteenth century. Ranged against the South was the North: not fully industrialized in the 1850s to be sure, but bourgeois, liberal, more entrepreneurial than the South, and straining to industrialize and to reduce the backward-looking Southern influence in Washington. At some time, a clash between these two societies had to occur; and the direct result of that confrontation, whether intended or not, was the further advance of industrialism in America.

This basic model of profound social antagonism between North and South has been refined in different ways. Charles Beard — a 'progressive' historian who exerted great influence from the 1910s to the 1940s — at one point argued that economic issues alone brought on the Civil War. Northern industrial interests sought to subordinate the agricultural South and its political leaders to their own need for tariffs, a national railway, and more encouragement for Northern farmers to settle in the West; these policies were implemented during the war. More recently, the idea that fundamental social and economic differences between North and South led to war has been put forward by Barrington Moore, a sociologist interested in the way in which the basic incompatibility between agrarianism and industrialism has produced revolutions in modern Western history. To other historians equally fascinated by the interplay between social incompatibilities — notably Eugene Genovese — the initiatives leading to war came from the South. The slavocracy, in this view, engineered Southern secession, and so provoked war, because it feared that its entire way of life, based on slavery and agriculture, was threatened by the industrial and commercial North.[6] So the conflict becomes a manifestation of that troubled passage from feudalism or agrarianism to modernism or industrialism which is crossed by all developing societies.

A good deal of evidence can be drawn from the 1850s to support this view of ante-bellum America as consisting of two distinct societies. Various Southern publicists liked to portray the South as peculiarly civilized and presided over by a cultured and gentlemanly class of planters. Much of this verbal boasting was intended either to boost Southerners' self-respect or to counter Northerners' criticisms of Southern society.[7] There is, however, very little hard evidence to support the notion that literature, art, architecture, or learning in general were more commonly or more energetically patronized in the South than in the North. Nor is it clear that the wealthier planters differed from

[6] Pressly, *Americans Interpret Their Civil War*, pp. 238–48; Barrington Moore, Jr, *Social Origins of Dictatorship and Democracy. Lord and Peasant in the Making of the Modern World* (Boston, 1966), pp. 111–55; Genovese, *Political Economy of Slavery*, pp. 13–36, 243–70.
[7] William R. Taylor, *Cavalier and Yankee. The Old South and American National Character* (New York, 1969 edn).

correspondingly wealthy Northern businessmen in seeking to acquire a certain measure of gentility, by building elegant country houses, purchasing objets d'art, and engaging in a leisurely social round. Too much has sometimes been made, both in the 1850s and since, of supposed sectional differences in social rituals amongst the wealthy, which in fact were superficial or non-existent.

The same contrast was sometimes drawn in political rhetoric. A Republican congressman characteristically affirmed in January 1859:

> Two antagonistic ideas underlie the political movements of the country and will be represented by its political organisations . . . the democratic and the aristocratic. The democratic affirms the equal rights of all men; while the aristocratic denies the existence of such rights, and divides mankind into classes – a governing and privileged class, and a governed and disabled class.[8]

Yet statements of this kind – and the critical ideas expressed here recur frequently in our story – were as much party propaganda as descriptions of reality. The Republican Party deliberately cast itself as the special defender of basic Northern beliefs against the planter élite in the South. Such rhetorical language was commonly used in America to advance a political cause. In the middle and late eighteenth century the British had been popularly cast as an aristocratic threat to American society. In the 1790s and 1800s the Federalist party was denounced by its opponents as representing aristocratic interests or even trying to establish a monarchy in America. In the 1830s the Democratic Party assumed the pose of 'people's party' by impugning the social and political motives of the Bank of the United States and its bosses: a 'nobility system' was about to be created in the land of the free. And the Democrats' political opponents adopted the name 'Whig' as one suitable for the foes of the Democratic leader 'King Andrew' Jackson.

The contrasting emphasis placed by the congressman quoted above on 'the equal rights of all men' and a 'privileged class' does, however, point the way to another refinement of the social model for the origins of the Civil War. Perhaps the North and South were not completely divergent societies; perhaps the Civil War was not a revolutionary struggle on the lines of other great revolutions of modern Western history, such as the English Civil War, the French Revolution, and the Russian Revolution; nevertheless, it might fit into the unfolding process of human improvement once believed to be manifested by the recent history of the Western world. The Northern struggle to smash the separate slave-owning republic thrown together in 1861 certainly contributed to progress, since it stemmed from, and furthered, respect for natural rights; apart from condemning the immorality of slave ownership,

[8] *Congressional Globe*, 35th Congress, 2nd Session (Washington, D.C., 1859), p. 299 (Israel Washburn, Jr of Maine).

Republicans argued that Southern poor whites were themselves oppressed by the planter class, and that slavery should therefore be set on the path to 'ultimate extinction'. Even though the vast bulk of Northerners were not abolitionists, they were by 1860 committed to a liberal, bourgeois ideology of enterprise, individualism, and evangelical morality which, according to Eric Foner, clashed fundamentally with Southerners' cherished assumptions about race and rigid hierarchy of class.[9]

That clash reflected two dramatic developments in Western thought. First, the steady growth in the late eighteenth and early nineteenth centuries of ideas of political representation and individual political rights – ideas securely translated into most American practice by the 1830s – was still not completed in the South, where, according to Republicans and many historians since the 1860s, a 'privileged class' continued to hold sway. Secondly, the Western European and Northern American attack on slavery made no headway in the South. Before 1760 slavery as an institution was hardly challenged in either America or Europe, but subsequent events left the South alone in condoning it. Thus, by the late eighteenth and early nineteenth centuries, slavery had been abolished in the Northern states, and both Britain and America had banned the slave trade; by the 1830s Britain had abolished slavery throughout its Empire and Northerners had turned in small but significant numbers to criticizing Southern slavery; finally, by 1860 Northerners were exasperated, if not nauseated, by the Southern Slave Power's refusal to recognize any hint of merit in the case against slavery, and by its insistence that slavery should be encouraged to expand into the western territories.

In two ways, therefore, the distinctive social order in the South had departed from the course of nineteenth-century progress: in terms of class politics and in relation to slavery. The Civil War, by destroying the Confederacy, both contributed to social improvement and drew the South back into the American mainstream, from which it had gradually been diverging. One important mechanism by which it was pulled back on course was the overturning of secession as a constitutional doctrine and a constitutional possibility.

Two genuinely disparate nations may not have existed in the 1850s, but would certainly have developed rapidly if secession had been permitted; indeed, the separation of other combinations of states was a real possibility. So the Civil War saved the nation itself, and this, in the eyes of Northerners in the 1860s and long after, was a signal contribution to world progress. Lincoln argued thus during the war, and many Northern historians have subsequently followed his line of reasoning.

---

[9] Eric Foner, *Free Soil, Free Labor, Free Men. The Ideology of the Republican party before the Civil War* (New York, 1970); Richard H. Sewell, *Ballots for Freedom: Antislavery Politics in the United States 1837–1860* (New York, 1976).

If historians see an event as contributing to social or political progress, they may naturally detect in its causes clear traces of its consequences. If the Civil War accelerated industrialization, then perhaps industrial interests played some key rôle in bringing war about. If the war represented an advance in American regard for natural rights, then perhaps we should look to abolitionist and civil libertarian thought for the crucial developments of the 1850s. If the war marked a triumph of nationalism, then perhaps expanding, dynamic ideas of nationality provide vital clues to the war's origins. The considerable literature on the origins of the Civil War demonstrates that it is easy in historical analysis to find evidence for what is believed – perhaps explicitly, perhaps intuitively – to be the truly significant factor at work.

What, however, can be lost sight of in these grand social or economic analyses of North–South differences is the very precise nature of the political crisis that ended in war. Of course, Northerners and Southerners competed for economic advantages in the 1850s and abused each other's social values. But what finally split the Confederacy and the Union was federal policy concerning slavery extension and the *long-term* implications of that policy. In order to understand the arguments over federal policy and slavery extension, one needs to discard inflated social stereotypes and grasp some essential characteristics of American politics.

North and South were both middle-class democracies, in the sense in which Richard Hofstadter has used the term 'middle-class' in describing the rural, as opposed to urban, society of America in the mid eighteenth century.[10] The South had a planter class, but this did not act as a political entity in the crisis of 1860–1; party politics and political activity reflected the attitudes and aspirations of the vast mass of ordinary Southern whites. What set Northerners and Southerners against each other in the 1850s was in fact a struggle to assert their respective constitutional rights, which came to include for Southerners the right to take slaves into western federal territories, and for Northerners the right to prohibit slavery in these same territories. Sectional animosity mounted because party leaders expressed deeply felt and rationally based fears for the future character of the federal territories – would they be slave or free? – which raised acute questions concerning the basic constitutional rights of both Northerners and Southerners.[11]

Disputed rights touched America's rawest nerves; for Americans expected equality of esteem and equality of opportunity.[12] Proper esteem was demanded by individuals for themselves, their communities, their states, and (increasingly from the 1830s) their sections. In federal

[10] Richard Hofstadter, *America at 1750: a Social Portrait* (London, 1972), pp. 131–42.
[11] William J. Cooper, Jr, *The South and the Politics of Slavery, 1828–1856* (Baton Rouge, 1978); J. Mills Thornton, III, *Politics and Power in a Slave Society. Alabama, 1800–1860* (Baton Rouge, 1978); see also Michael F. Holt, *The Political Crisis of the 1850s* (New York, 1978).
[12] Americans' ideas of equality may be further explored in: J.R. Pole, *The Pursuit of Equality in American History* (Berkeley, 1978).

politics, questions about slavery, its existence and especially its extension, swiftly raised sensitive issues about equality of esteem within the Union for citizens of both sections, but particularly those of the South. Southerners resented being cast as the pariahs of America, backward economically and shackled to a barbaric set of 'domestic arrangements'. As one English traveller noted in 1858: 'all slave owners are on the defensive and begin to defend themselves as if they stood at the bar, and so they do, the bar of intelligent opinion'.[13] Having to defend themselves was bad enough; to be found wanting was infuriating. Moreover, Americans of both sections began to believe that their equality of opportunity was threatened. Equality of opportunity for an over-whelmingly agrarian people largely meant guaranteed access to land. Northerners feared that the opportunities for ordinary farmers to migrate westwards and cultivate land there would be impaired if Southerners flocked into the western territories with their slave labour force. Southerners, on the other hand, insisted that they had a con-stitutional right to enter the same territories with all their property (including, of course, their slaves). So, while slavery was certainly at the root of the sectional debate, it provoked sectional outrage because of its implications for white Americans: equality of esteem for Southern whites in the Union and equality of opportunity for all in the western territories. Concern for constitutional rights thus stemmed from assumptions shared by Northerners and Southerners alike about what was due to ordinary citizens in an agrarian democracy.

So we return full circle to the dilemma earlier mentioned. Was the struggle a contest between two very different societies or a conflict over constitutional rights fought within one nation? How much was at stake in 1861: the position of the upper class in the South − the Slave Power − or the aspirations of a middle-class rural democracy? Did the political crisis of the 1850s arise from disputes over economic interests, concepts of natural rights, and the ultimate emergence of a great nation, or the acceptable distribution of power and constitutional respect between divergent sections? Was the Civil War a terrible accident that occurred through the bunglings of politicians in 1860−1, and which could and should have been prevented? Or did it emerge logically from differences and disputes long dragging North and South inexorably apart?

Such questions can be explored only through a study of politics; for what Southerners attempted when they tried to secede from the Union was a constitutional revolution. But politics cannot be understood in a social or intellectual vacuum. Any examination of American political problems in the 1840s and 1850s must be prefaced, therefore, by a brief consideration of some of the forces shaping American society at that time, by a brief description of the political system and by an analysis of what is meant by the terms 'North' and 'South'.

[13] Barbara Leigh Smith Bodichon, *An American Diary 1857−8*, ed. by Joseph W. Reed, Jr (London, 1972), p. 79.

Economic Growth, Religion, and Nationalism

The three great influences on mid-nineteenth-century American life were economic growth, religion, and nationalism. What effect did these have on the growth of sectional consciousness?

The American economy in the 1840s and 1850s grew at a rate unsurpassed in the country's history; rapid economic growth between 1843 and 1857 was perhaps the single most important fact of American life. In many respects, the economic activities of North and South complemented each other. But, at the extreme edges, North-eastern railway building and factory development set off that region quite markedly from the rural order of the Deep South; this striking contrast between industrial areas of New England on the one hand and the old-established slave states and the cotton states of the south-west on the other was repeatedly and graphically depicted and inflated in a flourishing pamphlet and newspaper literature on North–South differences. Fast economic growth fostered North-eastern pride in its achievement which readily turned to mockery of the South's economic backwardness. Such mockery was of course answered by rebuttals, and a running debate ensued. Northern disparagement of the South's economy and society was not entirely fanciful. Failing to attract foreign immigrants, the South lagged far behind the free states in population growth. Failing to build up major financial centres or heavy industry, the South fell behind the free states in railway building in the 1850s. Failing to diversify sufficiently at the local level, the South never rivalled the free states in urbanization and in nurturing a professional middle class. Yet, for white people at least, wealth and opportunity were widely spread and per capita income in the South was virtually the highest in the world *outside* the North. Southerners were, therefore, far from dissatisfied with their economic lot. Some Southern polemicists indeed urged their fellow-citizens to greater commercial efforts. Others, however, extolled the virtues of their distinctive agrarian society: it was pointed out that the South had escaped the horrors of the factory system, while plantation slaves were said to be far better treated than factory workers.[14] In more general terms, the country's rapid economic growth stimulated sectional consciousness in two main ways.

First, there was an upsurge of community competition. Consciousness of a community's identity of interests – especially economic ones – increased greatly with burgeoning trade and the commercial

[14] The rate of increase in net national product for 20-year intervals may be calculated from the indices in Lance E. Davis, et al., *American Economic Growth. An Economist's History of the United States* (New York, 1972), p. 34; Douglass C. North, *The Economic Growth of the United States, 1790–1860* (New York, 1966), pp. 101–14, 122–33, 204–15; Robert W. Fogel and Stanley L. Engerman *Time on the Cross* (London, 1974), I, pp. 247–57; Avery O. Craven, *The Coming of the Civil War* (Chicago, 1957 edn), pp. 272–82; Eugene D. Genovese, *The World the Slaveholders Made. Two Essays in Interpretation* (London, 1970), pp. 165–234.

development of small and medium-sized towns. Towns, states, regions, and sections – political, social, and geographical units drawing citizens' loyalties – struggled for economic advantage. One local newspaper described Iowa's railway mania in 1853:

> Every town, cross roads, and blacksmith shop in the state has held public meetings and passed resolutions demonstrating to all the world . . . the peculiar advantages of said village, cross roads, or blacksmith shop for a railroad route . . . . So furious has the zeal of each locality become in favor of itself, and so venomous against every other point coming in competition, that even political ties are sundered and the 'cohesive power of public plunder' proves too weak for the repulsion of railroad mania.[15]

When schemes for *federal* aid to railway building – or for banking – were devised, similar competition between sections exploded. Just as economists of the 1960s wrote of developing nations' 'crusade' for economic take-off into self-sustained growth, so, from the first two decades of the nineteenth century, American communities and later regions and sections strove increasingly and ever more self-consciously for economic advance. That competition for economic growth accelerated with time: any graph of business incorporation rises steadily during the early part of the century and swings sharply upwards in the late 1840s and 1850s. While it cannot be said that specific economic grievances caused the Civil War, the spirit of economic development and competition certainly heightened community awareness at all levels as the century progressed, and meant that sectional consciousness had a more urgent and practical meaning by the 1850s than it had offered in the 1820s.

Second, the pursuit and attainment of fast economic growth confirmed and strengthened older habits of American enterprise. Americans had long been sturdy exponents of self-help. But in the mid nineteenth century commercial opportunities increased job mobility and social fluidity: fewer Northerners remained farmers, and Northerners tended more than ever before to move from place to place and job to job. As this process set in, so the notion of 'self-help' flourished and spread. Before 1850 self-help had been lauded, but mainly in pamphlets; after 1850 self-help literature became lengthier and more sustaining.[16] When Northerners adopted the self-help philosophy, they also more readily criticized Southern society – or the popular image of Southern society – as class-ridden, caste-bound, lethargic, immobile, and destructive of opportunity for poorer whites. So, too, a people dedicated to

[15] Quoted in Morton M. Rosenberg, *Iowa on the Eve of the Civil War. A Decade of Frontier Politics* (Norman, Ok., 1972), p. 78. The idea of community consciousness is well explored in Stuart M. Blumin, *The Urban Threshold: Growth and Change in a Nineteenth-Century American Community* (Chicago, 1976).

[16] Irvin G. Wyllie, *The Self-Made Man in America: the Myth of Rags to Riches* (New Brunswick, N.J., 1954), pp. 10–20, 126–30.

improvement through self-help and the work ethic became disposed to frown upon forced labour. Work, it was felt, should flow willingly from an inner desire to toil and should legitimately result in fair reward for the labourer. The more fully the 'capitalist' work ethic was expressed and manifested, the more frequently would slavery be regarded as an aberration from acceptable practice. As Abraham Lincoln said, 'There is no such thing as a man being bound down in a free country through his life as a labourer'. The spirit of nineteenth-century laissez-faire directly contradicted slavery; and the doctrines of laissez-faire gained wider currency and apparent relevance with the attainment of high levels of economic growth in the 1840s and 1850s.[17]

Religious sentiment similarly strengthened sectional consciousness in the mid nineteenth century. It is easy to forget in that land of conspicuous piety that the United States when founded was deistic and even agnostic, rather than devoutly Christian. Christian religion, however, revived and burgeoned in the first two decades of the nineteenth century, and by the 1850s America was arguably the most vigorously Christian country in the world. It had 20 denominations each possessing over 100 churches, and many other lesser denominations. In 1860 its 54,000 churches could seat 19,129,000 people, at a time when a large proportion of the total population of 31 million consisted of young children, and of course 4 million slaves, often informally churched.[18] The influence exerted by this large number of churches is difficult to define precisely, but certain themes seem clear.

Slavery split the leading churches themselves into Northern and Southern wings during the 1840s. Religious conviction and enthusiasm forced men, North and South, to justify their attitudes towards slavery in religious terms. Defenders of slavery invoked Biblical justification for enslavement; and just as a sense of religious mission led some Northern evangelicals to assert their responsibility to the oppressed slave, so religious concern led many Southerners to formulate a sincere if also self-serving notion of moral stewardship as the dominant element in master-slave relations. Evangelical ardour thus worked to heighten sectional attitudes towards slavery.[19]

That ardour was more noticeable and more effective in the 1840s and

[17] Howard Temperley, 'Capitalism, Slavery and Ideology', *Past and Present*, LXXV (1977), pp. 94–118; Foner, *Free Soil, Free Labor, Free Men*, ch. 1; Roy P. Basler (ed.), *The Collected Works of Abraham Lincoln: Supplement, 1832–1865* (Westport, Conn., 1974), p. 44; Daniel W. Howe, *The Political Culture of the American Whigs* (Chicago, 1979), pp. 265–9, 280–1, 291.
[18] Henry F. May, *The Enlightenment in America* (New York, 1976), pp. 223–7, 230–6, 263–73, 278–302, 315–24; *Statistics of the United States (Including Mortality, Property, etc.) in 1860; Compiled from the Original Returns and Being the Final Exhibit of the Eighth Census* (Washington, D.C., 1866), pp. 497–501.
[19] Louis Filler, *The Crusade Against Slavery, 1830–1860* (New York, 1960), pp. 123–6; William S. Jenkins, *Pro-Slavery Thought in the Old South* (Gloucester, Mass., 1960 reprint of 1935 edn), ch. V; Drew G. Faust, *A Sacred Circle. The Dilemma of the Intellectual in the Old South, 1840–1860* (Baltimore, 1977).

1850s because the churches enjoyed a new sense of power and purpose after their successful battle in the first two or three decades of the century against the legacy of late-eighteenth-century scepticism. By the 1830s the Protestant denominations overcame that legacy, and by the 1850s they had won their internal battle to secure a better educated, more highly organized clergy. Probably more militant and more effectively managed by the 1840s, the churches could also appeal to a larger body of literate followers than ever before. Wider literacy played a vital part in the growth of sectionalism, for like all American political upheavals, the political debates of the 1850s were accompanied by a sustained and thunderous war of words. Finally, Northern evangelical Protestant clergymen campaigning against slavery in the early 1850s found further cause for alarm in the political alliance between Southern slaveholders and the Northern Democratic party, which tolerated the Roman Catholic Church. As one congressman from New York declared in July 1856:

> where the conscience is enslaved by the priest, the civil rights of the subject are abridged by the despot; and on the other hand, where the conscience is free in matters of religion, political freedom prevails. In other words, Protestantism results in civil enfranchisement; Jesuitism, on the contrary, affiliates with and tends to political despotism. As in the empires of the Old World, Jesuitism allies itself with kingcraft, so in the New, it strikes hands with slavery.[20]

Catholics in the North — poor, uneducated, Irish, and politically docile — gave essential support to the Democratic party, thereby helping to maintain the party's hold on national power.

Americans did not divide denominationally on sectional lines: in both North and South, Methodists, Baptists, and Presbyterians were the leading denominations with only minor sectional differences. But the denominations split internally into sectional organizations in the 1840s, and Protestant evangelicalism, working through the denominations, intensified sectional consciousness and awareness of the slavery question in the 1850s. Just as a common and voracious appetite for economic growth encouraged sectionalism, so shared religious values impassioned sectional debate.

Against these centrifugal forces it might be thought that nineteenth-century nationalism would have tugged the sections closer together. In fact, nationalism, like many political ideas, was sometimes stronger in its negative than its positive aspects. Americans first defined themselves in the 1770s and 1780s as being 'more British than the British': more libert-arian, more parliamentary in their governing habits, more insistent on their constitutional rights. Britain's political system during the

[20] *Appendix to the Congressional Globe*, 34th Congress, 1st Session (Washington, D.C., 1856), p. 957.

Revolutionary period was increasingly regarded as corrupt, decadent, and despotic; it was drifting inexorably away from its original representative, libertarian path.[21] American nationalism was thus initially defined in strictly political terms: there was none of the swelling undercurrent of cultural pride that flowed so effectively into various European nationalisms in the nineteenth century. Americans received a boost of political nationalism from the war of 1812 with Britain, and thence onwards national sentiment rose, perhaps reaching an apogee of sorts in the 1830s, when leading literary men such as Ralph Waldo Emerson and George Bancroft proclaimed the need for Americans to free themselves culturally as well as politically from the 'courtly muses of Europe'.[22] Even at this time anti-British feeling formed a major ingredient in American national pride. The politician most readily identified with the rash of American nationalism in the 1820s and 1830s, President Andrew Jackson (1829–37), had won his national spurs as the victor of the battle of New Orleans (1814) against the British. From the early 1840s, however, nationalism ceased to be as strongly unifying a sentiment as it had been earlier.

One reason for this was that Americans, as they grew closer together, found slavery an increasingly irreconcilable difference between themselves. In terms of communications, America in the 1840s, and still more so in the 1850s, was a far more tightly knit country than it had been a generation earlier. In the 1780s it had been possible to accept differences over slavery for the common good of white men's republicanism; and the population was so widely dispersed that slavery did not impinge too obtrusively on Northerners' consciousness. By the 1840s, however, the situation had changed considerably. The Northern states had themselves abolished slavery; communications bound the country more closely together; one country could be said to exist. And in intellectual and political circles a more strident insistence on 'the nation' was perhaps heard during the 1840s than had prevailed in the past. The more Americans lived and thought nationally, the more conscious some became of the sectional difference over slavery. Patriotic boastfulness about America's achievements against British despotism in the 1770s and grandiloquent enthusiasm for 'the Union' remained to keep Americans together in the 1850s. But nationalism alone had a divisive as well as a unifying effect.

This apparent anomaly emerged particularly clearly in the debate over territorial expansion. During the two decades before 1860, but most eagerly during the 1840s, the Democrats had tried to sustain their

[21] Discussion of nationalism centres on David M. Potter's essay 'The Historian's Use of Nationalism and Vice Versa' reprinted in his *The South and the Sectional Conflict* (Baton Rouge, 1968), pp. 34–83; for Revolutionary ideology, see Bernard Bailyn, *The Ideological Origins of the American Revolution* (Cambridge, Mass., 1967).

[22] Marcus Cunliffe, *The Literature of the United States* (London, 1961 edn), p. 44; Arthur M. Schlesinger, Jr, *The Age of Jackson* (London, 1946), pp. 318–21, 374–86.

national party and its national appeal by pursuing an actively expansion-ist foreign policy. Antipathy to Britain and to alleged British designs was one aspect of this policy, and territorial expansion into Central America and the Caribbean region was its over-riding objective. Yet the expansionist drive of the 1840s, accompanied by a riot of nationalistic ballyhoo (the term 'Manifest Destiny' and the emphasis on 'Young America' both date from the mid 1840s) fanned sectional rivalries and sectional rhetoric as much as it fostered national spirit. Because the national government acquired vast new territories into which Southerners wished to send slaves and from which a considerable body of Northerners insisted that slaves be excluded, national expansion simply produced a violent controversy over national policy in the new territories.

There is, therefore, a sense of inevitability about the coming of the American Civil War. Although Americans were united by their quest for economic growth, in their religious pursuits and in their national pride, they seemed at every turn to be divided increasingly into North and South by those same forces as the 1840s and 1850s progressed. And during these two decades the very expressions 'North' and 'South' became a staple ingredient of political discourse and took on a new force and meaning. Yet this inevitability was not apparent to most Americans during the 1850s, and as late as 1860 an armed conflict between North and South did not strike the vast majority of Americans as unavoidable. This was because the American political system permitted sectional debate without destroying all hope for the continued survival of the federal Union.

2 The Political System

The Functions of Government

Although North–South differences grew in the 1840s and 1850s and increasingly affected all aspects of American life, the federal system of government helped to contain as well as encourage North–South rivalries. First, the system lodged much authority and responsibility with the individual states, while burdening the federal government with few duties; during the 1850s all governments were limited, but the federal government was more limited than others. Clashes of interest between North and South in the federal Congress were not necessarily felt in ordinary citizens' lives. Secondly, sectional jealousy did not, as is sometimes misleadingly claimed, throttle all federal government initiative and thereby further intensify Northern resentments of the South, or Southern resentments of the North, for reducing the federal Congress to paralysis. Occasions arose when the federal government proved incapable of legislative action. But these often resulted from the sheer multiplicity of different regional interests involved in a promotional scheme and not simply from North–South antagonism.

A classic example of a congressional impasse in the 1850s was the repeated failure of federal politicians to agree upon aid for constructing a railway from the Mississippi valley to the Pacific coast. This failure was hardly surprising: the project was enormous and costly; Atlantic seaboard states were not much interested in subsidising a railway that would greatly promote trade and settlement in the Mississippi valley and be of but mild benefit to themselves; different states and regions in the Mississippi valley bickered over the selection of a precise route; and many politicians doubted the wisdom of pumping public funds into the bottomless coffers of a giant, private corporation. North–South rivalry was therefore but one of many reasons why the federal Congress failed to agree on a Pacific railway in the 1850s. And, more generally, congressional debate on promotional plans brought out a whole range of local, state, and regional, as well as simply sectional, struggles for power and advantage. Active or inactive, the federal Congress fostered particularism as well as sectionalism in the 1850s.

It is worth remembering that the federal government in the nineteenth century was relatively unimportant. Most historical work now read concerning the origins of the Civil War has been written since the early

1930s – written, that is, in a period when the functions and responsi-bilities of the federal government in general and the presidency in particular have expanded enormously. Yet, while Americans today expect the president and Congress to bear the greatest burdens of governing, their forebears in the mid nineteenth century did not share that assumption.

The federal government of the 1850s was an unimpressive, indeed a somewhat ramshackle, affair. Its duties were few. Foreign policy was important, and most presidents devoted a great deal of their annual messages to Congress to their own conduct of foreign affairs; a number of presidents, notably Franklin Pierce (1853–7) and James Buchanan (1857–61) sought fame by notching up somewhat nebulous achievements in this field. British restlessness and robustness in the world at large, and in the Caribbean in particular, perennially attracted American suspicion and distrust. Yet foreign affairs did not dominate American domestic politics and did not draw the United States actively or conspicuously on to the world's stage. America in the mid nineteenth century was not a Great Power and never passed as one, this lack of diplomatic ambition being reflected for instance in the smallness of America's armed forces. The United States Army varied in strength from 10,572 men in 1853 to a high point of 17,678 in 1858. The expansion in numbers occurred mainly between 1854 and 1855 when western territorial commitments (containment of Indians and supervision of settlers) became more pressing, and in 1858, when extra forces were required to control the Mormons in Utah. Nevertheless, in relation to a population numbering 23.3 million in 1850 and 31.5 million in 1860, such an army was minuscule.[1]

Aspects of economic policy perhaps exercised the federal government more than foreign policy. For much of the nineteenth century, congress-ional discussion of economic policy amounted to little more than a quest for panaceas that would either open up boundless prospects for material advance or, equally magically, dispel the effects of economic slumps. But more practical questions were also raised by the pursuit of prosperity. The most important of these was how far the federal government should provide tariff protection to encourage American industrial growth. In 1828 a high protective wall had been erected, but in 1833 this was partially dismantled. Again, in 1842 tariffs were built up only to be knocked down after 1846. The modestly protectionist Walker Tariff of 1846 was further lowered in 1857; otherwise no further changes were made until the Civil War, although federal tariff policy was periodically discussed, especially after the panic of 1857. Similarly, in the field of banking policy, federal activity in the 1830s and 1840s was followed by quiescence in the 1850s. This inaction resulted from the Democrats'

[1] US Bureau of the Census, *Historical Statistics of the United States. Colonial Times to 1957* (Washington, D.C., 1960), pp. 737, 7.

political ascendancy, for the Democratic party opposed protective tariffs and sought to restrict the federal government's interference in banking and currency matters. Thus, in the 1830s the Democrats refused to recharter a national bank, the Bank of the United States, and in the 1840s they established the Independent Treasury to handle the federal government's fiscal dealings outside the banking system. Once the Independent Treasury was firmly created – for the second time – in 1846, the federal government, under Democratic influence, largely withdrew from banking affairs. Banking and currency were left to the individual state governments, with the result that America in 1860 had almost as many banking systems as it had states; and there were 33 states by that year. Assigning banking and currency policy firmly and clearly to the several states merely confirmed and reinforced their power and autonomy.

Until the Civil War American citizens regularly encountered the federal government only in the shape of their post offices. In 1861 the federal authorities, responsible before secession for 31.5 million people, employed only 36,672 civil servants, of whom a mere 2,200 worked in Washington and the vast majority (30,269) were employed by the Post Office. No federal agencies or departments existed to lay down rules or even guidelines concerning a host of social relationships and problems such as child labour, hours of work, or local provision of education; nor was federal action or initiative urged in these spheres before the Civil War. In 1860 the federal government spent a grand total of $63,131,000, of which nearly half went to the army ($16,410,000), the navy ($11,515,000), and interest on the national debt ($3,177,000). To meet such expenditures, the federal treasury department raised $56,065,000, nearly all of it in customs receipts, and secured the remainder through short-term borrowing.[2]

In contrast, all the state and local authorities in America together raised a grand total of $94.2 millions in taxes.[3] Their spending bore directly on social welfare, especially education, but also on public health and poor relief. Virtually all matters relating to business – transport, government financial aid for economic development, the incorporation and regulation of companies – came under the aegis of state government. If – as some historians have contended – there was an unprecedented spate of reform in the 30 years before the Civil War, that reformist activity and the reform agitation preceding it centred on the state governments.[4]

State government was bustling, contentious, and creative in a number of ways. First, states indulged in prolific constitution-making in the 1840s and 1850s. Constitutions were drawn up for each new state entering the

[2] *Ibid.*, pp. 710–12, 718.
[3] *Statistics of the United States, (Including Mortality, Property, etc.) in 1860; Compiled from the Original Returns and Being the Final Exhibit of the Eighth Census* (Washington, D.C., 1866), p. 511.
[4] See, for example, the collection of documents: Walter Hugins (ed.) *The Reform Impulse, 1825–1850* (New York, 1972).

Union: Florida and Texas in 1845, Iowa in 1846, Wisconsin in 1848, California in 1850, Minnesota in 1858, and Oregon in 1859. But, equally important, many states in the 1840s and early 1850s revised and redrafted their constitutions in a spasm of constitutional reform unmatched since the 1780s.[5] These changes were especially notable for extending the number of state offices open to election, thus enhancing voters' power and confirming ideas of individual citizens' rights to representation. Secondly, state legislatures acted vigorously in the early and middle 1840s to reform, and usually restrict, their banking systems, and then, at the end of the 1840s and in the early 1850s, to expand them once more in tune with the strong economic revival of those years. During the 1850s state legislatures worked hard at chartering, consolidating, and sometimes even regulating railway companies. State and especially local governments provided strong financial underpinning for some railways: for instance, they supplied 55 per cent of the $245 millions invested in Southern railways by 1860. The same decade witnessed an unprecedented surge of business incorporation by state legislatures throughout the country.[6] Thirdly, state legislatures, irrespective of section, came under intense pressure (to which they often succumbed) to curtail or ban the manufacture and sale of alcoholic liquor. The temperance issue was particularly prominent in the early and middle 1850s after Maine led the way in 1846 and 1851 with a prohibition law; 13 states passed various prohibition laws from 1852 to 1855. Also of national import was the drive to extend public schooling through state government initiative; state expansion of education was a marked phenomenon of the 1840s and 1850s.[7]

Finally, the governments of the free states in the 1850s found themselves under great pressure to legislate against the rendition of runaway slaves to their Southern owners. The demand arose from the provisions of the federal Fugitive Slave Act of 1850 which severely infringed the civil rights of blacks claimed as runaway slaves, and it became especially forthright in 1854–5, following the repeal of the Missouri Compromise, and after the Dred Scott decision of 1857.[8]

[5] William G. Shade, *Banks or No Banks. The Money Issue in Western Politics, 1832–1865* (Detroit, 1972), pp. 112–13; Michael F. Holt, *The Political Crisis of the 1850s* (New York, 1978), pp. 106–10.

[6] Shade, *Banks or No Banks*, chs. 5–7; Holt, *Political Crisis of the 1850s*, pp. 110–19; Carter Goodrich, *Government Promotion of American Canals and Railroads 1800–1890* (New York, 1960), p. 268; Douglass C. North, *Growth and Welfare in the American Past* (Englewood Cliffs, 1966), pp. 98–9; Thomas C. Cochran and William Miller, *The Age of Enterprise. A Social History of Industrial America* (New York, 1942), p. 70.

[7] Alice F. Tyler, *Freedom's Ferment* (New York, 1962 edn), pp. 347–8; Albert Fishlow, 'The American Common School Revival: Fact or Fancy?' in H. Rosovsky (ed.), *Industrialization in Two Systems: essays in honor of Alexander Gerschenkron* (New York, 1966), pp. 40–67.

[8] Norman L. Rosenberg, 'Personal Liberty Laws and Sectional Crisis, 1850–1861', *Civil War History*, XVII (1971), pp. 25–44.

So, state governments throughout the country were highly energetic during the 1840s and 1850s, and their activities had considerably more potential relevance to ordinary citizens' everyday affairs than those of the federal government. Even so, government of any kind was hardly significant in most individual Americans' lives. Aggregate spending by all levels of government totalled only $150 million in 1860, from a gross national product estimated at $4,170 million for 1859.[9] The social and economic impact of government was minor compared with its impact in late-twentieth-century America. Why then did Americans argue so furiously over federal power?

Territorial Government

The federal government held ultimate responsibility for the territories, that is, parts of the United States not yet raised to statehood. In the 1840s and 1850s, far from being quiescent, Congress was highly active in erecting semi-autonomous territorial governments, thereby provoking fierce and protracted inter-sectional and intra-sectional debate.

Governing the territories had long been a leading and onerous federal chore.[10] When the American colonies rebelled against British imperial rule in 1776 they sought rapidly to establish a large confederate government. General acceptance of that form of government was delayed, however, by disputes over who ruled areas outside the boundaries of the various rebellious colonies: the confederation or individual states? In 1784 the issue was settled when the confederation government founded the North-West Territory as a national domain. Domestic administration for that region was then arranged by the North-West Ordinance of July 1787.

The Ordinance did two far-reaching things. It banned slavery from the North-West Territory — why Southern politicians permitted this prohibition is unclear — and it provided a system of territorial government subsequently copied in absorbing all new lands into the USA. The national government directly ruled all areas within the confederation's (and, after 1789, the USA's) boundaries that did not form part of any *state*. As the national government saw fit, it opened such lands to white settlement. These organized territories became constitutional dyarchies with a mix of federal supervision and local representation. While the inhabitants of organized territories elected territorial legislatures to deal with domestic questions, acts passed by these legislatures were subject to the approval or veto of territorial governors and of the federal Congress; governors, together with other important territorial officials, were

[9] Robert E. Gallman, 'Gross National Product in the United States, 1834–1909', in *Output, Employment, and Productivity in the United States after 1800 (Studies in Income and Wealth*, xxx) (New York, 1966), p. 26.
[10] The following section draws heavily upon Don E. Fehrenbacher, *The Dred Scott Case. Its Significance in American Law and Politics* (New York, 1978), pp. 74–138.

appointed by the US president. Thus local representation and federal supervision jostled uneasily in the government of organized territories.

Once an organized territory gained a reasonably large (but not defined) population, it could apply to Congress for admission to statehood and then submit a draft state constitution for Congress's approval. With the consent of Congress and president, the territory became a state, so shedding the great bulk of federal restraints on its activities. States decided for themselves which officials were to be appointed or elected; state legislatures made laws on all subjects not clashing with the very narrow federal responsibilities; states determined their criminal and most of their civil laws; they provided the educational and social services they desired; they sent voting representatives to the two houses of Congress; and they enjoyed, irrespective of size or population, equal representation in the Senate, where each state returned two senators. Because organized territories were expected to become states, their social and political character was a topic of some concern to the country as a whole. And in the mid 1840s that topic centred on one question: should, and could, slavery be introduced into or excluded from the federal territories?

As early as 1787–90 the confederation and then the US Congress plumped for a dual policy towards slavery in the territories. Slavery was explicitly banned from the North-West Territory. The ban was not total in its effect, since slaves already in the territory were not freed. And when the vast expanse of the North-West Territory was later sub-divided, two of the new territories – Indiana and Illinois – adopted short-term, but renewable, indenture systems which closely resembled slavery. When Illinois finally became a state in 1818 it nearly legalized slavery. But Illinois' refusal to permit black servitude meant that slavery was excluded from the whole of the North-West Territory, largely as a result of the national government's initiatives of 1787. At the same time, however, Congress in the early 1790s allowed territories south of the Ohio river to decide for themselves whether or not they wanted slavery. Congressional action here was perhaps made possible because the line between slavery and freedom had not been conclusively drawn. When the new slave territory of Mississippi was created in 1798, Southern congressmen willingly admitted that slavery itself would eventually end. So, while the early republic forbade slavery in territories north of the Ohio and adopted a policy of laissez-faire for territories south of the Ohio, it acted thus when sectional feelings over slavery extension were restrained. Many Northerners felt sincerely hostile to slavery; but they did not believe anti-slavery to be *the* great, or indeed *a* great, issue in politics.[11] And, although Southern congressmen as early as 1798 were united in pressing for slavery's extension, they did not yet insist – as they did increasingly adamantly from the 1830s – that slavery was a positive

---

[11] *Ibid.*, p. 18.

good rather than a necessary evil.

The dual policy of 1787–90 prevailed also in 1820. Anti-slavery congressmen in the House of Representatives attempted in 1819 to prevent Missouri's admission as a fully-fledged slave state. But the senate blocked proposals to stop the entry of further slaves and to emancipate (at the age of 25) all slaves born in Missouri after it became a state. Very reluctantly, therefore – by 90 to 87 votes – the House of Representatives accepted in March 1820 the famous Missouri Compromise, by which two concessions were tossed to Northern waverers in return for Missouri's admission as a slave state. A further free state was created in Maine, so maintaining a senatorial balance of free and slave states. And Southern congressmen – or, at least, half of them – conceded that in future territorial arrangements slavery would be prohibited north of the line of latitude 36°30′ and permitted in the organized federal territories south of it. Thus Florida territory – established in 1822 – was automatically open to slavery, and Iowa territory – organized in 1838 – was automatically closed to slavery. In this way, the national government's policy for slavery in the territories – discovered fairly accidentally in 1787–90 – was both pragmatic and widely accepted for 50-odd years after the passage of the North-West Ordinance. That territorial policy was undermined by three developments in the 1830s and 1840s.

First, Northern attacks on slavery became more militant after 1831. By the early 1840s a growing body of Northern politicians objected to any further extension of slavery anywhere. Secondly, in response to such attacks, Southerners became more assertive in defending slavery, so that by 1837 abolitionist societies ceased to exist in the South. Thirdly, these two developments acquired immediate political force in 1846–8 when America invaded Mexico. Many Northerners wanted no more territories added to the USA or wanted slavery explicitly excluded from any territories snatched from Mexico. In turn, a leading Southern politician, John C. Calhoun, urged that Congress could not prohibit slavery in *any* federal territory. Since slaves were property, he argued, US citizens could settle anywhere in US territories with their property (including slaves); any federal government interference with slave-owners settling in federal territories would be unconstitutional. A policy which had worked for over 50 years thus became, in the mid 1840s, increasingly unacceptable to many Northerners on moral grounds and to many Southerners on constitutional grounds. Almost from the beginning of the Mexican war in 1846 until the beginning of America's Civil War in April 1861, federal power and policy in the federal territories was at the centre of a protracted, complex, baffling, and passionate sectional and intra-sectional debate.

Nor, unfortunately, was there any lack of demand for territorial government. Just at the time when the federal government raised a number of territories to statehood, in 1845–8, so it acquired vast new lands from conquered Mexico. Throughout the period 1848–61 the push and shove of westward settlement made territorial policy a vital and practical aspect of the federal government's work.

Table 1: Population in 1860 of territories organized from 1848 to 1861[12]

		White	Free Coloured	Slave
Colorado	(1861)	34,231	46	–
Dakota	(1861)	576	–	–
Kansas	(1854)	106,390	625	2
Minnesota	(1849)	169,395	259	–
Oregon	(1848)	52,160	128	–
Nebraska	(1854)	28,696	67	15
Nevada	(1861)	6,812	45	–
New Mexico	(1850)	82,924	85	–
Utah	(1850)	40,125	30	29
Washington	(1853)	11,138	30	–

The dates in brackets are those of territorial organization: population figures exclude Indians.

Sectional demands and expectations over slavery injected conflict and controversy into the whole business. From 1848 to 1861 inclusive the federal government organized 10 new territories and raised three of them (Oregon in 1858, Minnesota in 1859, and Kansas in 1861) to statehood. The movement of population westwards was appreciable; that fact – and the creation of such a large number of new territories – expanded the federal government's rôle. The geographical position of some of these territories on the route to California added further problems for the federal government. With gold-rich California incorporated into the American realm, how was the Pacific coast to be connected securely to the Mississippi valley? Various proposals to construct a continental railway – with federal aid – deeply affected the fate of the federal territories lying between the Mississippi river and California. Yet settlement and railway-building of themselves did not inflame discussion of territorial policy. The place of slavery in all these new territories did.

The collapse of the pragmatic dual policy laid down in 1787–90 and reaffirmed more formally in 1820 opened up a wide range of constitutional questions. Did all US citizens enjoy access to all territories, irrespective of the possessions they wished to take with them? Or could Congress prohibit the entry of a very peculiar form of property (slaves, that is) into some or all of the territories? Should the ban upon slavery in certain territories be extended, on the lines of the North-West Ordinance of 1787, to all territories? Or should all territories be left to decide for themselves whether or not they wanted slavery: as territories south of

[12] *Population of the United States in 1860; Compiled from the Original Returns of the Eighth Census* (Washington, D.C., 1864), pp. 598–9.

the Ohio river had been left to do in 1790? Moreover, because government in the territories was dyarchic – a large measure of self-government tempered by ultimate federal responsibility – a further bone of contention was the power available to territorial legislatures over slavery. Matters of territorial governance were of their very nature complex, and they became in the 1840s highly contentious. Simultaneously, governing the territories became an expanding federal concern: hundreds of thousands of settlers moved into the western territories; territorial development intertwined with possible railway links to California; and the West broadly and imaginatively conceived loomed ever larger in many Americans' thinking about their country's economic future. As the federal government set about expanding, ordering, and developing its western territories, it thus came under intense pressure to implement a number of thoroughly irreconcilable policies towards slavery in those territories.

The Federal Government

The federal government was regarded in the 1840s and 1850s with a mixture of pride, expectation, suspicion, and distaste. To most Americans it was the embodiment of democratic virtue; to many it offered the expectation of economic promotion; to others it contained an ever-present vulnerability to favour vested economic interests; to a few it represented a loathsome compromise with forces of evil – slavery at one extreme and abolitionism at the other. This focussing of popular attention on the federal government was not entirely novel to the mid nineteenth century, but it had not characterized previous generations as strongly. After the furore over federal powers and responsibilities in the 1790s, the federal government had not attracted keen public scrutiny in the 1810s and 1820s. Only at the end of the 1820s did more men begin to vote in federal than in state elections and only in the following decade was the federal government's primacy in the public imagination – as manifested consistently and markedly in higher turnout at federal elections – firmly established. Yet the federal government itself often appeared to operate in a cumbersome and incomprehensible way.

The various branches of the federal government very rarely worked harmoniously together; indeed they were not necessarily intended to do so. During the whole period 1828–60 only one president (James K. Polk in 1844) was elected with a precise programme and actually carried that programme to a successful conclusion. Other presidents were either elected on generalities and formulated policy in response to events, or were frustrated in their plans by reluctant or recalcitrant Congresses. While the presidential term of office was four years, the House of Representatives was elected every two years (to add to the confusion, these elections occurred at different times separated by up to a year). This meant that presidents regularly entered office with majorities in the

House but found themselves confronting a House of Representatives dominated by the opposition party or parties after only two years in office, as happened for example in 1847–9, 1855–7 and 1859–61.[13] Moreover, the upper house, the Senate, was elected by state legislatures and not at popular election-time; Senators therefore had constituencies different to those of the more humble Congressmen. With their stronger ties to state legislatures, their different times of selection, and their six-year terms of office, the Senators were a self-confident and distinctive group of politicians in Washington.

Cutting across the strong institutional divisions between presidency, House, and Senate were ties of party. From the 1830s until the Civil War, Congress divided fairly coherently and consistently along party lines; but the emphasis here should be on 'fairly', for the levels of party discipline were not strikingly high, by, say, British parliamentary standards. Persistent bargaining between leading Senators and Congressmen and the President, heavy use of presidential patronage, and strenuous invoking of party loyalty were required for legislative success. The wide divergencies of interest represented in the federal government – where Senators represented states, but Congressmen, enjoying office for a mere two years, were subject to intense and narrow constituency pressures – and the differences which often existed in party identification between different houses in the Congress or between one house of Congress and the President, partly explain Congress's legislative ineffectiveness.

Too much should not be made, however, of the general lack of creative legislation in the 1850s. That paucity is sometimes ascribed to the all-consuming nature of sectional strife. Allan Nevins, for example, concluded:

> Throughout the dozen years after 1848 . . . no laws except those pertaining to the slavery issue really counted; and Congress became less and less an implement for legislation, more and more simply a grand central forum for debate – a place where fears, hopes and hatreds of the colliding parties and sections might be stated.[14]

Yet Congress's relative effectiveness in passing bills presented to it was not much lower in the 1850s than in the 1840s or in the period 1865–73, when the Republicans controlled both Congress and the presidency (see Table 2 below). Moreover, the proportion of bills introduced that were actually passed varied considerably between Congresses in the 1840s and 1850s; numerous measures fell by the wayside simply because of their private or local character; and some schemes for federal economic promotion were killed by regional or sectional jealousies. Even so, in 1850, 1853, and 1856 the federal government granted large amounts of

---

[13] David M. Potter (completed and ed. by Don E. Fehrenbacher), *The Impending Crisis, 1848–1861* (New York, 1976), pp. 385–6.
[14] Allan Nevins, *Ordeal of the Union* (New York, 1947), I, p. 163.

public land to individual states to aid railway building. If Congress failed in the greater task of financing a railway to the Pacific coast, this failure did not result simply from neglect or pre-occupation with North–South antagonisms. It was simply impossible for representatives from rival regions or sections to agree on a single route. Unless the federal government spent on an unprecedented scale, thereby meeting rival claims, it was inevitably incapable of action on projects of bold internal development.

Table 2: Legislative activity of selected congresses, 1827–75[15]

Congress	Total number of bills introduced	Percentage passed
1827–9	612	36.9
1833–5	946	46.9
1839–41	1,081	12.9
1841–3	1,146	43.2
1845–7	956	27.5
1849–51	978	14.2
1851–3	1,011	26.6
1853–5	1,552	31.6
1857–9	1,544	17.7
1867–9	3,003	20.2
1869–71	4,446	12.3
1871–3	5,725	17.4
1873–5	6,252	13.3

The real problem of the 1840s and 1850s was not federal inertia but federal activity. Where it was competent, and under pressure, to act, the federal government was highly creative, as territory after territory was brought into being or to statehood. This, however, produced a clutter of Frankenstein's monsters which threatened to maul or destroy their creators. For tensions within the territories between pro-slavery and anti-slavery men made some territories virtually uncontrollable by the mid 1850s. Congressional ingenuity was flawed because congressmen had incompatible blue-prints for bringing territories to working order. Southerners wanted to forge new slave societies; Northerners wanted to model the territories upon the free states. But why did congressmen stick so resolutely to their pre-conceived designs?

Much of the trouble lay in the nature of American political rhetoric. Very weighty importance was attached to the proper defence of political rights won so hard from Britain and extended so widely in the 50 years after the Revolution. Within the federal Congress especially, the defence of states' or sections' constitutional and political rights was required of elected politicians. Politicians (and voters) in turn advanced their states'

[15] *Historical Statistics of the United States*, p. 690.

or sections' rights by securing beneficial, or blocking harmful, legislation and by supporting allies or fellow-believers for high office. As one Southern intellectual noted in 1860: 'No party, no confederacy can be held together by abstract principle simply. The great body of politicians and people require some symbols which they couple with principles, and which they finally receive as a substitute for it [sic]. These symbols are our candidates for office'.[16] By the 1850s − if not long before − sectional groups within the national parties were working hard to secure Northern or Southern or Western candidates for key offices. These candidates were frequently associated with concrete legislative proposals. But perhaps equally often such token representation was exploited by those who used vague, general, even baseless and paranoid fears to press for greater protection of theoretical rights. Not surprisingly, therefore, territorial legislation became warped by the juddering tug and counter-pull of conflicting demands.

The situation may be briefly summarized. The federal government possessed limited responsibilities and was devised to articulate and accommodate all manner of interests and demands. It is easy to see why Americans looked upon the federal government with mixed and varied feelings and even perhaps regarded it as rather unimportant to their normal lives. Yet in the 1840s and 1850s one area of federal activity − territorial policy − attracted detailed, powerful, and sustained scrutiny. Given the symbolic significance attached increasingly − and for whatever myopic or selfish reasons − to slaveowners' and Northerners' rights in those territories, the paradoxical juxtaposition of heated sectional controversy and generally limited federal powers and activities may be understood. What remains unclear, however, is the extent to which the battle over symbolic rights reflected a genuine and complete schism between North and South.

[16] Steven A. Channing, *Crisis of Fear. Secession in South Carolina* (New York, 1970), p. 233.

3 The North

An Agricultural People

Nothing about mid-nineteenth-century America is more difficult to discern than the reality behind sectional identities and the right balance to strike between peculiarly Northern or Southern, as opposed to generally American, characteristics. President Lincoln just after the beginning of the war, in July 1861, stated his view of the difference in a typically uplifting if rather general pronouncement:

> This is essentially a people's contest. On the side of the Union it is a struggle for maintaining in the world that form and substance of government whose leading object is to elevate the condition of men — to lift artificial weights from all shoulders; to clear the paths of laudable pursuit for all; to afford all an unfettered start, and a fair chance in the race of life.[1]

This is stirring stuff: but what did it mean? Certainly not that Lincoln's Republican party, or Northerners in general, believed that the federal government could or should abolish slavery; nor that the 'artificial weights' of racial discrimination and exclusion should be removed entirely from the shoulders of the free blacks in their midst. Some historians have argued that the Republican party embodied a progressive ideal to be translated into reformist action, and there is a certain amount of evidence for Republican reformism in the Northern states that they controlled in the late 1850s and in the mid 1860s. But the speeches of Republican governors in the late 1850s, the voting records of Republican state legislators, and Republican policy in a state such as Michigan where the party commanded strong support, reveal no clear or powerful reformist thrust.[2]

---

[1] Henry S. Commager (ed.), *Documents of American History. Vol. I: to 1898* (New York, 1963 edn), p. 395.
[2] Eric Foner, *Free Soil, Free Labor, Free Men. The Ideology of the Republican Party before the Civil War* (New York, 1970); B.W. Collins, 'The Politics of Particularism: Economic Issues in the Major Northern States of the U.S.A., 1857–1858' (Unpublished Ph.D. thesis; Cambridge University, 1975); Bruce Collins, 'Economic Issues in Ohio's Politics During the Recession of 1857–58' *Ohio History*, 89 (1980), pp. 46–64; Ronald P. Formisano, *The Birth of Mass Political Parties: Michigan, 1827–1861* (Princeton, 1971).

Nor could the attitudes expressed by Lincoln be described as peculiarly Northern. Southern state governors in the 1850s similarly urged that opportunity — for whites — be open and extended, and Southern politicians, like those in the North, spoke of the prevailing need to promote economic advance and public education and to remove artificial distinctions between white men.[3] The North–South contrast was narrowly, but perhaps accurately, drawn in 1857–8 by a visiting British anti-slavery feminist. Mrs Bodichon described a governor's message sent to Alabama's legislature in November 1857: 'All the opinions expressed on other things seem to me remarkably sound — how distorted every view becomes where slavery is concerned, I leave you to judge. He speaks of the possibility of the severance of the Union, the necessity of warlike preparations'. Yet Mrs Bodichon read no deep sociological distinctions into these separatist yearnings or leanings. Her keenest impression of America was recorded while she was visiting the Deep South:

> This is really a free country in the respect of having no privileged class — excepting the class of white over black. White men are free in America and no mistake! . . . One is so little used to freedom, real freedom, even in England that it takes time to understand freedom, to realise it. Nothing sent from upper powers to be worshipped or humbly listened to, no parsons sent by a class of born rulers to preach and lecture to another class born to submit and to pay. No race of men with honours they have not earned and power over others which the others have not consented them! . . . Here all who hold power are heaved up by the people, of the people.[4]

This description, when set against Lincoln's speech of July 1861, suggests that Lincoln's claims do not tell us very much about sectional differences within white society in ante-bellum North and South. What was expressed was instead a general American aspiration, deftly turned into sectional propaganda.

Contemporary Americans breathed hot and cold in rapid succession about sectional differences: at one moment, they enthused about their united country and their shared aspirations with patriotic and hyperbolic nationalism; at the next, they narrowly dissected local and sectional distinctions. The vast majority of Southerners who travelled to the North visited one or more of the three great cities — New York, Philadelphia, and Boston — or one of a small number of spa resorts. Their impressions of the North — dynamic, bustling, urban, profiteering — were hardly based on an understanding of the broader patterns of Northern life. So, too, foreign visitors tended to acquaint themselves with the major cities

[3] J. Mills Thornton, III, *Politics and Power in a Slave Society: Alabama 1800–1860* (Baton Rouge, 1978); William J. Cooper, Jr, *The South and the Politics of Slavery, 1828–1856* (Baton Rouge, 1978), ch. 2.

[4] Barbara Leigh Smith Bodichon, *An American Diary 1857–8*, ed. by Joseph W. Reed, Jr (London, 1972), pp. 117, 72.

and to observe the vast stretches of the rural North only as background scenery. When they did venture into rural and small-town America, foreign visitors tended to remark on the natural beauty of the surroundings and the languid pace of life in North and South alike. Much emphasis was, of course, laid on Southern whites' brutality towards and exploitation of slaves. But British travellers often noted that Northerners appeared to avoid menial labour as far as possible, relying instead on the 'lumpen proletariat' of Irish immigrants to provide navvies, labourers, and domestic servants – and this despite the favourite Northern argument that slavery debased the value of manual toil amongst the whites.[5]

But how far were North and South diverging economically in the mid nineteenth century? Certainly, an industrializing and eagerly commercial North was increasingly different from the overwhelmingly agricultural South. But the North–South contrast was not so sharp and simple as is sometimes intimated. The North was very far from being a fully industrial region in 1860, while Southern agriculture was advanced in organization and closely geared to expanding world markets.

Manufacturing industry grew quickly from about 1810, receiving an immediate and sudden stimulus from the war of 1812 with Britain. However, even by 1860 only four manufacturing sectors in the entire country employed more than 50,000 people. Of these sectors, the most productive – boot and shoe manufacture – employed 123,000 people; this sector was followed by cotton goods and men's clothing with 115,000 each, and lastly lumber industries with 75,000 employees. These leading manufacturing sectors scarcely accounted for a significant proportion of the 8,287,000 free Americans in employment in 1860 and represented a tiny fraction of the total population of 31 million.[6]

Moreover, industry in 1860, rather than being uniformly dispersed throughout the North, was concentrated in small establishments and was distinctly localized: half America's output of boots and shoes came from Massachusetts, while one third to half the country's output of various iron and steel products came from Pennsylvania.[7] No manufacturing sector supplied world markets; American industrial production was geared to the needs of a limited, albeit expanding, home market, and had to be supplemented by steady imports, mainly from Britain, of manufactured

[5] John Hope Franklin, *A Southern Odyssey. Travelers in the Antebellum North* (Baton Rouge, 1976), pp. 5, 17–18, 22–44; Max Berger, *The British Traveller in America, 1836–1860* (New York, 1943), pp. 31–3, 43–4, 54–8; William Ferguson, *America by River and Rail; or Notes by the Way on the New World and Its People* (London, 1856), chs. 32, 35; Bodichon, *An American Diary*, pp. 110, 113, 125–6.

[6] Figures taken from: *Population of the United States in 1860; Compiled from the Original Returns of the Eighth Census* (Washington, 1864), pp. 656–80.

[7] Figures are available in: *Manufactures of the United States in 1860; Compiled from the Original Returns of the Eighth Census* (Washington, D.C., 1865), pp. 251, 540–1, 543, 733, 737, 741. Cf. David Montgomery, *Beyond Equality. Labor and the Radical Republicans, 1862–1872* (New York, 1972 edn), ch. 1.

goods. The leading economic pursuits of Northerners, and of Americans in general, lay elsewhere.

In the North, as in the nation at large, the leading occupations in 1860 were farming, labouring, farm labouring, and domestic service. Of those gainfully employed in the *free states* in 1860, 55.5 per cent were engaged in such basic occupations. The actual numbers were 1,567,000 farmers, 702,000 labourers, 550,000 farm labourers, and 461,000 servants in a work force of 5,908,000. Although the South was more heavily committed to agriculture than were the free states, both North and South were agricultural producers: in both the majority of occupations were rural and urban employment consisted largely of small-town craft skills serving agricultural needs. This agricultural specialization is well shown by the poor distribution of really substantial towns. In 1860 most states in the country (ten slave and seven free) each possessed only *one* town with more than 20,000 people, even though the states themselves were usually at least 35,000–40,000 square miles in area. Many, largely newer, states (five slave and five free) did not have even one town of such modest size. Only six (free) states each possessed more than one town of over 20,000 people: New Jersey and Connecticut two each, Ohio three, Pennsylvania four, and New York and Massachusetts eight each.[8] Given the huge land area involved, America was poorly equipped with moderate-sized commercial towns.

Rather than being generally industrialized, the North can be more accurately perceived as a highly efficient agricultural producer containing isolated pockets of heavy industry and scattered, small centres of commercial activity. American farmers were rural businessmen, directing their efforts to the demands of regional and industrial markets and dependent upon a far-flung network of canals and railways for the transport of farm produce. They speculated intensely in land, often feeling little attachment to particular localities or communities, but eager to sell their farms when property values rose and to move farther westwards where larger tracts could be purchased at a lower price per acre. Although it was so largely agrarian in character, Northern society evinced none of the spirit of inertia and resolute traditionalism that is associated with peasant societies. Northerners appeared to be in constant motion during the nineteenth century and their energy had markedly visible effects. Areas that were sparsely populated, open prairie in the 1820s, were covered with profitably organized farms and supported thriving, if small, commercial towns connected by networks of railways only a generation later. Commercial values and the 'capitalist ethos' pervaded Northern society in the 1850s. Yet, while close attention was paid to the best use of time and raw materials and the diligent manipula-

---

[8] Figures taken from: *Population of the United States in 1860*, pp. 656–80; Stuart M. Blumin, *The Urban Threshold. Growth and Change in a Nineteenth Century Community* (Chicago, 1976), pp. 223–4.

tion of property and commodities markets, concentrated industrialism and urbanization had not spread far from the eastern seaboard.

The Regions

The impact of industrialization may be best illustrated by a breakdown of the North into its major regions. This analysis corresponds to contemporary usage; mid-nineteenth-century Americans spoke, wrote, and thought in regional as much as sectional terms, and one key stage in the growth of purely Northern consciousness was the forging of stronger economic and political links between two of those regions — Middle Atlantic seaboard and the Midwest — during the 1840s and 1850s. But whether these various regions were tightly wed together by their economic endeavours and opposed to Southern interests is open to question.

Even in the longest settled region of the Atlantic seaboard, New England, the industrial interest was not paramount. By the nineteenth century its numerous small towns had developed a vigorous community life and fostered a distinctive puritan morality; the progressive attitudes and philanthropic impulses of Massachusetts which so impressed Charles Dickens during his visit of 1841 manifested themselves in social reform and in the ample provision of orphanages, prisons, and schools.[9] Here, apparently, was the ideal type of 'modern' society. Yet New England was not industrialized, urban, socially homogeneous, and by its very nature different from the rural South. Instead, it was a region of startling social contrasts often glossed over by its urban political leaders.

In 1860 only about one American in ten — 3,135,000 — lived in New England, even though the region's cultural and economic influence far exceeded that simple numerical ratio.[10] Manufacturing especially was well advanced in those states, with 262,834 males and 129,002 females finding employment in some 20,671 manufacturing establishments. Such a level of manufacturing employment was impressive indeed, absorbing as it did nearly 40 per cent of New England's work force of 1,104,000. And many workers toiled in large factories possessing well-developed and elaborate technology. Concentrated industrial production was found in Boston and its hinterland, in Rhode Island, and in some towns in Connecticut. Yet the majority of New England's people were rural folk in 1860; 64 per cent of them lived in communities whose populations were under 2,500. And town-life was not synonymous with advanced industry. Even in towns whose populations exceeded 2,500, many people had agricultural interests, while factory workers often took

[9] Charles Dickens, *American Notes* (London: Chapman & Hall edn), pp. 25–7, 39–46 (ch. 3).
[10] Figures in this paragraph are taken from: *Population of the United States in 1860*, pp. 656–80; *Manufactures of the United States in 1860*, pp. 677–86; J. Potter, 'The Growth of Population in America, 1700–1860', in D.V. Glass and D.E.C. Eversley, *Population in History; Essays in Historical Demography* (London, 1965), pp. 680–7.

Table 3: Population and area of the states, by region, in 1860

	Total population (in '000s)	Slave population (in '000s)	Area in square miles (in '000s)
New England			
Connecticut	460		5
Maine	628		35
Massachusetts	1,231		8
New Hampshire	326		9
Rhode Island	175		1
Vermont	315		10
Middle Atlantic			
Pennsylvania	2,906		46
New Jersey	672		8
New York	3,881		47
Midwest			
Illinois	1,712		55
Indiana	1,350		34
Michigan	749		56
Ohio	2,339		40
Wisconsin	776		54
North Central			
Iowa	675		55
Minnesota	172		83
Pacific West			
California	380		189
Oregon	52		95
Border States			
Delaware	112	2	2
Kentucky	1,156	225	38
Maryland	687	87	11
Missouri	1,182	115	65
Upper South			
Arkansas	435	111	52
North Carolina	993	331	51
Tennessee	1,110	276	46
Virginia	1,596	491	61
Lower South			
Alabama	964	435	51
Florida	140	62	59
Georgia	1,057	462	58
Louisiana	708	332	41
Mississippi	791	437	47
South Carolina	704	402	34
Texas	604	183	274

Table 3 (cont.)

	Total population	Slave population	Area in square miles
Others			
All organized territories	327		all territories and D.C.
District of Columbia	75	3	1,287
Total USA	31,443	3,954	3,010

Note: Totals are affected by rounding all figures to the nearest thousand.
Source: Population of the United States in 1860, pp. 598–9; *Statistics of the United States (Including Mortality, Property, etc.) in 1860; Compiled from the Original Returns and Being the Final Exhibit of the Eighth Census* (Washington, D.C., 1866), p. 339.

on farm jobs during industrial recessions or winter slack spells. Only in larger towns were the seasonal rhythms associated with agriculture overwhelmed by technology. Many factory workers, notably the women workers in the cotton textile mills, returned to farm life after only a brief sortie into urban employment.[11] Furthermore, the aggregate figures for workers in 'manufacturing establishments' include village craftsmen and small-scale entrepreneurs, as well as many urban artisans whose labour in small work-shops and plants was highly traditional in character. Perhaps, therefore, the figure provided by the census-takers in 1860 of only 62,000 people in New England being factory-hands offers a truer impression of the impact of industrialization than the figures for workers in 'manufacturing establishments'. But this urban proletariat, and urban culture in general, were not spread uniformly throughout the region. Granted, 60 per cent of Massachusetts' people were 'urban', as were 63 per cent of Rhode Island's. Yet these were the highest proportions of urban inhabitants in America in 1860, and the other New England states' inhabitants were overwhelmingly *rural*: 74 per cent in Connecticut, 78 per cent in New Hampshire, 83 per cent in Maine, and 98 per cent in Vermont. Such divergent habits of residence and occupation can clearly not be lumped together under the facile description of 'industrial New England'.

Differences of interest between rural and urban New England were not thoroughly reconciled in the 1850s, and emerged in at least two political issues in that decade. The first of these was the federal tariff. Industrial New England and the agricultural South are sometimes thought to have been at loggerheads over a protective tariff. Most Southern politicians insisted on free trade or the imposition of low import duties for revenue purposes only, since free trade would permit Southerners to buy

[11] Norman Ware, *The Industrial Worker, 1840–1860* (Chicago, 1964 edn), p. 149; Bodichon, *An American Diary*, p. 156; Blumin, *The Urban Threshold*, pp. 73–4.

manufactured goods from the cheapest market, Britain. In contrast, textile manufacturers especially desired tariff protection against imported British goods and protectionist sentiment therefore flourished in the major textile producing states, Massachusetts and Rhode Island. The tariff issue, however, was also a cause of contention within the North. While New England farmers benefited from the urban growth of the region, agricultural and urban interests in the region did not necessarily work hand in glove. One example of such divergent interests was the perennially brusque treatment of sheep farmers by industrialists. Scant concession was made to sheep farming interests when, in 1857, New England woollen textile manufacturers went to great lengths, including liberal bribery, to secure congressional reduction of import duties on the desired grades of foreign raw wool. So the tariff issue was not one that united New England or that set New England on an inevitable collision course with the South.[12]

Secondly, political tension arose because New England enjoyed no comfortable ethnic unity. Country folk — the majority of the region's inhabitants — and residents of traditional small towns regarded industrial centres with suspicion: physically overcrowded, ethnically and religiously heterogeneous, and centres (it was popularly believed) of disorder, squalor, and vice. In the region as a whole, some 15 per cent of the people were foreign-born immigrants, largely concentrated in the towns; in Massachusetts, Rhode Island, and Connecticut in 1860 about one person in five was foreign-born. These immigrants, largely Irish, although a considerable number were of German origin, aroused fierce native American hostility in the early and middle 1850s. Within industrial towns, foreign immigrants — especially the Irish — were often residentially segregated and had to endure sustained abuse. In addition, the criticism of immigrants often took the form of more general nativist denunciations of the great cities and their attendant ills. Native Americans — including artisans, middle-class businessmen, and professionals — established anti-foreign political parties in the 1850s to bridle the alleged excesses of intemperate, uneducated, and largely Catholic immigrants. Attempts to limit by legislation the sale of alcoholic liquor and to prolong the period of residence required before immigrants could become United States citizens were common and popular in New England.[13]

An image of New England as a Weberian ideal type of industrialized society has sometimes been starkly contrasted with the social character-

[12] F.W. Taussig, *The Tariff History of the United States* (New York, 1964 edn), pp. 149–52; Roy F. Nichols, *The Disruption of American Democracy* (New York, 1967 edn), pp. 193–4; Fred H. Nicklason, 'The early career of Henry L. Dawes, 1817–1871' (unpublished Ph.D. dissertation, Yale University, 1967), pp. 134–9.
[13] Potter, 'The Growth of Population in America', p. 686; William G. Bean, 'Puritan Versus Celt, 1850–1860', *New England Quarterly*, VII (1934), 70–89; Oscar Handlin, *Boston's Immigrants: A Study in Acculturation* (New York, 1972), pp. 88–101, 180–92, 201–6; Michael F. Holt, *The Political Crisis of the 1850s* (New York, 1978), pp. 156–75.

istics and attributes of the ante-bellum South. In fact, as has been seen, New England was divided between rural and urban interests, and between the Protestant native-born and Catholic immigrants. It was the centre in the 1850s not only of anti-slavery and abolitionist sentiment, but also of anti-foreign, anti-immigrant agitation. Its nationally important industrial sector was counter-balanced by a wide commitment to agriculture. Its proud traditions of local self-government and political effervescence contrasted with striking examples of electoral apathy; between 1843 and 1861 no more than 50 per cent of adult white males in Massachusetts voted in any state election, at a time when turnouts of 70 to 80 per cent were common elsewhere.[14] The true picture, then, is one of internal contrast, tension, and diversity, even in the decade when many publicists and politicians seemed to believe that New England was an homogeneous unit in sharp contrast with the society of the South.

After New England, the most industrialized region of America was contained in the Middle Atlantic seaboard states of New York, New Jersey, and Pennsylvania. Again, however, industry tended to be locally concentrated rather than diffused throughout any state. New York, with 3,881,000 people, Pennsylvania with 2,906,000, were the nation's most populous states: indeed, they provided homes for rather more than one in five Americans. New York City, Philadelphia, Buffalo, Pittsburgh, and Albany were leading industrial and commercial centres, but, apart from the widely scattered iron, coal, and textile production in eastern Pennsylvania, industrial activities stood isolated from the surrounding small towns and the countryside. In New York State 61 per cent of the population, and in Pennsylvania 69 per cent, resided in the countryside; and state politics revolved much around rural–metropolitan antagonisms provoked by the contrast of New York City and Philadelphia with the agricultural and small-town social milieu and economic pursuits of their hinterlands.[15]

The great metropolitan centres of New York and Philadelphia shared at least one common interest with numerous smaller up-state towns and agricultural communities; this was a desire to exploit the natural resources of the trans-Appalachian region, and to open the states' back-country to commerce. Against this common interest must be set the fact that New York City and Philadelphia were both genuinely national centres of manufacturing, banking, and commerce. They possessed a strong and profitable Southern connection, and they depended upon

[14] The figures are in J.R. Pole, *Political Representation in England and the Origins of the American Republic* (Berkeley, 1971 edn), pp. 550–2. It might be added that many white adult men were not qualified to vote and therefore the comparison I make is misleading. It would be useful to know whether the legal restrictions on voting were actually enforced. Nothing is said of this problem of turn-out in the important article by Dale Baum, 'Know-Nothingism and the Republican Majority in Massachusetts: the Political Realignment of the 1850s', *Journal of American History*, LXII (1978), 959–86.

[15] For population figures, see Potter, 'The Growth of Population in America', pp. 684, 686.

Southern as much as up-state and Midwestern markets. Thus the mercantile and business élite in these two Northern cities was very far from hostile to the South *per se*, and during the crisis winter of 1860–1 it strenuously hoped and worked for peace.[16]

Of course, some metropolitan interests objected to the free trade policies promoted and supported by Southern politicians. Textile manufacturers in Philadelphia, and iron, steel, and coal producers in eastern Pennsylvania and the Pittsburgh area desired tariff protection, especially after the economic recession of 1857–8. The appeal for tariff protection, however, did not stem from or exacerbate tension on simply sectional lines, but reflected other, purely Northern, antagonisms, and failed to win unanimous support. The tariff issue was in fact closely bound up with the stubborn, bitter ethnic hostilities that seethed in the largest industrial cities during the 1850s. The nativist party, the Know-Nothings, remained active, influential and popular in New York City, Philadelphia, and Buffalo until 1857–8, whereas they lost ground in most other areas in 1855 and 1856. Nativist sentiment in Pennsylvania was appeased after the final disappearance of the Know-Nothing party nationally by the adoption of tariff protection as a campaign pledge by the Republicans in 1858. The Republicans in Pennsylvania then stressed the need to protect American goods and American workers from competition by foreign labour and imports.[17] While, therefore, the call for tariff protection in Philadelphia and many other parts of Pennsylvania met the long-term needs of certain economic interests, it appealed also to nativist resentment against foreign immigrants. And it was a response to disquieting short-term economic adversity, rather than to structural economic dislocation. For the broad mass of farmers in the Middle Atlantic states and in the Midwest, and in areas lightly troubled by nativist activity, the tariff question was hardly a major bone of contention with the South.

Lying beyond the Appalachian Mountains was the Midwest, comprising Ohio, Indiana, Illinois, Michigan, and Wisconsin. It had been cut off from white settlement until the mountain barrier was pierced in the late eighteenth century; but by the 1850s most of the region was, by contemporary American standards, well populated, thoroughly cultivated, and commercially developed. In Ohio, for example, about 80 per cent of the land area was absorbed into farms. Some concentrations of industry existed, although the major cities of Cincinnati and Chicago were perhaps more notable as centres of transport, finance, and commerce than as industrial forcing-houses. Generally, manufacturing establishments were small, with an average of only about six employees

[16] Philip S. Foner, *Business and Slavery: The New York Merchants and the Irrepressible Conflict* (Chapel Hill, 1941), chs. 9–15; Philip S. Klein and Ari Hoogenboom, *A History of Pennsylvania* (New York, 1973), pp. 159–60.
[17] William Dusinberre, *Civil War Issues in Philadelphia, 1856–1865* (Philadelphia, 1965), p. 78; Foner, *Free Soil, Free Labor, Free Men*, pp. 173–6.

per firm, while most industrial enterprises were engaged in food processing or other activities closely related to an agricultural economy whose large surpluses were sent to the eastern seaboard or to Europe. Economic ties with the South were weakened between 1840 and the 1850s, when the bulk of Midwestern produce ceased to be transported along the southerly river routes and moved instead eastwards by lake and rail. Although the advent of the railways thus shifted the direction of inter-regional trade, it created no radical changes in Midwestern society. In 1860, only 14 per cent of the population of 6,927,000 were town-dwellers, and most of the towns were small market centres locked tightly into an agrarian economy rather than engines of social transformation.[18]

Midwestern farmers had little interest in urbanization or industrialization, except as far as both processes provided them with markets, however distant or foreign. What then did Midwesterners hold against the South?

Midwestern resentment was provoked on four principal topics, in which the South was believed to exert a constrictive and conservative influence on federal policy. The first, perhaps most strongly justified, complaint concerned internal improvement. Midwestern politicians urged the federal government to provide financial aid for the improvement of harbours and rivers, to protect the former from silting and to dredge and canalize stretches of the latter. Such use of federal largesse was opposed by the Southern Democrats in particular, and in 1846, 1854, and 1860 Democratic presidents vetoed internal improvement bills widely desired in the Midwest. A second subject of Midwestern complaint against the federal government under Southern influence was Congress's refusal to commit federal resources to the vigorous promotion of a transcontinental railway; in the 1850s Congress became bogged down in considering the construction of a railway from the Mississippi valley to the Pacific. The force of this grievance was perhaps reduced by the fact that Congress (with at least the Senate controlled on each occasion, in 1850, 1853, and 1856, by the Democrats) granted substantial amounts of federal land to the state governments of Iowa, Michigan, Wisconsin, Illinois, Louisiana, Mississippi, Alabama and Florida for use by the states in promoting railway building.[19]

The Midwest had a more popular grievance against the stout refusal of Democratic federal administrations to grant homesteads free, or

[18] *Statistics of the United States (Including Mortality, Property, etc.) in 1860; Compiled from the Original Returns and Being the Final Exhibit of the Eighth Census* (Washington, D.C., 1866), p. 339; Fred Bateman and Thomas J. Weiss, 'Comparative Regional Development in Antebellum Manufacturing', *Journal of Economic History*, xxxv (1975), 182–208; Douglass C. North, *The Economic Growth of the United States, 1790–1860* (New York, 1966), pp. 101–10; Potter, 'The Growth of Population in America', pp. 684, 686.
[19] Joel H. Silbey, *The Transformation of American Politics, 1840–1860* (Englewood Cliffs, 1967), pp. 24–5; *Report of the Secretary of the Interior*, House Executive Documents, 39th Congress, 1st Session, (Washington, D.C., 1865), pp. 32–4, 165–7.

virtually so, to settlers in the territories. Such a proposal was vetoed by President Buchanan in 1860, on grounds that were numerous and not unreasonable. Homesteads, it might be objected, could already be obtained cheaply (the price at this time was $1.25 per acre) and a reduction in price would clearly be unfair to various interests, notably settlers who had bought land at the higher price, farmers in the western states where land values might be depressed, and citizens of eastern seaboard states who would be unlikely to participate readily or in significant numbers in such a scheme. In addition, there were objections on the grounds that Congress could invoke no specific constitutional provision for such an arbitrary use of federal resources, and that such a reduction of federal revenues from sales of public lands would coincide with a period (1859–60) when the federal government's finances were shaky, following a fall in customs receipts after the panic of 1857.[20] But, whatever the cogency of the case against free or very cheap homesteads, the demand for a new homestead bill was widely supported in the Midwest by both political parties, and opposition to such legislation was seen to stem from Southern Democrats' unnecessarily restrictive view of federal powers.

Embracing the homestead issue, however, was a far larger, more powerful, ever present, and more urgent concern: the settlement of the western territories. The Midwest, created by migrants, long continued to be a migrant society. Access to land was the basis of a regional society in which 86 per cent of the population lived outside towns. Virtually all of the Midwest had been mere frontier two generations before the 1850s, and Midwesterners continued to believe that their own and their children's prospects for future material improvement depended upon assured access to lands even farther west. So Midwesterners were united by a desire for the federal government to facilitate settlement in the western territories; and even more strongly by a fear that their opportunity for self-advancement would be impeded if slaveowners, with their secure labour supply, flooded into the same territories. Despite the disparagement of the South as an economic backwater in the scornful view of Northern publicists of the 1850s, the logical core of the anti-Southern case (the slaveowners' capacity to compete with Midwesterners) was, ironically, quite flattering to Southerners' ability as agricultural entrepreneurs.

Given this preoccupation with access to land, the Midwest reacted more immediately and directly than the rest of the North to renewed threats of the extension of slavery which emerged in 1854. New England and the Middle Atlantic states responded more slowly to alleged Southern aggression and, for the rest of the decade, tended to be more confused in their domestic political attitudes. But in one respect the antipathy felt by Midwesterners for the South after 1854 was paradoxical, for of all the

[20] For Buchanan's veto message, see Silbey, *The Transformation of American Politics, 1840–1860*, pp. 100–2.

regions in the North, the Midwest most resembled the South in being agrarian in character and overwhelmingly engrossed in the purchase, sale, and exploitation of America's rich endowment in land.

Northern Society

Land, the key commodity in the nineteenth-century North, was clearly the focus of most of its citizens' activities. Did this preoccupation foster any peculiarly Northern social values?

The ready availability of land stimulated the average citizen's belief in the probability that he could enhance his economic position during his own lifetime. Hereditary ownership of vast estates was rare in the North, although it was known in some regions, such as New York's Hudson Valley. Land speculators flourished in the west, but their objective was profitable sale, not estate-building. Western landlords accumulated holdings of 10,000 to 20,000 acres; occasionally great estates were created, such as William Scully's, which eventually amounted to 250,000 acres in the Midwest and Louisiana, and which survived into the twentieth century. But the typical Northern farmer was not a tenant to a great landowner on the European model; he was an owner-operator. In Illinois and Iowa in 1860, for example, between 75 and 90 per cent of farmers, the proportion varying according to locality, were such agrarian businessmen.[21] Their lives were often harsh, monotonous, demanding, and frugally managed, but nurtured a sense of individual worth, autonomy, and achievement.

Wide availability of land encouraged both a sense of stern individualism and a high degree of physical mobility within society. Impatient to succeed, Northerners moved from place to place and from job to job with considerable rapidity. The incidence of business failure among the North's numerous small entrepreneurs and craftsmen was high; but business failure simply spurred men to seek opportunity elsewhere or in a different line of enterprise. Such individualism and fluidity meant that, while the spread of commercialism in the early and middle nineteenth century encouraged a broader sense of community in small towns across the nation, those small towns also lacked strong continuity of population, leadership, or political attitude.[22] Northerners, while certainly

[21] Allan G. Bogue, *From Prairie to Corn Belt. Farming on the Illinois and Iowa Prairies in the Nineteenth Century* (Chicago, 1968 edn), pp. 42–3, 57–66.

[22] Clyde and Sally Griffen, *Natives and Newcomers. The Ordering of Opportunity in Mid-Nineteenth Century Poughkeepsie* (Cambridge, Mass., 1978), pp. 15–18, 50, 104–5, 108; Stephan Thernstrom, *The Other Bostonians. Poverty and Progress in the American Metropolis 1880–1970* (Cambridge, Mass., 1973), pp. 61–6, 233–5; Peter R. Knights, *The Plain People of Boston, 1830–1860: A Study of City Growth* (New York, 1971), ch. 4; Blumin, *The Urban Threshold*, pp. 187–9, 207–9, 212–22. Physical mobility was not a feature only of town life; Western farmers and farm labourers were highly mobile in the 1850s. Bogue, *From Prairie to Corn Belt*, pp. 25–6; Rebecca A. Shepherd, 'Restless Americans: the Geographic Mobility of Farm Laborers in the Old Midwest, 1850–1870', *Ohio History*, 89 (1980), pp. 25–45.

prodigious community-builders, were also energetic disputants. The communities which they founded were frequently rent by party battles, ethnic hostilities and multitudinous denominational disputes. Moreover, towns by their very nature were distrusted and criticized by rural Americans.

A major contradiction therefore existed between the rural reality of the North and the popular image of the North as an urban and industrial contrast to the agrarian South. This contradiction may perhaps be explained by the inequality of wealth in the free states. While Northerners expected American life to offer a rough and ready equality of opportunity, very few of them demanded an equality of distribution or outcome; and material attainments were indeed very unequally shared. In 1860 the wealthiest 10 per cent of all adult male Northerners owned 68 per cent of their section's aggregate wealth, whereas the poorest 70 per cent owned a mere 8 per cent. This glaring inequality partly, though by no means entirely, reflected the age distribution of the population at the time. In 1860 two thirds of Northerners (and of all Americans) were under 30 years of age.[23] American society consisted mainly of young people who were only just embarking on life's typical process of steady material accumulation. Older Northerners could therefore be expected to have become more amply endowed with land, farm stock, houses, and chattels. Even so, and making due allowance for the bias towards youth in the population distribution, the inequalities of wealth remained striking. Equally striking was the fact that the most lucrative careers were urban; successful Northerners were merchants, real-estate agents, urban lawyers, corporation promoters, manufacturers, and bankers.[24] Thus the image projected by the North's favoured, if not always favourite, sons was urban, in sharp contrast to the close association of leading Southerners with plantation agriculture, and in equally sharp contrast to the overwhelmingly rural nature of Northern society.

The social values described and defended as being distinctly Northern by many Northern politicians during the 1850s were doubly misleading. The North did not, despite the claims of these politicians, possess a vastly more egalitarian social structure – among whites – than did the South; nor was the North free of those social inequalities between whites that many Northern publicists ascribed to the existence of a wealthy planter élite, and to the peculiarly Southern disdain for manual labour as being fit only for slaves. The North undoubtedly possessed a darker side. Social mobility in cities and towns was neither rapid nor assured. Men clawed their way up the social ladder rather than leapt ahead; and while there existed a firm belief in the possibility of material improvement, the

[23] Lee Soltow, *Men and Wealth in the United States 1850–1870* (New Haven, 1975), p. 99; Potter, 'The Growth of Population in America', p. 687.
[24] Abner Forbes, *The Rich Men of Massachusetts* (Boston, 1852 edn), p. 233; James H. Madison, 'Businessmen and the Business Community in Indianapolis, 1820–1860' (unpublished Ph.D. dissertation, Indiana University, 1972), p. 216.

accretion of wealth was in fact a rather hit-or-miss affair, with Northern townspeople enjoying perhaps only slightly more than a 50/50 chance of increasing their wealth during any one decade in the nineteenth century. Residential mobility was very high, as the quest for improvement led Northerners from job to job; and the least attractive product of this high mobility was a group of people at the bottom of the Northern social scale, footloose, indigent labourers who drifted from town to town seeking casual employment in small factories or with nearby farmers. Their cheerless and apparently threatening collective presence was recorded in many ante-bellum Northern towns, even if their individual, unsettled, and occasionally unsettling lives have been lost to history. More is known of the urban poor who huddled in ethnic and religious ghettoes. In 1860 foreign-born immigrants accounted for 21 per cent of the population in the Middle Atlantic states, 17 per cent in the Midwest and 15 per cent in New England. Of these, the Irish and Germans, particularly the Catholics among them, were often derided, discriminated against, and denied opportunities available to native Americans.[25]

Yet even if wealth was unequally distributed and poverty in places was acute, opportunity remained appreciably greater than it was in contemporary Europe, and the enormous expanses of land to the west offered the promise of individual economic improvement in the future. As Horace Greeley, editor of a leading New York City reformist newspaper, periodically reminded the metropolitan poor: 'Go West, young man!'

The pressures and aspirations of a youthful population could be satisfied, and the antagonisms between ethnic groups resolved, only if economic opportunity, based on fast economic growth, continued to be available in the future as it had been, or had been perceived to be, in the past. Opportunity and growth, which had enabled America to cope with the expansion of its population from three million in 1790 to 31 million in 1860, were, however, dependent upon (and extremely wasteful of) the supply of land. Because the prolific availability of land was the central fact of economic life to nineteenth-century Northerners, the question of future settlement in the west acquired momentous real and symbolic importance; it was not surprising that Northerners' access to the western territories became the leading federal issue during the 1850s.

[25] Blumin, *Urban Threshold*, pp. 90–102; Griffens, *Natives and Newcomers*, pp. 39–43, 50–72, 84–108, 137–8.

4 The South

The South as a Section

In November 1861 Karl Marx noted: ' "The South" . . . is neither a territory strictly detached from the North geographically, nor a moral unity. It is not a country at all, but a battle slogan'.[1] Like many terms used by historians, 'the South' is a broad generalization which, confusingly, denotes different phenomena at different times. Customarily, however, it is used in three crucial senses.

First, it designates the area in which slavery was legally permitted in the nineteenth century. The legalization of slavery had been a matter left entirely to the individual states to decide for themselves; for most of the eighteenth century slavery had been condoned throughout the American colonies, but had been abolished in the northern states in the last quarter of the century, starting with Vermont in 1777. Emancipation marked a revolution in European racial thinking: revulsion against enslavement was a departure in the treatment of African peoples hitherto regarded as both morally and biologically inferior. But since so radical a process took place gradually, some slaves remained in seven of the eleven free states as late as 1820, though they were numerically significant in only two of them.[2] Moreover, the abolitionist impulse – especially inspired by Quakers and other evangelical Protestants – did not entirely capture Northerners' political imagination; from the 1790s to the 1830s there was little concerted Northern criticism of Southern slavery, and in 1818 the new state of Illinois (in the old North-West) actually came very close to permitting slavery in its constitution.

After 1818, however, slavery was generally confined to the states south of Pennsylvania and the Ohio River. Geographical demarcation was strengthened in 1820 by the Missouri Compromise, in which Congress declared that slavery should never spread north of latitude 36°30' in the federal territories. Strictly speaking, therefore, the South, as a region corresponding with the area where slave ownership was condoned by law,

---

[1] Karl Marx and Frederick Engels, *The Civil War in the United States* (New York, 1961), p. 72.

[2] The best account of this process is: David B. Davis, *The Problem of Slavery in the Age of Revolution, 1770–1823* (Ithaca, 1975); Louis Filler, *The Crusade Against Slavery, 1830–1860* (New York, 1963 edn), p. 13.

began to have meaning only in the late eighteenth century, and acquired real force only in 1818–20.

Even so, by the 1850s the westward extension of slavery meant that Missouri, Arkansas, and Texas had been added to the 'South'; yet these states had strong economic ties with other, more northerly, Western states and possessed many of the social and economic characteristics of Western rather than Southern states. What they shared with the other Southern states was, of course, an appreciable stake in slave-ownership; and, in relation to this common interest, the expression 'the South' became an emotive and frequently used slogan in politics from the 1830s. The rights of the South to slave ownership were to be vigilantly guarded against all Northern criticism or attack either implicit or explicit, and were to be guaranteed by ensuring that slavery could expand into the western territories. The emphasis on Southern rights developed into a standard component in slave-state politics, particularly when public interest in federal affairs increased tremendously in the 1830s; federal election campaigning then began to include exaggerated promises to defend the South's special interest in slavery. In 1828 and 1832 Andrew Jackson's party (soon called the Democrats) totally dominated the presidential elections in the slave states. But in 1834–5 when the Democrats seemed unlikely to nominate another slaveholder for the presidency, an opposition arose in the South denouncing the Democrats as insufficiently Southern.[3]

Secondly, 'the South' took on a wider meaning in the 1850s as Northern publicists enlarged the scope of their attack on the slave-owning region. No longer did the South simply represent a collection of states allowing slavery. Increasingly, the South was criticized as essentially un-American, a section where economic opportunity was not widely available to ordinary citizens, where a rigid social order stretching downwards from baronial plantation-owners flourished on the sorry basis of slave-holding, and where the rapid and diverse economic growth typical of the rest of America was not achieved.[4]

The extent of the South's economic backwardness has long divided historians, just as it divided contemporaries. At one extreme, it has even been argued that Southern plantation agriculture was more efficient than the Northern yeoman agriculture of the 1850s.[5] In a more widely accepted view, North and South are said to display respectively the contrast between economic growth (increasing economic diversity and industrialization) and economic expansion (more and more of the same).

[3] William J. Cooper, Jr, *The South and the Politics of Slavery, 1828–1856* (Baton Rouge, 1978), chs. 1–3.

[4] Richard H. Sewell, *Ballots for Freedom: Antislavery Politics in the United States, 1837–1860* (New York, 1976), pp. 101–6; Eric Foner, *Free Soil, Free Labor, Free Men. The Ideology of the Republican Party before the Civil War* (New York, 1970), ch. 2. There were earlier precedents for this line of analysis, Davis, *The Problem of Slavery*, p. 339.

[5] Robert W. Fogel and Stanley L. Engerman, *Time on the Cross. The Economics of American Negro Slavery* (London, 1974), i, pp. 191–209, 247–57.

Even when the Southern economy expanded and the slaveowners made considerable profits, this expansion and profitability contributed nothing to future growth and to the diffusion of economic benefits throughout white — let alone black — society. In this essential respect, not in its potential ability to expand and to generate wealth, the South differed profoundly in economic character from the North.

Such a description is more convincing than the claim that Southern agriculture was more efficient than that in the North, but its validity depends heavily on an unprovable premise: that specialization in cotton distorted the economy and rendered it incapable of adjusting to changed patterns of world demand for raw cotton.[6] This premise is difficult to prove because when cotton declined as a highly profitable primary crop between 1860 and 1890, the South was no longer a society amenable to the sort of economic *dirigisme* possible under slavery. A whole cluster of circumstances — not simply the habit of cotton culture — following the Civil War and emancipation turned the South into a semi-peasant agrarian order, with all its attendant sluggishness, unresponsiveness, and relative poverty.

Finally, the South signifies the political entity created in 1861. Yet the Confederate States of America included only 11 of the 15 slave states and 2 of these — Virginia and Tennessee — were deeply divided over their adherence to the rebel cause. Moreover, during the war itself, Southern loyalty was sometimes qualified by state pride and selfishness. And when the war began to drag on after 1861, much disaffection with the war effort spread within the Confederacy, notably in non-slave-owning areas.[7] Once the war ended, however, such internal questionings and hesitations were banished by nostalgia for the Lost Cause and patriotic veneration for the Old South.

The South of the 1850s was divided politically into states, geographically and in terms of slave ownership into three broad belts, and economically into smaller sub-regions. The political division was obvious and important; state pride was intense before the war, when attempts to foster Southern unity almost invariably failed outside Congress or national party nominating conventions. Eager Southern separatists initiated exclusively Southern commercial conventions; but these had lost support by the late 1850s, and even when they were relatively successful earlier in the decade, they tended to attract large delegations only from the states in which they were variously convened.[8] The belief entertained by many Southern separatists that a Southern union could be created only by

[6] Gavin Wright, *The Political Economy of the Cotton South. Households, Markets, and Wealth in the Nineteenth Century* (New York, 1978), esp. chs. 4,6.
[7] Frank L. Owsley, *State Rights in the Confederacy* (Chicago, 1925); Robert L. Kerby, *Kirby Smith's Confederacy: The Trans-Mississippi South, 1863–1865* (New York, 1972); David D. Scarboro, 'North Carolina and the Confederacy: The Weakness of States' Rights during the Civil War', *North Carolina Historical Review*, LVI (1979), pp. 133–49.
[8] Robert R. Russel, *Economic Aspects of Southern Sectionalism, 1840–1861* (Urbana, Ill., 1924), pp. 123–50.

co-operative action among the slave states never came to fruition: the Confederacy was formed by chain-reaction as successive states seceded.

A broad geographical division of the South into three tiers reflects some central social realities and is also useful in illuminating Southern politics, provided that we take due account of economic sub-regions. The three major regions − the border states, the Upper South, and the Deep South − in 1860 contained 12 million people, of whom 4 million were slaves. Some free blacks lived in the South, as in the North, but everywhere their social and political status was degraded.

The border region − Delaware, Maryland, Kentucky, and Missouri − had 2,710,000 whites and 430,000 slaves. It possessed three major cities − Baltimore in Maryland, Louisville in Kentucky, and St Louis in Missouri − all of which were ports and manufacturing centres. Baltimore and St Louis experienced the same social tensions and occasional disorder aroused by ethnic differences and the obtrusive presence of numerous immigrants as did the cities of the North. Throughout the 1850s the four border states enjoyed vigorous and evenly balanced party politics with no single party attaining easy ascendancy. None of these states seceded from the Union in 1860−1, and one possible reason for their continued faith in it was their full and constant experience of the possibility of political change. Accustomed to genuine and effective two-party competition − as the Deep South in the 1850s was not − the border states perhaps regarded the Republican victory in the presidential election of 1860 as a less irreversible political development than did Democrats in the Deep South, who became in the 1850s increasingly unfamiliar with the regular ebb and flow of party fortunes.[9] Similarly, although the border states would have been the first to be affected by the spread of abolitionism from the North, they had the smallest economic commitment to slavery of any broad area of the South and the least substantial potential black threat to white numerical dominance. This is not to say that the border states possessed internal unity or consciousness. They were simply less committed to slavery and to support of the Southern Democratic party, and more northward-looking, than any other area of the South.

The second broad division of the South − Virginia, North Carolina, Tennessee, and Arkansas, making up the Upper South − was much more strikingly subdivided by geography than the border states. This region stretched from America's first permanent settlement at Jamestown to the most recent frontier in Arkansas. The states themselves displayed pronounced local contrasts. The plantation belts of coastal Virginia and North Carolina, and of the Mississippi valley in Tennessee and Arkansas, differed considerably in economic pursuits and social habits from the back-country of these states, which was in places very mountainous and

---

[9] Michael F. Holt, *The Political Crisis of the 1850s* (New York, 1978), pp. 229–37, 248–56.

distinctly impoverished. The region as a whole contained no major city, and was more firmly committed to slavery than were the border states; there were 2,925,000 whites and 1,210,000 slaves in the Upper South in 1860. Divergent economic interests, efforts to promote better communications, and perhaps the varying distribution of slave ownership encouraged a vigorous political life for most of the 1840s and 1850s. Party competition, while not as lively as in the border states in the late 1850s, was certainly more active in the Upper than in the Deep South.

The stereotyped image of the ante-bellum Deep South depicts a region carved up into extensive estates whose opulent, cultured owners controlled politics through their domination of a single party lodged firmly in power. Poorer whites deferred to the plantation-owning élite, and despite that élite's lack of attention to their material and educational needs, these poorer whites failed to support any party other than the entrenched Democrats. This political acquiescence stemmed from the poorer whites' desire for proper social control of the blacks. Without slavery and the plantation order, the blacks would compete with them for jobs and would become generally rowdy, socially disruptive, and sexually self-indulgent at white women's expense. The rule of the planters was accepted, and the Democratic party, which the planter class depicted as representing Southern interests and Southern patriotism, was supported, because of the poorer whites' craving for security.[10] This model of a stratified society bound together by common racial fears had a good deal of plausibility to it, but its description of agriculture, distribution of wealth, class differences, and political power is open to severe qualification.

The Deep South in 1860 stretched in an arc at least 1,000 miles long from the Atlantic coast to the brash frontiers of Texas. It comprised the seven states — South Carolina, Georgia, Florida, Alabama, Mississippi, Louisiana, and Texas — that joined together to form the initial Confederacy in February 1861. In 1860 the Deep South's 2,580,000 white inhabitants only just outnumbered its 2,310,000 slaves, while in South Carolina the 301,000 whites were in a distinct minority against 402,000 slaves. It is little wonder that fears of a drift to emancipation were so intense and that South Carolina led the secessionist stampede.

White society in *parts* of the Deep South had certain distinctive characteristics, very boldly presented in South Carolina. The coastal region of this state consisted of substantial estates handed down from generation to generation whose owners distributed state legislative seats heavily in favour of their own region. The planters of South Carolina maintained the most reactionary political system in nineteenth-century America; the state legislature, dominated by the planters, chose virtually

---

[10] See, for example: Eugene D. Genovese, *The Political Economy of Slavery* (New York, 1965), chs. 1, 10; Frederick Law Olmsted, *The Cotton Kingdom. A Selection*, ed. by David F. Hawke (Indianapolis, 1971), pp. 191–2.

all state officials from the governor down to the local road commissioners, and cast the state's presidential vote. Only very rich planters held the highest public offices.[11] The members of the planter élite often and rather self-consciously aspired to aristocratic status. Yet despite their well-developed sense of lordly dignity, their solemn claims to Cavalier ancestry, and their robust and assertive notion of honour, the great planters possessed somewhat circumscribed power and prestige. They were obliged to ally themselves politically with up-country interests. Their conspicuous consumption was modest by European aristocratic standards. Country houses were ornate but not palatial in size or furnishing. The scene of their elaborate, ritualized social round and of most summer residences, Charleston, was a picturesque town, but moderate in size (40,522 people in 1860)[12] and fulfilled a whole range of business functions; Charleston's Broad Street, with its banks and lawyers' offices, was the Wall Street of the coastal plantation strip. However much they hankered for independence, Southern planters were forced into daily compromises with a national political party – the Democrats – and with Northern and British financial and trading interests. This contrast between the aristocratic self-image of aloofness and independence and murkier mundane realities was much resented.

But South Carolina was no microcosm of the Deep South. In 1819, for example, Alabama's planter élite drew up the most liberal state constitution of that time, and thereby opened the way to truly democratic politics. Texas and Mississippi were also highly democratic states.[13] The south-west generally – Alabama, Mississippi, Louisiana, and Texas – was far less socially stratified than South Carolina. Although individual planters in these states may have been scions of eminent planter families in the older states of the Atlantic seaboard, most of them were probably self-made men, and many were ruthless entrepreneurs.[14] Slave ownership in itself obviously bred more autocratic habits in affluent whites than were to be found in the Northern rich. But slave ownership, like land-owning, was not open merely to the few in the ante-bellum South, nor did it concentrate wealth exclusively and disproportionately – by comparison with the North – in the hands of an élite.

[11] Ralph A. Wooster, *Politicians, Planters and Plain Folk. Courthouse and Statehouse in the Upper South, 1850–1860* (Knoxville, Tenn., 1975), p. 126; *The People in Power. Courthouse and Statehouse in the Lower South, 1850–1860* (Knoxville, Tenn., 1969), p. 55.
[12] *Population of the United States in 1860; Compiled from the Original Returns of the Eighth Census* (Washington, D.C., 1864), p. 452.
[13] Duncan J. MacLeod, *Slavery, Race and the American Revolution* (Cambridge, 1974), p. 73; J. Mills Thornton, III, *Politics and Power in a Slave Society: Alabama, 1800–1860* (Baton Rouge, 1978), pp. 13–14. Roger W. Shugg, *Origins of Class Struggle in Louisiana* (Baton Rouge, 1939) argues that the planter élite ignored the poorer masses' needs, but fails to show that the poorer classes pressed for benefits from the slaverholders in power: Wright, *Political Economy of the Cotton South*, p. 41 (n. 43).
[14] Willie Lee Rose (ed.), *A Documentary History of Slavery in North America* (New York, 1976), pp. 155–6, 291.

Any Southerner who accumulated savings — a striving farmer, a successful lawyer, or a prosperous merchant — bought slaves as sound investments, useful guaranteed labour, visible signs of material affluence, or invaluable domestic servants. Just as middle-class Northerners enlisted Irish immigrant girls or free blacks as household servants — domestic service being the fourth most important occupation in the North in 1860 — so both urban and rural middle-class Southerners purchased slaves. Poorer Southerners generally accepted this system as a way of controlling the loathed blacks; and they aspired themselves to owning more land and a slave or two. Such hopes were not fanciful. In 1860, 19 per cent of Southern adult white males owned slaves, and given the youthfulness of the American population at the time, this figure signified a wide distribution of human chattels. Moreover, the general distribution of wealth among white Southerners, precisely resembled that amongst Northerners if slaves are counted as property, as indeed they were in the 1850s. The vast majority of Southern whites, who owned no slaves, corresponded closely to the poorest 70 per cent of Northern adult males, who owned only 8 per cent of Northern wealth.[15] By the standards of nineteenth-century Europe, however, the opportunities throughout the country for acquiring land and then achieving affluence through slave ownership (in the South) or employing workers and investing in company stocks and bonds (in the North) were impressive indeed. For the Southern white population, slave ownership did not distort the general pattern of opportunity or the distribution of wealth prevailing in the 1850s. Perhaps 65 per cent of Southern whites owned their farms: a proportion lower (but not vastly so) than that in the Midwest. One need not romanticize the position of these plain folk to say that tangible rewards for agricultural effort were widely available in the ante-bellum South. Furthermore, about the same proportion of the white labour force (65–70 per cent) was engaged in the basic occupations of farming, labouring, and domestic service in, for example, the Southern states of Missouri, Virginia, Tennessee, and Georgia as in the populous Midwestern states of Ohio, Illinois, and Indiana.[16] Of course, because the

[15] Otto H. Olsen, 'Historians and the Extent of Slave Ownership in the Southern United States', *Civil War History*, XVIII (1972), pp. 101–16; Lee Soltow, *Men and Wealth in the United States, 1850–1870* (New Haven, 1975), pp. 99–101. Comparing the Northern distribution of wealth with the Southern distribution is fraught with difficulties. Comparison between the distribution of agricultural wealth in the two sections distorts the picture since Northern wealth tended to be more urban than was Southern wealth. If Southern slaves are counted as people, then the mal-distribution of Southern wealth becomes very striking. I have taken figures for total wealth in both sections and counted the slaves as chattels: that, after all, is how they were used in the mid nineteenth century. But for a different approach, see Wright, *The Political Economy of the Cotton South*, pp. 25–7, 37–40.

[16] The basic information on occupations by state is tabulated in *Population of the United States in 1860*, pp. 656–80. For farm-ownership in the South, see Fabian Linden, 'Economic Democracy in the Slave South,' *Journal of Negro History*, XXXI (1946), pp 140–89, esp. 143–4.

overwhelming bulk of the slaves were also employed in these occupations, the South was more agricultural in economic character than even the Midwest; but for Southern *whites* alone the opportunities available seemed remarkably similar to those offered in the great farming regions of the North.

What of the élite? The Southern upper class was perhaps more visible and politically aggressive than the corresponding Northern upper class, but it was no more exclusive or socially and politically united. The Southern pyramid of slave ownership was broad-based and not very high in relation to its breadth. In 1860 there were 1,470,000 white families in the slave states; 150,000 people owned between 5 and 19 slaves, and 48,000 planters held 20 or more. A few of these possessed over 500 slaves, and a mere handful had as many as a thousand. Thus within the planter class there were no great magnates corresponding to the thousand or so Russians of the 1850s who each held more than 1,000 serfs, or even to leading British textile manufacturers, some of whom employed as many as 5,000 or 6,000 workers.[17]

We do not know very much about social connections within the planter class, but access to it appears generally to have depended only on suitable financial credentials.[18] The great planters' wealth, position, and prestige were much resented by poorer whites, but the riches, power, and social predominance of Northern metropolitan lawyers and financiers was similarly resented by ordinary Northern labourers, farmers, artisans, and small businessmen. In neither section was such resentment strident enough to activate class politics. Southern planters certainly failed to act politically as a single class, divided as they were between Whigs and Democrats. Nor were they responsible for all Southern shortcomings. To take one example, the educational backwardness of the South seems to have been aggravated by the strenuous and continuous resistance to state and local government spending on education put up by representatives from the poorer areas of the South; frugal government was the highest end of statesmanship to poorer Southern whites.[19]

Geographical segregation between different classes of white was somewhat limited. The most fertile stretches of river valley indeed tended to support the very largest plantations; slaves in such areas sometimes constituted 70 to 90 per cent of the population. At the opposite extreme, wide stretches of infertile or heavily wooded country were inhabited by poorer pastoralists; although such people disliked the planters, they also

---

[17] John Vincent, *The Formation of the British Liberal Party 1857–1868* (London, 1972), p. 76; Richard Pipes, *Russia Under the Old Régime* (London, 1977), p. 178.

[18] There are no detailed studies of local communities in the slave South comparable to a number of sophisticated modern monographs on Northern towns in the mid nineteenth century. We can safely say, however, that the slaveowners did not form a political oligarchy in the sense used by Marx in 1861: Marx and Engels, *Civil War in the United States*, pp. 68–71.

[19] Thornton, *Politics and Power in a Slave Society*, pp. 83, 87–9, 115–16, 299–304.

despised the blacks, and so acquiesced — albeit ambiguously — in the prevailing social order.[20] But most Southerners lived in socially more mixed areas, where owners of widely different holdings in land and slaves co-existed. It is difficult to detect in these broad sub-regions (though detailed research may further illuminate such relationships) any sharp social divisions or any class politics. This was probably because differences in wealth were not translated into stark distinctions of social class, and because political office was open to all manner of modestly affluent white men.

Political office was not monopolized by the planters, even in the Deep South. Of all state legislators in 1860, 54–76 per cent were slaveowners in six states of the Deep South, and 82 per cent were slaveowners in the seventh state, South Carolina. But only 18–29 per cent of legislators were planters (owners of 20 or more slaves) in four states, and 41–55 per cent were planters in three; the only state legislature in which a majority of representatives were planters was South Carolina. Beyond South Carolina, the great planters did not necessarily dominate even the highest reaches of office. For example, of Georgia's four governors in the 1850s, one was a middling planter, but the others owned only 11, 7, and 5 slaves respectively, evidence of prosperity and substance but not lordly splendour. Outside the Deep South in 1860, planters provided more than 20 per cent of legislators in only two states. Moreover, those elected to office did not sit comfortably entrenched in power. Throughout the South — as throughout the North — state legislators customarily served no more than two terms of usually two years each. In Arkansas between 1835 and 1861, only 6 per cent of members of the state's lower house served more than one term; in Virginia between 1849 and 1861 only 18.3 per cent of those in the House of Delegates served more than two terms. The well-connected lawyer-planters undoubtedly grasped a disproportionately high share of state and federal offices, but the social group they belonged to was relatively large and open throughout the antebellum South. And the political system they helped manage was distinctly middle-class in character: a band of self-important, often boisterous, middling farmers and lawyers each with a handful of slaves crowded in and out of political office; and conflicts within the states — even in the Deep South — often reflected regional quests for economic advantage or poorer areas' objections to costly schemes of state government action.[21]

One obvious political distinction was that the Deep South was very markedly Democratic. South Carolina was little more than an oligarchic backwater, and in Texas political competition was largely a matter of rivalries and tensions within the Democratic party. In Alabama, the Democrats throughout the 1850s won more than 55 per cent of the vote in

[20] Frank L. Owsley, *Plain Folk of the Old South* (Chicago, 1949), chs. 2 and 5.
[21] Wooster, *Politicians, Planters and Plain Folk*, pp. 42–4; *The People in Power*, pp. 33, 39–42, 55–60; Thornton, *Politics and Power in a Slave Society*.

presidential and gubernatorial elections. In Georgia, in Mississippi, until 1855, in Florida and in Louisiana, until 1856, the opposition sometimes secured over 45 per cent of the vote; but only in certain parts of these states did party competition remain relatively buoyant throughout the 1850s.[22]

Why the Democratic party prevailed over its opponents so readily throughout most of the Deep South is far from clear. The heartlands of Democratic popular strength were often the poorer back-country areas where Jackson's appeal in the 1830s had been to the yeoman farmers and poorer whites. The Democracy had been the faith of proud, assertive, ordinary rustics. It was not simply the planters' creed; in 1843 the future wife of Jefferson Davis described him in amazement; 'Would you believe it, he is refined and cultivated and yet he is a Democrat'.[23] In the 1840s and early 1850s, however, the Democrats enlarged their appeal by identifying themselves as the special defenders of Southern rights in the nation, and as the opposition to Northern financial and commercial power centred in New York City and expressed in legislative schemes at Washington.[24]

On all counts, then — the rich plantation agriculture, concentrations of slave ownership, a powerful class of planters, and one-party politics — the Deep South corresponded to the stereotype already described far more closely than did the other broad regions of the slave states. But on all counts, also, the extent of so-called Southern-ness can be exaggerated. The planters did not form an exclusive social class and did not control politics as an oligarchic club; one-party politics were not universal in the Deep South and did not stem from the planters' political control. Most importantly, the ownership of land and slaves was widely distributed amongst the population, and wealth was perhaps no more narrowly concentrated among whites in the South than it was in the North. Opportunity for economic advance was available to ordinary white Southerners, just as to Northerners. The key to opportunity was the acquisition of land and slaves.

---

[22] *Congressional Quarterly's Guide to U.S. Elections* (Washington, D.C., 1975), pp. 269–71, 397, 403–4, 416.

[23] Clement Eaton, *Jefferson Davis* (New York, 1977), p. 24. For changes in the Democrats' support see Thornton, *Politics and Power in a Slave Society*, and Holt, *Political Crisis of the 1850s*.

[24] It used to be argued that the Southern movement of the 1850s was deeply inspired by states' rights ideas. This point is well made, for example, in Dwight L. Dumond, *The Secession Movement, 1860–1861* (New York, 1931), ch. 1. Later historians have tended, however, to see states' rights doctrine as a convenient rhetorical device, used by Southerners in the 1850s as a respectable constitutional formula to cover their main concern: the defence of slavery. Yet an understanding of why the Democrats and not the Whigs emerged as the leading party in the South during the early 1850s, at a time when *both* parties in the South defended slavery and 'Southern rights', perhaps requires some consideration of the greater plausibility, for the South, of the Democrats' traditional rhetoric in favour of a pluralistic Union and against major concentrations of financial and economic power.

Southern Ideology

Increasingly important differences between North and South were apparent in the attitudes, aspirations, and economic pursuits of the top people in each section. In the South, the rich and the powerful were planters by birth or by purchase, whereas the wealthiest and most influential men of the North tended to be urban lawyers, bankers, and entrepreneurs. In contemplating the general direction of nineteenth-century social and economic change, the South's leaders, spokesmen, and intellectuals naturally appeared conservative, even reactionary, by comparison with leading Northern politicians and publicists, eager for urbanization and industrialization. Secondly, Southerners regarded slavery as a positive element in their bustling, expanding, and profitable economic order, while Northerners in growing numbers looked on the presence of blacks with disfavour and on slavery as immoral, or at least as threatening to white labour in the western territories.

Poorer whites accepted the prevalent distribution of wealth and status — such as it was — partly because they hoped to rise in the farming hierarchy, but also because the existing order reinforced their belief in themselves as infinitely superior to the one third of Southerners who were black. Under abolitionist attack from the 1830s onwards, Southerners increasingly united in a comprehensive defence of slavery.

Slavery — and fears of any racial adjustment or increased restlessness among slaves — united Southerners and created a sectional consciousness as nothing else could have done. The vigorous Southern reaction to the abolitionism of the 1830s dismayed Northern gradualists, who hoped that slavery would one day cease to exist. Until the 1820s slavery had commonly been justified as a necessary evil that would end naturally at some date in the future, but after the 1830s the apologetic tone disappeared entirely from Southern pro-slavery rhetoric. As Dr Johnson said, 'Where there is yet shame, there may in time be virtue'.[25] Not only did the sense of shame about slavery decline; slavery's defence was conducted with all the scientific and scholarly skills that the Southern upper and middle classes, intent on rational self-justification, could supply.

Southern intellectuals and scientists in the 1840s and 1850s toiled to produce evidence for black inferiority. Anthropologists and medical doctors exploited the phrenological craze then current in attempts to show that the black man's brain was peculiarly small. They also argued that blacks suffered congenitally from certain psychological and physiological afflictions that rendered them incapable of voluntary application to work. Complex physiological explanations were offered for the slaves' habit of running away (a disease described as 'drapetomania') and for

[25] *Johnson's Journey to the Western Islands of Scotland and Boswell's Journal of a Tour to the Hebrides with Samuel Johnson, LL.D.*, ed. by R.W. Chapman (Oxford, 1970 ed.), p. 6.

their natural propensity to rascality (the well-known disease 'dysaesthesia Aethiopica'). Scientists variously asserted that the blacks belonged either to a different animal species from Europeans, or to a distinctly lesser sub-species; this issue was a matter for heated scientific controversy. Biblical and classical scholars meanwhile contributed to this thorough defence of slavery by providing plentiful precedents for the enslavement of black by white.[26] The unhappy paradox arose in the South that the spread of education and scientific learning in the early and mid nineteenth century merely strengthened support for slavery.

Very few nineteenth-century Northerners would have quibbled with the proposition that blacks were inferior to whites, although Northerners rarely carried the analysis and description of this inferiority to the extremes reached by their Southern compatriots. The difference between Northerners and Southerners in fact was the difference between believing that blacks were inferior and contemptible, and believing that they were so inferior, contemptible, and potentially dangerous that they had to be enslaved. Southerners emphasized the inherent bestiality of blacks to support the argument that blacks posed what might be termed an innocent threat: innocent, that is, in that they self-consciously pre-meditated no evil, but threatening in that they were by nature lascivious, violent, and uncontrollable. The justification of slavery lay in containing this threat, while also Christianizing pagan Africans and setting a naturally lazy people to fruitful labour. In this last respect, slave-owners persuaded themselves that they were answering the highest call to moral stewardship, for, in the Calvinist perspective so pervasive in nineteenth-century America, the provision of honest work and the dispelling of idle habits was a vital Christian duty. To reinforce this aspect of their defence of slavery, Southern writers pointed to the deplorable economic consequences of black emancipation in the Haitian Republic and the British West Indies: where blacks were free, they refused to labour.

Harsh moral stewardship was seasoned by paternalistic benevolence. Slaveowners justified their position — or had it justified for them by Southern intellectuals — as one promoting both the religious salvation and the material comfort of the slaves. Slaveowners furnished adequate, indeed in their own eyes generous, housing and clothing, medical care, food and sustenance in old age to people who would be wantonly lazy and self-indulgent if left to their own devices. Many wealthy planters, by encouraging the development of this paternalistic ethos and by adopting in their private lives an exaggeratedly aristocratic pose, projected a public image very different from that developed by the upper classes in the Northern states. It was perhaps ironic that much of the moral impulse behind such benevolent paternalism came from the same Calvinist

[26] William S. Jenkins, *Pro-Slavery Thought in the Old South* (Chapel Hill, 1935), chs. 2, 5, 6; J.D.B. De Bow, *The Industrial Resources of the Southern and Western States* (3 vols.: New Orleans, 1852–3), I, pp. 322–3.

religious sentiment that inspired many of the South's most active Northern enemies.[27]

It is relatively simple to detect the central ideological difference between North and South in regard to slavery. But when and why that difference became urgent, all-embracing, and politically vital is a far more difficult matter to define.

Up to 1820 North and South were not sharply distinguished by their contrasting attitudes to slavery. Many Northerners believed that a gradual scheme of abolition would be set in train by the ending of the overseas slave trade in 1807; many believed that abolition would be socially acceptable if freed slaves were sent out of the USA, an idea pressed by the American Colonization Society from its establishment in 1816, first put into practice in 1820, and given a further boost with the founding of Liberia in 1822. But these beliefs were partly based upon a delusion exposed in 1819–20 during the Missouri crisis. Many Northerners had assumed that the soul-searching over slavery that had occurred in the Upper South in the 1780s would continue and grow. Instead the South became more *united* in defence of slavery by 1820. The slave rising in 1791 in St Domingue, leading to the creation of the black republic of Haiti in 1804, intensified and multiplied earlier fears of slave rebelliousness. The economic boom of the 1810s and the phenomenal spread of cotton cultivation and the plantation system after the War of 1812 reinforced the whole South's economic stake in slavery. By 1820 racial prejudice had hardened against the blacks. Free blacks were more systematically constrained than they had been in the South before the 1790s. Courts throughout the South became much tougher during the 1810s and 1820s in their treatment of blacks petitioning for freedom on the grounds of distant and partial white ancestry. Scattered foundations had been laid for the later scientific argument for blacks' innate and complete inferiority. Most importantly, earlier doubts about the moral acceptability of slaveholding were fast receding. One Southern politician informed Congress in 1806: 'A large majority of the people in the Southern States do not consider slavery as even an evil'. When an attempt was made in 1819 to block the possible extension of slavery into the new state of Missouri, even the Upper South – and notably Virginia '– vehemently refused to countenance such an infringement of Southern rights. Already in 1818, a Southern senator had provided a foretaste of the coming era by emphasizing the benefits of slavery to the complete exclusion of any evils inherent in the institution. The congressional struggle over the admission of Missouri as a slave state stiffened such attitudes and revealed to the North a South firmly committed to the full

---

[27] Eugene D. Genovese, *The World the Slaveholders Made* (New York, 1969), part 2; *Roll, Jordan, Roll. The World the Slaves Made* (London, 1975); Drew G. Faust, *A Sacred Circle. The Dilemma of the Intellectual in the Old South, 1840–1860* (Baltimore, 1977).

protection and extension of slavery.[28]

Even so, with the admission of Missouri as a slave state in 1821 and with the creation of a national party system in the 1830s, sectional differences were at least contained for another 20 years. Indeed, in the early 1840s an intense economic depression pushed economic issues to the forefront of political debate and lessened the importance of sectional consciousness. However much North and South were seen to be different sections in the 1830s, those differences were actively and successfully suppressed or camouflaged by party politicians. Abolitionists' meetings in the North were riotously disrupted in 1835–7, and Northern Democrats in particular worked hard to keep slavery questions out of politics. The political defence of slavery provoked many Northerners' anger: especially at interferences with personal liberty, when Congress prevented debate on abolitionist petitions from 1836 to 1844 and when the Supreme Court in 1842 strengthened the legal position against fugitive slaves. But Northerners' antagonism against the South did not burst into widespread sectional attacks until the institution of slavery became intertwined with western extension in 1844–8.[29] The quest for western lands exacerbated North–South rivalry because both North and South were expansive agricultural economies in which white social mobility depended upon land speculation and rural enterprise.

Cheaper lands and consequent economic opportunity were widely desired by the South's poorer farmers, who moved to the south-west in large numbers in the 30 years before the Civil War. Such mobility meant that, as early as the 1830s, the white population of some Atlantic seaboard states was growing at a relatively low rate. But eastern stagnation was outweighed by western effervescence and expansion in the slave states. The Northern traveller and writer Frederick Law Olmsted noted the constant trekking of poorer, land-hungry farmers through the back-country of Louisiana and Texas during the 1850s.[30] The durability of white society, in the South as in the North, depended on social mobility: and social mobility very often depended (or was thought to depend) upon geographical mobility.

An appetite for land, shared by all Americans, underlay the political crises of the 1840s and 1850s. The long-term need for *lebensraum* encouraged Southern politicians to look increasingly to Mexico, to Cuba, and to the territories of Kansas and Nebraska for areas into which slaveowners could move. No immediate pressure for land existed in the South, and most of the area under dispute between North and South was

[28] MacLeod, *Slavery, Race and the American Revolution*, pp. 12, 36, 152–4, 158, 40–1, 162–3, 113, 117–19, 180, 46–7, 60, 104; Davis, *The Problem of Slavery*, pp. 336, 340–2; Filler, *Crusade Against Slavery*, p. 20.

[29] Cooper, *The South and the Politics of Slavery*, chs. 5, 6; Filler, *Crusade Against Slavery*, pp. 64, 72, 76–80, 90, 99, 102–3, 166, 169–72.

[30] Olmsted, *Cotton Kingdom*, pp. 141–3, 145–6, 149. The political consequences of heavy demand for land are well discussed in William L. Barney, *The Secessionist Impulse. Alabama and Mississippi in 1860* (Princeton, 1974).

unsuitable for plantation agriculture. But the need to keep wide areas open for potential settlement by Southern small farmers, possessing perhaps a few slaves, assumed immense symbolic importance to a Southern, white, agrarian electorate as young, as mobile, and as aspiring as its Northern counterpart. Because America in the 1850s was a society of young people, and because that society had spread so rapidly and widely within two generations, discussion of the future fate of the western territories, seemingly so legalistic, recondite, and irrelevant to practical needs in the mid nineteenth century, disturbed and challenged deeply-held hopes and assumptions; political disputes over the western territories touched the very nerve-centres of American society.

The quest for new lands became closely intertwined in the 1840s and 1850s with Southerners' full assertion of constitutional rights. Between 1844 and 1854 Southerners pressed so hard and so persistently for their right to extend slavery — and for their right not to be condemned for slaveownership — that in 1854–6 a purely Northern anti-slavery extension party was established in reaction to Southern truculence. After that, sectional consciousness took firmer shape and sectional conflict seemed genuinely possible.

Despite contrasts and divisions within the South, two of the three basic meanings of 'the South' had come into prominent political play by the mid 1850s. By 1856 a majority of Northerners wanted the South to remain the *only* area in which slavery would be permitted in America. And this increasing Northern determination to hedge in slavery partially stemmed from a heightened Northern feeling that the South was economically backward, and socially and culturally deviant from the American norm. Yet Southerners, in turn, took up the 'battle slogan', the South, more frequently during the 1850s because they saw themselves as fighting for their typically American rights of gaining access to western lands and of being properly esteemed and respected as full citizens by their fellow countrymen in the North.[31] Their 'battle slogan' thus encapsulated, in varying degrees, the defence of a racist order, the protection of economic opportunity, the maintenance of constitutional rights, and the struggle for national approval. Starting life as a somewhat vague description of a heterogeneous section, 'the South' by the mid 1850s bore an increasingly onerous emotional and political weight. Southern-ness acquired this burden from the territorial expansion and Northern anti-slavery sentiment of the 1840s.

[31] Thornton, *Politics and Power in a Slave Society*, pp. 205–9, 217–19.

5 Territorial Expansion, 1844–1848

The Growth of Sectional Consciousness

Sectional antagonism grew as America expanded between 1845 and 1848. The steps by which this antagonism increased are easy to pin-point. In 1844–5 America annexed Texas, voluntarily, to the Union and in so doing provoked both a rash of Northern objections to the absorption of a new slave state and Southern enthusiasm for territorial extension. In 1846 America went to war with Mexico and thereby set Northerners and Southerners arguing whether or not slaves would be introduced into the lands that everyone expected would be – and indeed subsequently were – grasped from the Mexicans. The place of slavery in the Mexican Cession was not finally settled until 1850, after much bitter squabbling and the first serious threats of Southern secession. In 1854–8 a further effort to extend slavery – this time into the more northerly region of Kansas and Nebraska – ended in the creation of a purely Northern political party, the Republicans, and in a frustrating, painful, and, to many, humiliating defeat for Southern politicians. By 1858 the Republicans had established themselves as the North's majority party and insisted that slavery should extend no further. Southerners by 1859 very nervously pondered how they should respond to a Republican victory in the presidential election of 1860. These stages by which sectional antagonism deepened are easily discerned; yet the reasons why sectional identity submerged a host of regional and particularist loyalties, and why politicians variously intent upon maintaining the Union failed in their self-appointed task, are more difficult to unravel.

For seven years after the financial panic of 1837, federal politics revolved around economic questions. Why prosperity had been lost and how prosperity could be regained preoccupied politicians. In 1844, however, the problems of territorial expansion and slavery extension burst upon the country with sudden force: should America acquire new territories in the West – or in the Caribbean – and should slavery be admitted to those territories? Should territorial and slavery expansion proceed jauntily together, separately in Indian file, with slavery lagging lamely and far behind, or not at all? The moral, religious, political, and material considerations that bore upon these interrelated questions confounded straightforward analysis. The answer was complicated by

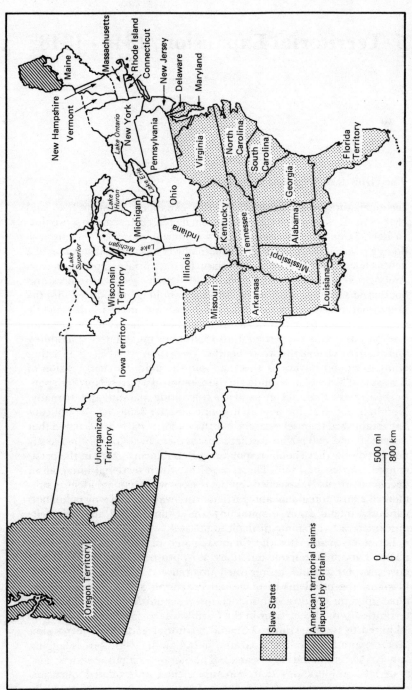

America in 1840

Slave States

American territorial claims
disputed by Britain

0   500 ml

0   800 km

developments beyond politicians' control. Even during the years of economic recession and recrimination sectional consciousness had grown; and by 1844 the future status of Texas had become a problem of some urgency. It is worth considering each phenomenon in turn.

The elusive concept of sectional identity came to seem increasingly real and important to individuals, to group organizations, and to state politicians in the second quarter of the nineteenth century. Southern consciousness in particular deepened as national discussions about slavery became more common and more intense. In 1819–20 sectional animosity was kindled in congressional efforts to decide whether the new state of Missouri should be admitted as a slave state. But this political crisis soon receded; and even at its height probably left the mass of Americans unmoved.[1] Again, although fears for the future protection of slavery inspired the efforts of South Carolina in 1831–2 to nullify a federal law, the nullification crisis was equally speedily resolved, and the South Carolinian claim that states individually – in special conventions – enjoyed the constitutional right to nullify objectionable federal laws was not taken up by Southerners *en masse*.[2] Moreover, in 1831 the legislature of the most populous slave state, Virginia, actually debated the feasibility of emancipation. The sense of 'Southern-ness' was therefore still uncertain and incomplete by the early 1830s.

The development of 'Southern-ness' was much accelerated by militant abolitionism, which provoked Southerners into an extreme defence of their sectional position. The newly energetic, radical, and uncompromising attack on slavery made by abolitionists can be dated from the founding of William Lloyd Garrison's *The Liberator* in 1831 and the establishment of the American Anti-Slavery Society in 1833. The abolitionist hall-mark was immediatism: there was to be no moderate tampering with slavery, no utopian quest for a gradual wearing down of slavery's bonds. The immediatist cause was strengthened in 1833 with the emancipation of slaves in the British Empire; and during the 1830s the British government became more watchful and active in the international restriction of slave-trading and of slavery itself. Belaboured and beleaguered in this way, slaveowners naturally became wary of all criticism, sensitive to potential reductions in their political influence, and intolerant of doubts about slavery nearer home.

Furthermore, differences of sectional economic interest had begun to emerge by the 1830s and led politicians to speak in sectional terms of the different lines of economic development that might be followed by North, South, and West. While these sections did not in fact possess strikingly divergent economic interests, by the 1830s the contrast between the Cotton Kingdom of the Deep South and the more commercial and

---

[1] Eric Foner, 'Politics, Ideology, and the Origins of the American Civil War' in George M. Frederickson (ed.), *A Nation Divided* (Minneapolis, 1975), pp. 17–22.

[2] William W. Freehling, *Prelude to Civil War. The Nullification Controversy in South Carolina, 1816–1836* (New York, 1965).

industrial North-East was considerably stronger than it had been 20 years earlier; since the 1810s the cotton trade had burgeoned, with the South becoming heavily committed to cotton-growing, while manufacturing in the North-East boomed when war with Britain in 1812 cut off British exports to the USA. The contrast was, however, simplified in popular rhetoric. It took a firmer hold on political consciousness as American nationalism became more clearly articulated in the 1820s and 1830s. As Americans thought of themselves in increasingly national terms, so the difference between the broad economic pursuits of the Deep South and the slave states in general, and the North-East and the free states in general, was more fully described, emphasized, and exaggerated. From the mid 1830s, it has been suggested, Southerners were so sensitive about their place and their rights in the nation that the safeguarding of Southern interests became the central theme of Southern party politics. Indeed, the emergence of a two-party system in the South in 1835–6 can be partly ascribed to fears that the Democratic party (when its leadership went to the New Yorker Martin van Buren) would be excessively influenced by Northern, anti-slavery sentiment.[3] The abolitionist movement can therefore be seen as basic to the development of Southern consciousness.

What precisely was the abolitionist movement of the 1830s and early 1840s? Abolitionism, to many observers then and since, was a pack of angry, howling, and snapping factions, which, instead of hounding the slaveowners to earth, wasted much energy, enterprise, and initiative in pursuing and savaging each other. Yet, above this din of internal antagonisms, the factions' frequent bayings against slavery rose in volume and intensity in the 1830s and 1840s, and were widely heard.

When the abolitionist movement divided formally in 1840, the schism partly resulted from the very successes achieved in the previous seven or eight years: how to proceed from solid foundations already laid was of great significance. But the split followed also from endemic diversities of outlook, temperament, politicial interests, and short-term objectives within the movement. Abolitionists included patrician philanthropists, religious persuaders, aggressive agitators on the make, and simple moralists disgusted at the blot of slavery upon the republic's self-image and world reputation. Yet such diversity of membership, short-term tactics, and propagandizing technique may well have enhanced the movement's appeal to a larger public.[4]

Founded in 1833, the American Anti-Slavery Society itself had always been a somewhat loose organization; in 1840 disagreements over political

[3] William J. Cooper, Jr, *The South and the Politics of Slavery, 1828–1856* (Baton Rouge, 1978), ch. 3.
[4] This is the central theme of a convincing analysis by Ronald G. Walters, *The Antislavery Appeal. American Abolitionism after 1830* (Baltimore, 1976), esp. pp. 3–18. Further reading on abolitionism should start with Walters and proceed from his bibliographical note, pp. 187–8.

strategy led to the final schism. Three main groups emerged: the passionate Garrisonians who continued to run the society; the more politically active and pragmatic Liberty party; and those who opposed Garrison for tactical and personal reasons and who deplored Garrison's enthusiasm for women's participation in anti-slavery campaigning. This last group subsequently established the American and Foreign Anti-Slavery Society. The three groups differed considerably on ideological as well as strategic grounds. To Garrison and his followers, the struggle against slavery was an intense contest against sin. Only a general purification of the body politic would lead to the abolition of slavery. Religious and spiritual improvement took priority over mere political action, for all American political institutions suffered moral deficiencies – authority restrained the free operation of individual conscience – and political life was tainted by individual corruption and mere striving for office. Following the opposite tack, the Liberty party was established in 1840 with the aim of promoting the abolitionist cause within the normal political system; Liberty party men were prepared to compromise and to accommodate other issues in their quest for political influence, a quest that had been largely frustrated in 1837–40.

The Liberty party men's basic dilemma may be readily understood. During the 1830s abolitionists were highly successful in spreading anti-slavery sentiment, though not immediatism, in the North, and provoked widespread discussion in pamphlets, newspapers, and religious circles about the morality of slavery. But despite this work, and despite their petitioning federal and state legislatures in 1836–7 and their efforts to persuade Northern political candidates to condemn slavery, many abolitionists by 1840 were driven to organize a separate party by the stern resistance of the political establishment to their moral invocations. The national party system helped to contain and muffle sectional extremism. Abolitionists' hopes of gaining greater influence in the Whig party – more abolitionists and anti-slavery men were Whigs than Democrats – were dashed in February 1839 when a leading Whig contender for the following year's presidential nomination bitterly denounced abolitionism. While declaring himself to be 'no friend of slavery', Senator Henry Clay added: 'The liberty of the descendants of Africa in the United States is incompatible with the safety and liberty of the European descendants'. Thereafter the pressure for a separate abolitionist, or at least anti-slavery, party mounted. Yet the old ties of party remained strong. Whig abolitionists and anti-slavery men believed it more important to thwart the Democrats, with their powerful Southern wing, than to support a pure anti-slavery presidential candidate who would be certain to lose. Even in 1844, Clay – as the Whig presidential candidate – seemed worth supporting, because, for all his refusal to condemn slavery, he was reluctant to embark on further slavery extension. Not surprisingly, therefore, despite great effort, enormous propagandizing, and furious discussions with other abolitionists over strategy, the Liberty party made little direct political impact. Its leader, James G. Birney, was occasionally driven to despair. In 1842 he wrote:

> There is no reason for believing that the virtue of our own people would ever throw off Slavery. Slavery has corrupted the whole nation, so that it seems to me we are nearly at the point of dissolution. I must say — and I am sorry to believe it true — that our form of government will not do.[5]

Yet the Liberty party's contribution to sectional dispute was a portentous one. Liberty party men tried to force anti-slavery to the centre of public attention and to foster working partnerships with existing parties. By capturing a slice of political power they might exert considerable influence in a situation where the Whigs' and Democrats' shares of the political cake were often virtually equal. Yet the Liberty party also sought allies within the South, for hostility to slavery was not in Liberty men's eyes bluntly sectional; it was directed in South as well as North against a conspiratorial and privileged class. As the party's journal stated in 1842:

> We do not go for a *Northern*, but an American party. We war not against the South, but the Slave-Power. This power does not occupy the whole South, nor is it confined by southern limits. A large portion of the people of Kentucky, Western Virginia, Eastern Tennessee, Maryland, and Missouri, will deeply sympathise with the Liberty Party, whenever they can understand its principles and objects. Their interests are really oppressed by the Slave-Power.[6]

This was a potent and fateful argument; for here were the central themes adumbrated only a decade and a half later by the majority party — the Republicans — in the North. First, slavery — odious in itself — was distinguished from the Slave Power, the social and political élite of the South, which imposed its values on the humbler orders and against the interests of the poorer whites. This stress on the peculiar and élitist Slave Power, harmful to much of the South as it was objectionable to the nation at large, became a constant component of criticism of the South in the 1850s. Secondly, denying that anti-slavery was a purely Northern impulse was essential to Union-minded anti-slavery reformers in the 1840s and 1850s. The Republicans followed the Liberty party in portraying themselves as nationally minded and as reformists with the true interests of poorer Southern whites at heart. In 1861 the slave states and parts of slave states listed in 1842 as 'oppressed by the Slave-Power' were indeed those opposed to secession. And in 1861 the Republicans asserted that those same areas and those same people would support them in crushing the Slave-Power's rebellion.

[5] Richard H. Sewell, *Ballots for Freedom. Antislavery Politics in the United States, 1837–1860* (New York, 1976), pp. 48, 122–3: and generally chs. 1–5.
[6] *Ibid.*, p. 87.

In the early 1840s, however, the Liberty party exposed another dilemma. It was all very well for abolitionists to declare slavery in America to be an affront to Christian morality, an absurd contradiction of republican principles, and a startling rebuke to national ideals when even a decadent monarchical and aristocratic régime had emancipated Britain's slaves in 1833; but what, abolitionists could rightly be asked, did they believe could be abolished? Virtually all American lawyers and politicians argued that the federal government possessed no powers to abolish slavery.[7] Even men of radical reputation in the Republican party in 1861, on the eve of war, denied any competence to the federal government over slavery in the states.[8] Slavery was, after all, introduced or prohibited by *state* governments and so beyond the federal government's control. The pragmatists' answer – and America in the 1840s struck abolitionists as a hotbed of pragmatism – was to leave uncriticized, if also unsung, all features of American society outside the reach of federal power. To surround slavery with the sounds of silence became a major task of statesmanship.

Garrisonians were exasperated with the federal government's eunuch-like character: capable of singing the sweet, harmonious praises of the Union as it existed, the federal government seemed thoroughly incapable of spawning a new and more perfect Union. So, Garrisonians denounced the Constitution of 1787 and urged their fellow-citizens to renounce their allegiance to it. They contended that the Constitution gave positive sanction to slavery and was drawn up with that very purpose in mind; this assertion ironically coincided with the Southern claim that the Founding Fathers approved of slavery. Garrisonians further believed that the emancipation of slaves would follow not from political pressure but only from a general improvement of American moral perceptions; abolition would be merely one element in the universal transformation of society from one ruled by men to one ruled by God. This perfectionist world-view made Garrisonians impatient at tinkering with the party system, and uninterested in the work of many anti-slavery lawyers and judges who attempted to ease the existing legal burdens and hardships imposed upon blacks both slave and free.

Against Garrisonian renunciation and perfectionism, some abolitionist theorists argued, with increasing intensity, that the Constitution itself vindicated the abolitionist stance. Although such arguments won little favour at the time, these theorists developed an impressive tradition of

---

[7] This problem is treated in William M. Wiecek, *The Sources of Antislavery Constitutionalism in America, 1760–1848* (Ithaca, 1977), chs. 9–11. I rely heavily on Wiecek in the following discussion.

[8] For example, Owen Lovejoy explained to the House of Representatives in January 1861 that he wanted slavery abolished throughout the USA, but realized that the federal Congress lacked the constitutional power to emancipate the slaves. *Appendix to the Congressional Globe*, 36th Congress, 2nd Session (Washington, D.C., 1861), p. 86.

libertarian constitutional analysis, dating from 1837 when Alvan Stewart interpreted the due-process clause of the Fifth Amendment — that no person be 'deprived of life, liberty, or property, without due process of law' — as empowering the federal government to abolish slavery. Stewart and other abolitionist lawyers continued to develop the dual argument that the Constitution afforded numerous grounds for federal action on slavery, and that the Declaration of Independence, with its ringing statement of the 'self-evident' truth that all men are created equal, was a substantive basis for constitutional interpretation and not merely uplifting rhetoric.[9]

Radical theorists insisted, then, on the natural rights of all blacks, and argued, both from the Declaration of Independence and from the absence of any positive federal law upholding slavery, that the federal government had a constitutional obligation to destroy the peculiar institution. These constitutional arguments made little impact in the 1840s and 1850s, but the stress on natural rights and the new constitutional significance attached to the Declaration of Independence, which preceded and was in spirit superior to the Constitution, greatly influenced numerous politicians opposed to the extension of slavery. In 1850, for instance, Senator William H. Seward referred to the disavowal of slavery by a 'higher Law' than the Constitution; and in 1858 Abraham Lincoln, campaigning for the Senate, made famous and prominent reference to blacks' natural rights. Very few political leaders, however, dared or cared to embrace the radical claim that the federal government possessed sufficient power to end slavery.

The Liberty party, then, entered the political arena at a time when abolitionists were, amongst other things, desperately trying to sort out what they could expect or urge any federal government to do about slavery. Liberty party men endorsed the prevailing orthodoxy that the federal government lacked the constitutional authority to abolish slavery; but they insisted on the corollary that the federal government equally lacked the authority to establish slavery anywhere. From its formation in 1840 to its demise in 1848, the Liberty party warred not against slavery as such, but against any federal contact with the institution of slavery. Slavery should not be condoned by Congress in the District of Columbia, or protected in any federal territories; nor should Congress erect new slave states or help to recapture fugitive slaves. With these practical objectives in view, the Liberty party was far more capable of co-operation with politicians in the two main parties than perfectionist Garrisonians or radical, abolitionist constitutional theorists. If it played down the moral impulse infusing abolitionism, the Liberty party did not, however, ignore the long-term aim; it believed that once a 'quarantine of slavery' was securely established by congressional surrender of all ties with the

[9] Wiecek, *Sources of Antislavery Constitutionalism*, pp. 254–7.

institution, then slavery would begin gradually to disappear.[10]

Clearly, therefore, the abolitionists were deeply and often bitterly divided. But they were also united by certain preoccupations.[11] They uniformly depicted the evil wrought by slavery in the nation and insisted, against the prevailing orthodoxy of existing parties, that this was important. They shared a common frustration at the churches' reluctance to turn their evangelizing energies against slavery. They urged a common war on the pseudo-scientific doctrines that were applied to dehumanize blacks; while agreeing that blacks might be biologically inferior, abolitionists stressed that blacks possessed moral perceptions and Christian impulses which could be succoured and promoted only when freedom was granted.

Abolitionists in general also worried about the sexual licence and depravity, widespread miscegenation, and lack of strict personal self-control allegedly found among both whites and blacks in the South. They argued that slavery distorted personal relationships, undermined respect for individuals, set up morally warping patterns of personal domination, destroyed the close-knit character of the family, and put the child − the embodiment of future aspirations both moral and social − at the mercy of irrational impulses. Family life for both whites and blacks was disrupted far more severely in the slave states than in the north. Growing concern for the family as a special ethical entity during the second quarter of the nineteenth century was reflected in Harriet Beecher Stowe's belief that the 'worst abuse of the system of slavery is its outrage upon the family'.[12] Given the youthfulness of the American population, this concern for proper sexual and moral order within the family was a natural preoccupation amongst evangelical reformers. Many anti-slavery men therefore encouraged the active participation of women in their movement, and contributed considerably to the 'cult of domesticity' by contrasting ideal family life with the emotional mayhem allegedly produced by slavery among blacks and whites alike.

Despite their fierce disagreements over political strategy and constitutional powers, abolitionist activity greatly heightened sectional consciousness in the late 1830s and 1840s. By injecting their language, ideas, and aspirations into Northern − and, negatively, Southern − awareness by the end of the 1840s, the abolitionists had achieved the first objective of any reformist group. Southern politicians in turn became increasingly sensitive to any criticism − however veiled − of slavery. In 1826 Congressman James Buchanan of Pennsylvania said, 'Slavery is a great moral evil . . . . It is, however, one of those moral evils, from which it is impossible to escape, without the introduction of evils infinitely

---

[10] *Ibid.*, ch. 10.
[11] For the following two paragraphs, see Walters, *Antislavery Appeal*, chs. 3–6.
[12] *Ibid.*, p. 95.

greater'.[13] Thirty years later when Buchanan was elected president, he could not have expressed even that degree of conservative helplessness – no Democratic leader in the 1850s could cast aspersions on slavery.

Sectionalism may thus have been intensified by the abolitionist campaign; but abolitionism won very little direct political support in the North. In the mid 1830s abolitionist meetings were violently disrupted by crowds of respectable citizens,[14] and in the presidential election of 1844 even the less provocative Liberty party won only 2.3 per cent of the national vote. If sectional rhetoric was increasing in volume, it did not immediately transform political behaviour.

The strongest force opposing sectionalism was party politics. Granted, parties often expressed, exploited, and encouraged sectional prejudices. Sectional consciousness was certainly increased by the necessary haggling over place and platform promises within the two great national parties; and a politician's prominence would be enhanced if he could portray both himself and his policies as representative of a sectional, rather than merely a state, interest. However, national consciousness operated in much the same manner. The emergence in the 1830s of a fully-developed national party system, with Whigs and Democrats fighting each other fairly evenly in every state in 1840, gave added weight to national considerations. The very stuff of party politics was national economic policy, concerning as it did banking, currency, internal improvements, and protective tariffs. Parties were also shaped by other forces – personalities, ethnic prejudices, local antagonisms, suffrage rights – but central to party debate were disputes over the rôle of the federal government in economic development.[15] Clearly, all these issues were of national rather than narrowly sectional interest.

Moreover, national and sectional loyalties interacted in odd ways. It did not necessarily follow that intensified loyalty to a part of the country should result in alienation from the whole. Quite the reverse occurred in the 30 or 40 years before the Civil War. As the market economy developed in the early and mid nineteenth century, towns and villages grew rapidly in population and wealth and competed fiercely with each other for commercial connections and advantages. As state and federal governments engaged in economic promotion – aiding the construction of canals, roads, and railroads and providing banking systems – so community leaders pushed their own community's special merits against those of rival localities and towns. Yet this pervasive and energetic spirit of local and state 'boosterism' coincided with – and did not detract from – an

[13] James A. Rawley, *Race and Politics. 'Bleeding Kansas' and the Coming of the Civil War* (Philadelphia, 1969), p. 141.
[14] Leonard L. Richards, *"Gentlemen of Property and Standing": Anti-Abolition Mobs in Jacksonian America* (New York, 1970).
[15] William R. Brock, *Parties and Political Conscience: American Dilemmas, 1840–1850* (Millwood, New York, 1979), chs. 1–3; Cooper, *The South and the Politics of Slavery*, ch. 5.

intensification of national pride and interest in national affairs.

So, while abolitionism undoubtedly increased Northerners' moral distaste for slavery, other factors deepened sectional loyalties without inevitably undermining nationalism. Economic issues, dealt with on an enlarged scale by the federal government in the 1830s and 1840s, sharpened the edge of competition between sections and raised the stakes of co-operation within sections. If the federal Congress formulated a tariff, devised a banking policy, or aided the building of roads, canals, and, later, railways, then co-operation between politicians from a particular region or section might yield vital economic benefits unobtainable by states or congressional districts struggling singly in Washington. Political (or interest-group) sectionalism was a marked feature of the early and mid nineteenth century which flourished side by side with nationalism and remained a notable characteristic in American life after 1865 without provoking any further civil war. Increasing sectional consciousness did not, therefore, flow solely from abolitionist efforts; nor did it lead inevitably to a snapping of national ties and national affinities.[16]

Instead, westward expansion turned sectional rivalries into a perilous and significant contest over fundamental rights. The crisis over territorial policy which arose in 1844 emerged partly from the nature of western settlement and economic growth in the 1830s. That settlement and growth had been achieved in a frenetic speculative burst. Between 1830 and 1840 the population of the eastern seaboard increased by 17 per cent; that of all trans-Appalachian states and territories by 73 per cent; and that of the western *free* states and territories by 100 per cent.[17] Whigs and Democrats divided over how best to control the destabilizing consequences of Western economic development. Western expansion, pushed forward recklessly and with entrepreneurial panache in the 1830s, helped create the new political conditions of the 1840s, for it whetted Americans' already strong appetite for new farmlands, and raised fundamental questions about the extent of federal power. If the federal government possessed the power to determine the future course of development in the West, by financial aid in opening transport routes or by distributing federal cash holdings to banks of its choice, might it not also, many Southerners feared, possess or seek to use the power to abolish slavery? Western expansion therefore increased sectional consciousness in two ways. By settling American domains to their geographical limits,

[16] Discussion of this problem flows from David M. Potter's essay 'The Historian's Use of Nationalism and Vice Versa' conveniently reprinted in his *The South and the Sectional Conflict* (Baton Rouge, 1968), pp. 34–83. The idea of growing community consciousness is ably developed in Stuart Bumin, *The Urban Threshold: Growth and Change in a Nineteenth-Century American Community* (Chicago, 1976). For the notion of 'boosterism', see Daniel J. Boorstin, *The Americans: the National Experience* (New York, 1965), esp. pp. 161–8.

[17] For basic figures, see: *Population of the United States in 1860; Compiled from The Original Returns of the Eighth Census* (Washington, D.C., 1864), p. 603.

while at the same time fuelling the desire for land, expansion in the West intensified Southern claustrophobia; for the Missouri Compromise had limited slavery to federal territories south of latitude 36°30', yet few such areas remained available for settlement at the end of the 1830s. Western expansion also stimulated political interest in a more active federal government, an idea that to Southerners seemed full of potential danger.

In summary, then, the intensified sectional consciousness which was so important an element in the territorial question resulted from the interplay of three main factors: economic expansion, and especially the diverging developments in the North-East and in the south-western part of the Cotton Kingdom; greatly increased abolitionist agitation; and the unprecedented pace of settlement and economic growth in the West.

Texas

The annexation of Texas opened the series of political crises which culminated in civil war. It shifted the attention of federal politicians from the economic issues of the late 1830s and early 1840s to a single problem, the extension of slavery. Although the Texas problem emerged quite suddenly in 1843–4, it was an inevitable result of the general westward expansion of the 1830s and had been looming ahead for a considerable time.

Opinions differ as to the cause of the crisis of 1844. Historians conventionally argue that Texas was brought to the forefront of political debate as a result of party in-fighting, internal divisions among Southern and Democratic leaders, and sheer political opportunism.[18] All this, though accurate enough, tends to minimize the very real difficulties that confronted America in the 1840s over both Texas itself and British ambitions in the New World. These difficulties may well have been exaggerated and pressed to an early resolution in 1844 by politicians seeking an advantage in domestic politics, but Texas would certainly have had to be dealt with sooner or later; while British intentions in the New World, however misunderstood and misinterpreted these may have been in America, were a genuine challenge to the aggressive American nationalism of the time.

Texas was the creation of American immigrants.[19] Between 1821 and

[18] A very lively account written from this perspective is James C.N. Paul, *Rift in the Democracy* (Philadelphia, 1951). Michael F. Holt in *The Political Crisis of the 1850s* (New York, 1978), ch. 3 also gives primacy of place to party politics, though his method and conclusions are very different from Paul's. There are difficulties, however, in explaining all developments in political policies and attitudes by reference solely to party and indeed narrowly 'political' considerations. Public issues exist and flourish: they are not simply created and manipulated by politicians.

[19] This account is based on: Jan Bazant, *A Concise History of Mexico from Hidalgo to Cárdenas, 1805–1940* (Cambridge, 1977), ch. 2; Daniel James, *Mexico and the Americans* (New York, 1963), pp. 51–9; Karl M. Schmitt, *Mexico and the United States, 1821–1973: Conflict and Coexistence* (New York, 1974), pp. 51–70; Charles A. Hale, *Mexican Liberalism in the Age of Mora, 1821–1853* (New Haven, 1968), pp. 188–214; Oakah L. Jones, Jr *Santa Anna* (New York, 1968), pp. 85–94.

1823 the Austins, father and son, won the privilege of settling. Americans in Texas from three successive governments – the Spanish imperial authority, the new Mexican empire, and the subsequently formed Mexican republic. In 1821 the region was scarcely touched by permanent settlement: 4,000 Mexicans lived precariously amongst hostile Indian tribes. From 1823, land-hungry American frontiersmen entered this large, neglected area, encouraged by generous offers of land: substantial farms here were considerably cheaper to buy than in the US territories. The Americans brought with them their slaves and also their own political assumptions. The Mexicans imposed complex stipulations about slavery and insisted that colonists convert to Catholicism; tensions between the Mexican government and the settlers mounted when the latter assumed simply that slavery existed in the same form as in the United States, and paid no heed to the requirement for religious conversion. In 1829, when Mexico abolished slavery in an effort to curtail American settlement, the settlers disregarded abolition. By 1835, with the population of Texas consisting of 30,000 immigrants and only 7,800 Mexicans,[20] trouble was clearly brewing. As early as 1830, a leading Mexican conservative writer predicted that Texas would become independent, or part of America, unless it were settled by Mexicans, or at least by American Catholics. Yet at least one prominent Mexican liberal, Lorenzo de Zavala, saw the infusion of American influence as a positive benefit, arguing in 1834 that two Mexicos would develop, leading to a cathartic civil war: 'upon the gothic rubbish of indefensible privileges, will arise a glorious and enlightened generation . . . the American system will gain a complete though bloody victory'.[21]

The privileged orders in Mexico, however, were determined to stem the tide of American liberalism. In 1834 General Santa Anna became president and set about dismantling the Mexican federal system. In 1835 the general crushed one state that resisted his plans for centralization; by October of that year he was confident enough to push through a decree abolishing all state legislatures and providing for state governors' appointments to be approved by the central government. The American settlers in Texas refused to accept Santa Anna's centralizing policies, with all their obnoxious connotations of military and clerical rule; they were also determined to retain slavery. Early in 1836 they therefore declared themselves independent of Mexico and in April won that independence by defeating Santa Anna at the battle of San Jacinto.

Although Mexico continued to claim suzerainty over Texas, the various Mexican regimes of 1836–46 scarcely regarded the Texas question as an over-riding national concern. Indeed, the Texas rebellion did not decrease admiration for American republicanism amongst

---

[20] Michael C. Meyer and William L. Sherman, *The Course of Mexican History* (New York, 1979), p. 336.
[21] Hale, *Mexican Liberalism*, p. 204.

Mexico's liberal intelligentsia, and one leading liberal, Zavala, actually served briefly as the first vice-president of Texas. Moreover, Mexican politics at this time were distinctly volatile; between 1829 and 1846 there were at least 19 different governments, and the search for a stable régime was the primary concern of Mexican politics.[22]

However, to the conservative leader Santa Anna, who returned to power in 1841, Texas was naturally a keenly sensitive issue. During his flamboyant, corrupt, and exuberantly militaristic dictatorship Santa Anna's intentions towards Texas were far from pacific. In 1843, for example, when further American settlers entered Texas, his government warned the USA that it still claimed title over the region, adding that annexation of Texas to the USA would be regarded as an act of war.[23]

The upstart republic, meanwhile, looked to the USA for settlers, for loans, and for political support. Within the USA, expansionists rapidly identified the very real problem of the disputed status and fragile financial and international position of Texas, and related it to American national aims. Texas would have to be provided with long-term security against her tumultuous southern neighbour, Mexico, an unstable hotbed of militarism always about to ignite. American expansionists in 1844, however, made greater political play of British designs.

British intentions in North America tended to be exaggerated and falsified by American expansionists,[24] but in the early and mid 1840s these intentions were in fact far from clear. The British government claimed a large portion of what Americans designated their own Oregon country. The boundary between Maine and British Nova Scotia was not firmly delineated and created diplomatic friction until 1842. Furthermore, the British government attempted in the early 1840s to revitalize the government of its North American colonies by establishing a single colony of Canada to incorporate present-day Ontario and Quebec. In theory at least, this reform was intended to swamp the discontented Quebeçois, who had staged a rebellion in 1837–8 and threatened to disrupt Anglo-American relations by their trans-border activities, and to galvanize the British colonies into greater economic efforts; in the original report urging reform written by Lord Durham, analysis was based on the unfavourable comparison between British North America's lethargy and the bustle of the United States. Administrative reform thus flowed partly from a sense of Anglo-American rivalry. The French Canadian rebellion and the tense local difficulties it created with America meant that Britain had 21,000 militia and volunteers and 10,500 regular troops on active service in North America by 1839. The fear of war perennially gripped British North American military circles

---

[22] Meyer and Sherman, *Course of Mexican History*, Appendix.
[23] Schmitt, *Mexico and the United States*, pp. 60–1; Jones, *Santa Anna*, pp. 85–7.
[24] Frederick Merk, *The Monroe Doctrine and American Expansionism, 1843–1849* (New York, 1972 edn), esp. pp. 285–9.

in the years 1838–42.[25] Finally, Britain's world-wide campaign against slavery raised the possibility of British meddling in Texan affairs to forestall future American annexation of the area and subsequent maintenance of slavery there. In 1842–4 there seemed a further likelihood of Franco-British diplomatic initiatives in the running dispute between Mexico and Texas. European intervention in the region was not an impossibility, given Mexico's chronic political instability. Spain, indeed, had launched a minor invasion of Mexico in 1829, and France sent an expeditionary force against Veracruz in 1838. Britain delayed recognition of the Texan republic until 1840 in the vague hope of persuading Texas to abolish slavery; but diplomatic recognition eventually came in a mild effort to head off supposed American designs.[26] So boundary disputes, the possibility of British interference in Mexican and Texan affairs, and a renewal of energy in Britain's North American colonies all pointed to instability in North America.

The two main facts of international life in North America in the early 1840s – Texan vulnerability and British restlessness – coincided with a veritable explosion of American nationalism. The doctrine of 'Manifest Destiny', with its emphasis on the inevitability of American continental sway, was vaingloriously disseminated in Democratic party journals in 1845. It was perhaps an inflated and unnecessary response to British plans, or imagined plans. But it stemmed naturally from the emphasis on 'American-ness' common throughout the 1830s. National pride, and Americans' insistence on western expansion as a virtual birthright, together focused attention on the desirability of annexing Texas to the USA: voluntary annexation would rescue a sister republic from possible disaster, while at the same time striking a blow against British pretensions.[27]

Although the Texas problem was undoubtedly genuine, the timing of annexation was manipulated by politicians. The issue arose between late 1843 and May 1844 as annexation became the overriding policy promoted by the administration of President John Tyler. For this reason, annexation has often been regarded by historians as a spurious issue, a confidence trick played by ambitious Southern politicians upon a gullible electorate.[28] The real statesmen of 1844, it has been argued, were two

---

[25] Kenneth Bourne, *Britain and the Balance of Power in North America 1815–1908* (London, 1967), see chs 4, 5 generally, but esp. pp. 75–83. Reginald Coupland (ed.), *The Durham Report* (Oxford, 1945 edn), pp. 105–13, 126–36. J.M.S. Careless, *The Union of the Canadas. The Growth of Canadian Institutions, 1841–1857* (Toronto, 1967), chs. 1–7.

[26] Bourne, *Britain and the Balance of Power*, pp. 124–5; Bazant, *Concise History of Mexico*, pp. 41–4, 54–5; Schmitt, *Mexico and the United States*, p. 59; Jones, *Santa Anna*, p. 87; Hale, *Mexican Liberalism*, p. 211.

[27] The fierce nationalism and Anglophobia of one leading western Democrat is well shown in Robert W. Johannsen, *Stephen A. Douglas* (New York, 1973), pp. 139–43, 146–7, 163–71.

[28] See especially Paul, *Rift in the Democracy*, chs. 4–5. The following discussion draws on the material in Paul's book, but adopts a different perspective on events.

leaders who renounced any intention of prompt annexation: Martin van Buren, the former Democratic president who sought his party's presidential nomination, and Henry Clay, who became the Whig presidential candidate. Both, however, were defeated in 1844, the former mainly as a result of a propaganda exercise specializing in patriotic boasting and scare-mongering about the British threat. Allowing for the distortions of propaganda, the problem of Texas was, however, real and immediate, particularly while the military dictator Santa Anna was in power in Mexico.

In 1844 three groups sought to use annexation for their own political advantage: the half-hearted Whig president, the expansionist Midwestern and Southern Democrats, and the Southern Rights fanatics. To President Tyler (a nominal Whig, but completely estranged from the congressional Whigs under Clay during 1841) annexation offered the opportunity of building up a huge Southern following, both Whig and Democrat, which would win him another term in office. This expectation, however, proved entirely groundless. Southern Democrats who supported Tyler's policy in 1844 were interested in Texas rather than Tyler, and the president was consigned to the political scrap-heap after 1845. Yet Tyler's motives were not wholly self-interested. When the treaty of voluntary annexation failed to win the necessary two thirds majority of the Senate in the summer of 1844, Tyler persisted in his efforts to secure Texas, eventually winning Congress's approval for annexation through resolution – not requiring the Senate's ratification by a two thirds majority – rather than treaty. So Texas entered the Union in the last days of Tyler's presidency, in March 1845. Tyler clearly believed in the cause, as well as the political expediency, of expansion.

To a large body of Southern and Midwestern Democrats, westward expansion was appealing in itself. These men were energetic promoters, land speculators, robust nationalists, and visionaries: self-interest and enthusiasm combined in leading them to foster the development of the West broadly conceived. Theirs was a crude, materialistic, and aggressive nationalism that looked upon Mexico as benighted and inferior, and chafed at restraints upon American expansion imposed by barbaric Mexico or imperious Britain. The outlook of men such as Senator Robert J. Walker of Mississippi or Congressman Stephen A. Douglas of Illinois – both prominent in politics in 1844, and both fierce expansionists – would be regarded as distasteful if not repulsive by most late-twentieth-century Americans. Yet, however self-centred and self-righteous, this nationalism was visionary and idealistic. To Walker and Douglas alike, the crucial points at issue were American – not simply Southern – expansion, and an American demonstration of national power for the benefit of the British. Walker argued indeed that Texas annexed might diffuse sectional differences over slavery, since it would provide a conduit through which slaves would pass steadily away from the eastern seaboard, and might well be funnelled off to freedom in Mexico.[29]

Douglas, in turn, saw an extended Mississippi Valley West as an entity in itself and a countervailing force to the North-East and to the eastern seaboard slave states.[30] Given the provenance of the Texas republic – as a region of American frontier settlement and as a salient of American liberalism in the dark bastion of Mexican militarism and clerical-ism – these attitudes are easy to understand. For many Democrats, expansion was an intrinsically attractive policy that offered a morale-booster for their party and a highly popular issue for an election year and for the future.

The third political advantage expected of annexation was far more narrowly, if just as idealistically, conceived. From the late 1820s and the period when federal mass politics arose, one major (some historians would say the major) theme in Southern political debate had been the defence of Southern rights within the nation, and especially state rights, upon which slavery was founded. In 1828 and 1832 Andrew Jackson's Democratic party was regarded as the supreme defender of this double and intertwined cause. In 1835–6, however, when the Democratic presidential nomination went to the Northerner, Martin van Buren, who was allegedly weak on slavery, Southerners flocked in large numbers to the opposition party, the Whigs, and created within that party a strong state-rights Southern wing. Party competition in the South then consisted of fierce arguments as to who best represented the Southern cause.[31] Especially notable in this verbal battle, and especially free-wheeling in his party affiliation during the 1830s, was John C. Calhoun.[32] Calhoun was the assured master of his own state, South Carolina, until his death in 1850, and his overwhelming concern during this period was to promote Southern consciousness and rally the South to a constitutional defence of slavery in the nation. By 1844 Calhoun and other state-rights South-erners – who were by this time working on the fringes of the Democratic party – saw in the annexation of Texas a golden opportunity for the advancement of their cause. This moment was particularly attractive, because debates over federal economic policy in the early 1840s had again displaced discussion of Southern rights as the leading topic in Southern party rhetoric. Calhoun's appointment as Secretary of State to President Tyler was secured by his friends in early 1844 to help reverse this drift, and to restore the defence of Southern rights to first place in Southern political discourse. Calhoun met these expectations by rounding off the treaty of voluntary annexation, while seeking also to manipulate Tyler for his own ends.

Texas annexation was thus the common denominator in the complex

---

[29] Paul, *Rift in the Democracy*, pp. 25–30, 97–101; Merk, *Monroe Doctrine and American Expansionism*, pp. 24–5.
[30] Johannsen, *Stephen A. Douglas*, pp. 139–147, 162–9, 280.
[31] Cooper, *The South and the Politics of Slavery*, chs. 1, 3.
[32] *Ibid.*, pp. 103–18.

political arithmetic of 1844. President Tyler sought to break down Whig—Democratic differences in the South in order to emerge as the Southern candidate for the presidential election. Calhoun, far more radical and determinedly Southern that Tyler, joined the president's cabinet to speed up annexation, but had his own plans for raising Southern consciousness and re-shaping the Constitution to provide maximum long-term security for slavery. Finally, a large body of committed Democrats, especially those from the states of the Mississippi valley, endorsed annexation for its own sake and because they hoped to turn the issue to Democratic advantage. Because of its very centrality to political manoeuvring and because of its consequences, Texas annexation marked a turning-point in American politics. The discussion of Southern rights took concrete, rather than theoretical, form: if Texas were annexed, slavery would be on the march once more.

The annexation of Texas was assured by the annexationists' seizure of the Democratic presidential nomination in June 1844 and by the Democrats' victory in the elections of November 1844. The annexationists prevented ex-president Martin van Buren from obtaining the Democratic nomination for a third time and installed as the party's candidate a much less imposing figure, a drab expansionist from Tennessee, James K. Polk. Sectional demands for the westward extension of slavery had been grafted upon the larger and more flourishing plant of national expansion. But would Northern Democrats succour this hybrid?

Two interpretations, diametrically opposed, are possible regarding the significance of the year 1844 to the Democrats.[33] One suggests that the events of that year deeply alienated an important group of Northern Democrats who yet remained loyal to the party hoping to regain control of it in 1848. When they failed in that aim, this group began to desert to the anti-slavery extension movement, continuing to do so — by fits and starts after Slave Power provocation — throughout the remainder of the 1840s and the 1850s. The alternative argument is that the Texas problem sharpened party competition and enhanced party morale: a choice was offered in 1844 between the annexationist Democrats and anti-annexationist Whigs. Despite the qualms, doubts, and fears felt by some Northern Democrats over expansion, the vast majority of Democrats in both North and South were happy, if not eager, to push the nation ever westwards and onwards. Did, then, the Southern Democrats' coup of 1844 irreparably split or actually invigorate the party at large?

Clearly, some Northern Democratic leaders were deeply troubled by Texas annexation and the possibility of slavery's subsequent spread; these men were both influential and active. Following the lead of ex-president van Buren, a group of Northern Democrats became alarmed in 1845–6 at the increasingly pro-slavery policy pursued by President Polk. They

---

[33] Paul, *Rift in the Democracy*, pp. 181–3; Holt, *Political Crisis of the 1850s*, pp. 40, 43–9.

were prepared to see Texas annexed and to have most of it admitted as a slave state. But they expected a portion of Texas – it was assumed that Texas would be divided into numerous states, so spacious was its extent – to become free territory. Feeling the effects of anti-Slave Power rhetoric coming from the Liberty party at home, these Northern Democrats began to resent 'the increase and predominance of slavery, as a distinct and exacting power in the confederacy'. The morality of slavery was less important to them than the growing sense that the North was being exploited politically by the Southern Democrats. Van Buren had long laboured to shut slavery questions out of national party debate; and so in 1845 he quite logically objected to the terms upon which Texas was annexed as a huge and exclusive addition to the Slave Power.[34]

Yet, despite such sectional suspicions, the bulk of Democratic supporters continued to vote for the party. Only in the presidential election of 1848 was the Democratic cause markedly weakened by defections occasioned by hostility to yet another bout of slavery extension. In the 1840s as a whole, and including state and congressional elections in 1849 and 1850, there was no pronounced drop in the Democratic percentage of the Northern popular vote. While most Northern Democratic voters stuck with their party even when it endorsed slavery extension, this continued party loyalty did not necessarily result from any positive endorsement of slavery; most Northern Democrats *probably* remained morally neutral on the subject. Voters sustained the Democrats for many other reasons.

Their party, after all, was not simply the instrument of slavery extension, but represented for its supporters a wide variety of prejudices, hopes, antagonisms, and policies.[35] Although territorial expansion consumed much attention in federal politics during the 1840s, Democrats in the federal Congress and, more particularly, in the state legislatures, were absorbed also in a whole range of other, largely economic, issues. President Polk's administration pushed a highly partisan legislative programme through Congress. For example, President van Buren had made the establishment of an Independent Treasury a party measure in 1837, as a means of keeping federal money out of the private banking system; in 1846 the national Independent Treasury was re-established to handle the federal government's financial transactions. In 1846, moreover, the Secretary of the Treasury, Robert J. Walker, produced a low tariff, which, with modifications in 1857,

[34] Eric Foner, 'The Wilmot Proviso Revisited', *Journal of American History*, LVI (1969), 262–79: quotation on p. 271.
[35] Lee Benson, *The Concept of Jacksonian Democracy. New York as a Test Case* (Princeton, 1961), chs. 12, 14: this argues in particular that Texas annexation had no discernible impact on voting in the presidential election in New York state, and in general that party images and values (however vaguely defined) and popular loyalty to party endure strongly over time. A similar conclusion about broad continuity in voting behaviour in the 1840s is reached in Ronald P. Formisano, *The Birth of Mass Political Parties: Michigan, 1827–1861* (Princeton, 1971), ch. 2.

remained in force until the 1860s: this was a traditional Democratic response to Whig demands for tariff protection. At the same time, Polk blustered against British claims in Oregon, threatening '54°40' or fight', but eventually settling for a more modest Anglo-American boundary at latitude 49°. In the state legislatures protracted tussles over banking legislation occurred, with Democrats favouring strict state regulation as a minimum requirement, or the actual abolition of note-issuing banks. And Democrats at state constitutional conventions in the late 1840s and early 1850s prided themselves on opening up an even larger number of state offices to popular election.[36]

Party morale and continuing party loyalties were not determined simply by the annexation issue, even though annexation and slavery extension were obviously and justifiably important to the federal government. The Democratic presidential nominee of 1848, Senator Lewis Cass, was described by a Democratic worthy from Georgia as

> a perfect embodiment of progressive democracy as opposed to what the Whigs call conservatism, which in plain English means putting the people in ward, to save them from their pretended ignorance and folly . . . . Cass went for 54—40, is now for the acquisition of Mexican territory, free trade, the independent treasury, and hates the British; and therefore must be worthy of democratic suffrage.[37]

In 1848 the Democratic party represented much more to a moderate Southern Democrat than slavery extension or the defence of Southern rights. Specific policies were important to this Southern Democrat as was the party's claim to oppose the oligarchic and patronizing Whigs, puffed with pretensions to be the guardians of those incapable wards, the people. Similarly, for most Northern Democrats, party loyalty was too complex an affair in the 1840s to be eroded suddenly or cleanly by disputes over slavery extension.

Yet some Northern Democratic politicians and voters – as well as a smaller minority of Northern Whig politicians and voters – scurried away from their party when the issue of slavery extension was squarely put. At the presidential election of 1848 the Democrats pulled out only 84 per cent of their vote of 1844 in the free states, whereas the Whigs secured 97 per cent of their vote.[38] This falling off in Democratic support was neither a permanent feature of presidential elections nor a characteristic of state as well as presidential elections; it may be attributed to rising

[36] Charles Sellers, *James K. Polk. Continentalist 1843—1846* (Princeton, 1966), pp. 213—14; Holt, *Political Crisis of the 1850s*, pp. 45—9, 101—13; James Roger Sharp, *The Jacksonians versus the Banks: Politics in the States after the Panic of 1837* (New York, 1970); William G. Shade, *Banks or No Banks: the Money Issue in Western Politics, 1832—1865* (Detroit, 1972), chs 4, 5; William J. Evitts, *A Matter of Allegiances: Maryland, 1850—1861* (Baltimore, 1974), pp. 31—42.

[37] Ulrich B. Phillips (ed.), *The Correspondence of Robert Toombs, Alexander H. Stephens, and Howell Cobb*, (Washington, D.C., 1911), II, 107.

[38] Holt, *Political Crisis of the 1850s*, p. 65.

Table 4: Third Party support in the presidential elections of 1844 and 1848

States in which the Liberty Party won over 5 per cent of the vote, 1844

	Liberty %	Democratic %
New Hampshire	8.5	55.2
Massachusetts	8.2	40.2
Vermont	8.1	37.0
Michigan	6.6	49.9
Maine	5.7	53.8

States in which the Free Soil Party won over 10 per cent of the vote, 1848

	Free Soil %	Democratic %	Change in Democratic percentage points
Vermont	28.9	22.9	− 14.1
Massachusetts	28.5	26.2	− 14.2
Wisconsin	26.6	38.3	*
New York	26.4	25.1	− 23.8
Michigan	16.0	47.2	− 2.7
New Hampshire	15.1	55.4	+ 0.2
Maine	13.9	45.9	− 7.9
Illinois	12.6	44.9	− 9.0
Ohio	10.8	47.1	− 0.7

*Wisconsin was not a state in 1844.

Source: *Congressional Quarterly's Guide to U.S. Elections* (Washington, D.C., 1975), pp. 267–8.

opposition to slavery extension. In 1844 the abolitionist Liberty party won 2.3 per cent of the vote; in 1848 the anti-slavery extension Free Soil party won 10.1 per cent of that presidential vote. As may be seen from Table 4, such gains were made substantially at Democratic expense. Of the nine states in 1848 that gave the Free Soldiers over 10 per cent of their presidential vote, five showed a marked decline in Democratic support from 1844; and one other was a new state. In only three of these states were substantial gains in third party support not broadly matched by striking losses in Democratic backing.

Although the immediate impact of the annexation issue did not enfeeble the Northern Democrats in 1844, the medium-term repercussions of annexation set anti-slavery groups adrift from the Democratic party in the free states. This estrangement was not permanent. Grudging reconciliation followed after 1848. But nagging claims of conscience and of Northern sectional interest had been injected into internal party debate by the rush for national expansion.

The annexation of Texas was distasteful to many Northerners. It had been done in what seemed an underhand way; and it linked the government of the Union − nearly always an object of pride and often of reverence − with the equivocal cause of slavery expansion.[39] This moral taint was bad enough, but worse was to follow. Texas entered the Union in March 1845 with a sovereign status disputed by Mexico and with characteristically bold boundary claims. When these claims − at Mexico's cost − were endorsed by President Polk, a North American war soon followed.

Responsibility for the Mexican War has been ascribed to President Polk. Polk was very impatient for gains and may well have engineered the confrontation. But negotiations were further complicated by Mexican instability: a revolution against Santa Anna lasted from October 1844 to January 1845, and a further revolution occurred in December 1845. Polk's brusque brinkmanship may have been appropriate to dealings with Britain, but clearly took no account of the periodic shifts in Mexican politics: the various Mexican factions − proud, and resentful of America − could themselves hardly risk discredit or worse by attempting a settlement with the USA. As Alamán, a leading conservative publicist, declared in February 1846:

> We are not a people of merchants and adventurers, scum and refuse of all countries, whose only mission is to usurp the property of the miserable Indians, and later to rob the fertile lands opened to civilisation by the Spanish race . . . . We are a nation formed three centuries ago, not an aggregation of peoples of differing customs.[40]

[39] Brock, *Parties and Political Conscience*, chs. 6, 7.
[40] Schmitt, *Mexico and the United States*, pp. 62–9; Jones, *Santa Anna*, pp. 91–4; K. Jack Bauer, *The Mexican War, 1846–1848* (New York, 1974), pp. 11–13; Hale, *Mexican Liberalism*, pp. 213–14.

Most Americans in turn scorned Mexico as a land of militarism, Catholic control, economic torpor, and blatant class exploitation. To American expansionists, Mexico had no moral right to Texas – which in any case had been created by American settlers – or to even larger regions to the west. These alluring expanses came into the diplomatic arena in 1845–6, for Polk demanded Mexican concessions in the vast area that became New Mexico and California. By 1845 California was already developing in much the same way as Texas had done: Mexican rule was weak, while American informal settlement was very active; the area's potential, hardly exploited, was evidently immeasurable if it could only be settled by an enterprising and energetic people. Various vague and semi-official schemes for French and British takeover had been mooted in the late 1830s and early 1840s, and Polk, in seeking to advance American influence in California, was also protecting an ever-growing American presence there.[41] Yet the president could hardly have expected to meet anything but stern Mexican resistance to these ever-widening American claims.

Whatever its true cause, however, the Mexican war provoked a fierce debate within the USA about the morality of a government both expansionist and energetically committed to the cause of slavery: had America degenerated into the bully boy of the Western world and the mindless hatchet-man for 'the lords of the lash and the loom'?

The Mexican War and Slavery Extension

From May 1846 to February 1848 the Mexican War revealed to many Northerners – Whigs and Democrats alike – the daunting prospect of the easy conquest of huge territories, all potentially open to the introduction of slavery. Northern Democrats especially in 1846 were exposed to the charge of being mere stooges to their Southern expansionist colleagues. To meet this criticism, a Northern Democrat, David Wilmot, drafted a proviso to an appropriation measure, granting that appropriation only if slavery were excluded from any territory gained from Mexico. Wilmot's Proviso, formulated in August 1846, passed the House of Representatives, was repeatedly rejected by the Senate, but remained a bone of political and constitutional contention for nearly 15 years. The annexation of Texas set in train a long series of political crises; but the Wilmot Proviso sparked off immediate and acute sectional alignments in Congress. Although Texas annexation proved no electoral liability to the Northern Democrats in 1844,[42] only 22 months later, in August 1846, Northern congressmen voted overwhelmingly against any further extension of slavery in the lands to be won from Mexico. The appropriations

[41] Kevin Starr, *Americans and the California Dream, 1850–1915* (New York, 1973), pp. 4–5, 9–11, 13–17, 26.
[42] Benson, *Concept of Jacksonian Democracy*, ch. 12; Formisano, *Birth of Mass Political Parties*, pp. 21–30; Johannsen, *Stephen A. Douglas*, pp. 150–1.

bill containing the proviso passed the House of Representatives by a virtually strict sectional vote. Even though the House in March 1847 bowed to Senate intransigence and accepted the appropriations bill shorn of the proviso, Northern congressmen persistently tried to obstruct slavery's further extension: with very tangled constitutional and political consequences.[43]

Some Northern Whigs regarded the exclusion principle alone as insufficient reparation for America's moral guilt. Believing the war itself to have been provoked unjustly and with sinister intentions by Polk's administration, they urged upon Americans a self-denying course of inaction whereby all gains made from a war so unfairly begun would be disowned. Not all Whigs, however, so forcefully bemoaned the nation's moral trespasses. When the Treaty of Guadaloupe Hidalgo, with its bounteous additions to US territory, was presented to the Senate, the Whigs failed to vote in unison. For most Northerners, excluding slavery from the lands wrenched from Mexico would be an adequate rebuff to the South. Indeed, the exclusion principle seemed audacious as well as adequate in 1846–8: after all, the Wilmot Proviso laid down the doctrine that Congress could and should exclude slavery from all the new territories, a position not formally urged so powerfully since 1787.

The exclusion principle challenged the South and sent shock waves through Southern political circles. Many Southern politicians expressed their alarm and outrage at the Wilmot Proviso by demanding the very opposite of total exclusion: slavery should of right go into all the territories. For Democrats in particular, the tussle between Wilmot Proviso Northerners and slavery expansionist Southerners severely threatened the party's ability to formulate federal policy. Party managers and moderates desperately searched for an alternative to the two extreme positions of slavery nowhere or slavery everywhere in the territories. Some hoped for an escape into the practice of the past and suggested that the Missouri Compromise line of 1820 (slavery permitted south of latitude 36°30′, but excluded north of it) be extended to the Pacific coast. The Calhounites and many Southern Democrats were, however, so agitated in 1847 that this compromise seemed unacceptable.[44] So what could the moderates do to quiet this tumult?

Many Northern Democrats in dealing with slavery extension resembled the maiden at the ball: they were far from eager to say yes, but they were unsure when, how, and whether to say no. In such circumstances, the easiest way ahead was to ignore morality and take things robustly as they came. So in 1847–8 a number of Midwestern Democrats devised a fresh formula for deciding slavery's status in new territories. Led by Senator

[43] Don E. Fehrenbacher, *The Dred Scott Case. Its Significance in American Law and Politics* (New York, 1978), pp. 129–31, 135.
[44] Fehrenbacher, *Dred Scott Case*, pp. 127, 136–40, 104–10; Robert F. Dalzell, *Daniel Webster and the Trial of American Nationalism, 1843–1852* (Boston, 1973), pp. 122–31, 137–45; Cooper, *The South and the Politics of Slavery*, pp. 232–44.

Lewis Cass of Michigan, these compromising if not compromised Democrats argued that Congress should leave territorial governments to decide matters relating to slavery for themselves. This doctrine of congressional non-interference, or popular sovereignty, became a central element in the Democratic claim to be a national party and conditioned Democratic thinking about territorial expansion and slavery extension for the next 13 years. Northern Democrats could assure their electorates that free labour would triumph in the territories because Northern settlers would predominate there. At the same time, Southern Democrats could insist that their party nationally guaranteed ordinary Southerners' constitutional right to enter new territories with their slave property.

The doctrine of popular sovereignty, while politically convenient, was illogical in two vital respects. First, Congress would under this doctrine delegate to territorial legislatures powers over the status of slavery that it declined to exercise itself and that, according to Southerners, it did not in fact possess. Congress had previously been held responsible for all territorial laws, but was now to abandon the supervision of territorial law-making, either for the national good, or through lack of constitutional competence, according to different interpretations of popular sovereignty. The federal government's new rôle was clearly described by Senator Douglas in 1848: control of slavery 'belongs entirely with the State or Territory which is called upon to determine upon what system or basis its institutions and society shall be organized. The general government cannot touch the subject without a flagrant usurpation'.[45] This, a radical departure in theory, left obscure the second problem of the popular-sovereignty doctrine: when would territorial sovereignty be exercised over slavery? Would slaves be permitted to enter the territories until such time as a territorial legislature was set up, its representatives elected, and a decision on slavery taken? Under such a lax timetable, slavery might exist, flourish, and spread for years even in a territory where the majority of inhabitants opposed it. Or did territories themselves, as Southern Democrats began to assert, enjoy the right to exclude slavery only when they were ready for statehood? In swerving to avoid a political impasse, the Democrats plunged themselves into a semantic morass of constitutional quibbles. The meaning of popular sovereignty was still not satisfactorily defined a full decade after the term was devised.[46]

These palpable ambiguities were very attractive to Democrats in the political context of 1847–8. For one thing, Congress in 1847–8 was incapable of deciding between exclusion, extension of the Missouri Compromise line, or the free entry of slavery into all territories. Applying the doctrine of popular sovereignty removed the burden of decision-making from Congress. Transferring that burden to the inhabitants of

[45] Johannsen, *Stephen A. Douglas*, p. 233.
[46] Fehrenbacher, *Dred Scott Case*, pp. 142–7.

the territories appeared timely and sensible in 1848, for politicians could not be certain whether the lands to be taken from Mexico were suitable for slavery or not, a matter still unclear when their boundaries were defined in February 1848; this consideration was strengthened because Southerners seemed more concerned to assert their theoretical right to take slaves into the territories than to rush headlong into the fastnesses of the distant West.[47] Moreover, politicians in Washington might well ask how soon settlement in those lands would oblige the federal government to erect territorial governments; alternative opportunities in the West were plentiful, and the pressure for settlement in the lands seized from Mexico (euphemistically called the Mexican Cession) might not be immediate or strong.[48] Delay, and a policy by which responsibility for the decision over slavery was left to the settlers themselves, seemed a politic means of avoiding interminable congressional conflict over what might prove to be merely abstruse rather than practical rights. Finally, the very phrase 'popular sovereignty' had an appealing connotation to Democrats in 1847–8, when the party sought to identify itself as more popularly responsive than the oligarchic Whigs.[49]

Popular sovereignty was strenuously opposed, however, by two groups, at the opposite extremes of sectional politics: Southern rights politicians and anti-slavery Northerners.

The first of these, Southern rights advocates, demanded two basic safeguards. One was the guaranteed right of slaveowners to go anywhere in the federal territories with their property, since Southerners' individual rights and national esteem for their section would otherwise be impaired.[50] This demand was most closely identified with the Calhounites and Southern Democrats in the late 1840s, but it did not, in essence, divide Southern opinion. Indeed the clue to Southern patriotism's increasing appeal in the 1850s was the extremists' success in intertwining respect for Southerners' individual rights with the fullest constitutional defence of property rights in slaves. This demand hit a responsive chord throughout the South, including the border South. As the revised state constitution of Kentucky in 1850 declared:

> The right of property is before and higher than any constitutional sanction; and the right of the owner of a slave to such slave, and its increase, is the same, and as inviolable, as the right of the owner of any property whatever.[51]

If slaveownership was based on straightforward property rights – themselves sacred to nineteenth-century liberals – then slaveowners could

---

[47] Cooper, *The South and the Politics of Slavery*, pp. 242–3.
[48] Allan Nevins, *Ordeal of the Union* (New York, 1947), I, 21.
[49] For Democratic pressure for constitutional reform, see: Shade, *Banks or No Banks*, pp. 112–15; *A Matter of Allegiances*, pp. 23, 31–3.
[50] Cooper, *The South and the Politics of Slavery*, pp. 255–8.
[51] Quoted in Brock, *Parties and Political Conscience*, p. 273.

not logically be prevented from settling anywhere in the federal territories.

In addition, Southern rights advocates wanted longer-term guarantees of Southern equality in the Union. Their anxiety arose from differences in the rate of population growth; the residents of the free states already outnumbered those in the slave states and, according to trend, the gap could only widen. Southern politicians responded in varied ways to this hankering for future safety. For many, it meant that more slave states should be created and more Senate seats be given thus to the slave interest; for an extremist few it fired feverish desires for disunion and Southern independence; for Calhoun and his ever proliferating following in 1848–50, it reinforced demands for new constitutional checks against any form of congressional anti-slavery and for a more militant, non-partisan *Southern* political movement. All agreed, however, in repudiating the Wilmot Proviso and in extolling slavery extension. Self-righteous, indignant, and insistent in 1848, Southern politicians of both parties wrung basic concessions from their colleagues. The Whigs' presidential candidate, General Zachary Taylor, was a slaveowner proclaimed in the South — misleadingly as it later transpired — as an apostle of slavery expansion. Southern Democrats fought the war-hero and slaveowner by underlining the special advantages offered by popular sovereignty for slavery's entry into the territories: trust in measures rather than men, was their defensive message in 1848.[52]

Yet the Wilmot Proviso would not die. A prominent group of Northern Democrats stood by the exclusion principle and in 1848 joined the Liberty men to form the Free Soil party. Although the precise timing of the defection of these Northern Democrats from their party in 1848 was contingent upon factional rivalries, it stemmed ultimately from a fundamental dispute over the extent to which slavery and slavery extension should be condoned by the North. Adding further support to the Free Soil cause, the so-called Conscience Whigs of Massachusetts, and elsewhere in New England, also refused in 1848 to abide by their national party's accommodating needs and rejected further truckling to the Slave Power. The Free Soldiers stalked their quarry somewhat indirectly: they aimed not to kill slavery outright but to wear it down gradually and relentlessly, and the first step in that process was to prevent its further spread. This caution could well be attributed to the triumph of interest over virtue; for new territories, if the Free Soilers had their way, would be open only to free men, largely Northerners, and not racially contaminated (so contemporaries held) by the blighting presence of black slaves. Yet, although the Free Soilers appealed to whites' self-interest and most sternly abused the Slave Power rather than slavery, their case against slavery extension was not inconsistent with virtuous foresight. As David Wilmot said in October 1847, 'Slavery has within itself the seeds of

[52] Cooper, *The South and the Politics of Slavery*, pp. 258–68, 272–6, 287–8.

its own dissolution. Keep it within limits, let it remain where it now is, and in time it will wear itself out'.[53]

Virtuous or self-interested, accidental allies or co-workers destined since 1844—5 to band together, the free soil Democrats, Conscience Whigs, and Liberty men who established the Free Soil party were vociferous and well supported, boasted illustrious leaders, and made an immediate impact on politics. Their national ticket in 1848 consisted of ex-president van Buren and Charles Francis Adams, whose father and grandfather had both been presidents. And the party won 10.1 per cent of the presidential votes, against the Democrats' 42.5 per cent and the Whigs' 47.3 per cent: an impressive beginning for a third party. More importantly, the Free Soilers lodged their men at the very heart of power. As early as the winter of 1845—6 dissident anti-annexationist Democrats in New Hampshire elected John P. Hale to the Senate; Hale became a leading Free Soiler. Between February 1849 and August 1851 the Free Soilers gained two more Senators: Salmon P. Chase from Ohio and the stern, self-righteous Charles Sumner from Massachusetts. From their special vantage point, these committed anti-slavery senators were alert to the earliest manifestations of Slave Power aggression; very tenuously linked to parties, they dramatically demonstrated their disruptive rôle at last in 1854.[54]

But while the Free Soilers gained a vital watch-tower in the Senate, their fortunes in the country at large were topsy-turvy. Their three Senate seats were won through temporary alliances with regular Democrats; the Democrats in return gained control of state legislatures to enact banking laws or set up constitutional conventions. But the Free Soilers' relationships with the Democracy were extremely unstable; in 1849, for instance, the majority of Free Soil defectors in New York trudged back into the Democratic fold from which they had strayed in the previous year. In some years, the Free Soilers concentrated solely on slavery extension; in others, they broadened their programme to include traditional Democratic economic issues. But by 1851, despite their voice in the Senate, the Free Soilers possessed a vigorous organization only in Massachusetts and Ohio, and solid electoral support also only in Wisconsin and in the New England states of Vermont, New Hampshire, and Maine.[55] This level of organization and support proved thoroughly inadequate to maintain their national vote of 1848. Even so, the Free Soilers' rejection of popular sovereignty shaped political debate in the 1850s; for, if the Free Soil *party* was fairly weak after 1848, the free soil Democratic *faction* was quite strong, openly anxious at the pro-slavery

[53] Sewell, *Ballots for Freedom*, pp. 148—52, 159, 189, 190—2, 199—201; David Donald, *Charles Sumner and the Coming of the Civil War* (New York, 1961), ch. 7.
[54] Sewell, *Ballots for Freedom*, pp. 128—9, 168, 210, 222; Donald, *Charles Sumner*, chs. 8—10.
[55] Sewell, *Ballots for Freedom*, pp. 202—5, 223—30; *Guide to U.S. Elections*, pp. 269, 412, 420, 433.

drift of national policy, and prepared, reluctantly, to go its own political way.

The doctrine of popular sovereignty had been formulated in late 1847 to make territorial acquisitions from Mexico acceptable to a majority of Americans, at a time when the lands obtained were of little immediate interest to new settlers. But, unfortunately for those who sought domestic peace through ambiguous constitutional formulae, parts of the 529,000 square miles grasped from Mexico in 1848 proved to be far richer and more urgently attractive to Americans than the most fervent expansionists had dreamed. By mid 1848 the Pacific coast was alive with rumours of California gold; by the end of the year official reports of vast gold discoveries had reached Washington.[56] So began the gold rush to California and a new phase in the federal crisis over territorial policy. A sequence of events, begun in 1821–3 with American settlement in the wild frontier of northern Mexico, led in 1849–50 to the most bitter sectional debate over the provision of government for California: and to a severe testing of republican theory.

Eighteenth-century Europeans who contemplated such matters had usually assumed that republican government would be suitable only for relatively small and perhaps homogeneous communities. In the 1780s Americans had rejected that orthodoxy and initiated a great experiment in politics. By 1850 the effervescence of far-flung communities, and the uncontrollable push for new lands in Texas and California, indeed endangered the balance between the old-established sections of the country, by pitting North and South against each other in pursuit of their respective 'rights' in the territories. Many Americans were now determined to vindicate republicanism and preserve the nation against this challenge induced by unbridled territorial expansion; to them the republic guaranteed cultural diversity and local rights. Yet for many Northerners a republican form of government embodied a progressive extension of natural rights; it was not just an umbrella protecting a hodge-podge of locally entrenched interests, privileges, or prejudices. When Charles Sumner in 1850 declared his objective 'that the Federal Government may be put openly, actively and perpetually on the side of Freedom',[57] he concisely defined for Northern men of anti-slavery conscience the point still to be secured.

---

[56] Nevins, *Ordeal of the Union*, I, 21, 217–18.
[57] Donald, *Charles Sumner*, p. 188.

6 The Compromise of 1850

America was enlarged and greatly changed between 1844 and 1850. Not only did the USA settle its Oregon boundary and acquire the Mexican Cession; attitudes changed. In 1844 politicians could legitimately and with detached thoughtfulness object to the hasty westward expansion of their country.[1] They could question the legality and morality of annexing Texas when it was still subject to Mexican claims. They could point to the dangers inherent in slavery extension. They could contend that the true centres for national development were the Atlantic seaboard, the Mississippi valley and the Ohio valley, and that westward movement would merely distract and dissipate American energies. Six years later such arguments were futile and wrong. The discovery of gold in California made the far west essential economically; and it forced the pace of political events. Senator William Seward of New York aptly remarked in March 1850, 'A year ago, California was a mere military dependency of our own . . . . To-day, California is . . . more populous than the least, and richer than several, of the greatest of our thirty States'. By 1850 the white population of the Mexican Cession totalled 165,498, concentrated mostly in California (92,600) and New Mexico (61,500); yet neither area had a formal civilian government and both sought admission to statehood; the Northern Whig leader added, ominously, 'This same California, thus rich and populous, is here asking admission into the Union, and finds us debating the dissolution of the Union itself'.[2]

The crisis of 1850 was a dress rehearsal for the show-down of 1860–1. Many of the arguments used were the same. Many of the participants were the same. And the ultimate threat of the allegedly aggrieved party – the South's secession – was first proclaimed widely in 1849–50. Yet in 1850 a significant body of Northern politicians recognized some validity in Southern demands and made significant and timely concessions to Southern opinion. Their handiwork, the so-called Compromise of 1850, has received short shrift from modern historians. It has been viewed as an 'armistice', a flawed, if not botched, stop-gap: illogical, impermanent,

---

[1] William R. Brock, *Parties and Political Conscience: American Dilemmas, 1840–1850* (Millwood, N.Y., 1979), pp. 120–6.
[2] *Appendix to the Congressional Globe*, 31st Congress, 1st Session (Washington, D.C., 1850), p. 261.

immoral, and perhaps corrupt.[3] Why, then, was so much conceded by some Northerners in 1850 and why was this alleged concoction and confidence-trick, the set of compromise measures, so generally supported and lauded in 1851–2?

First, one must be clear what was at issue in 1850. Practical problems in governing the Mexican Cession (which included California) had not been resolved when the USA obtained that region in 1848. The whole of the Mexican Cession was simply ruled by the US Army: a highly unsatis-factory state of affairs for California especially, with its rapidly growing and politically unruly population. Moreover, Texas claimed sovereignty over large chunks of one part of the Mexican Cession, New Mexico, including the populous area around Santa Fé. During the summer of 1850 the governor of Texas threatened to maintain his state's claims by force of arms, with the result that in June–July 1850 the federal govern-ment was preparing to defend New Mexico's territorial integrity against the truculent Texans. These practical problems were compounded by a more theoretical dispute over slavery.

In August 1848 Congress and the Democratic President had agreed to organize Oregon territory with the customary ban on slavery: customary, that is, since Oregon lay well north of the line 36°30′. This action marked something of a defeat for the radical new Southern doctrine, expounded by Senator Calhoun of South Carolina, that slavery could not be excluded by Congress from any federal territory. Worse – in Calhoun's eyes – was to follow. A young Northern Democrat, Senator Douglas, proposed in December 1848 that the Mexican Cession, or at least California, be admitted directly to statehood. Such a step would avoid prolonged congressional wranglings over slavery in the territories. But it would also effectively block slavery's extension into either the entire Mexican Cession or California. At the same time, the House of Representatives passed a resolution favouring the ending of the slave trade in the federal District of Columbia. Alarmed at this prospect, Calhoun early in 1849 sought to rally Southern politicians to oppose these and other interferences with Southern rights. His 'Southern Address' decidedly failed in the short run to win the mass support of Southern representatives and senators in Washington. Yet it was a brilliant propaganda ploy, immediately becoming the great debating point among Southern politicians in 1849. Calhoun's fanatical preoccupation with the long-term defence of slavery and the 'Southern cause' dramatic-ally raised the political and emotional stakes of territorial policy in 1849. For his 'Southern Address' was a broad diatribe against the North. According to Calhoun, Northerners opposed slavery in the District of

---

[3] For example: Roy F. Nichols, *The Stakes of Power, 1845–1877* (New York, 1961), pp. 28–30; David M. Potter (completed and edited by Don. E. Fehrenbacher), *The Impending Crisis, 1848–1861* (New York, 1976), ch. 5; Brock, *Parties and Political Conscience*, chs. 10–11; Holman Hamilton, *Prologue to Conflict: The Crisis and Compromise of 1850* (New York, 1966 edn).

Columbia; they failed to return fugitive slaves to their Southern owners; they tolerated and encouraged extremist attacks on Southern institutions; and now, in 1848–9, they were depriving Southerners of their proper, constitutional, and equal rights in the US territories. Piling grievance upon grievance and capping all with a self-righteous refusal to notice the moral mote in the eye of the South, Calhoun's address laid the essential basis for the extreme Southern claim of the next decade: slavery should follow the flag into all new territories.[4]

Northerners felt quite differently in 1849. By the end of the year most Northern state legislatures had supported the Wilmot Proviso's contention that slavery should be excluded from all new territories.[5] So, what was to be the fate of the Mexican Cession?

From December 1849, when it met, until September 1850 Congress bitterly and exhaustively grappled with the twin problems of the Mexican Cession and Southern rights. The new Whig president, General Zachary Taylor, sought a speedy solution to practical questions of government. Before Congress convened, Taylor encouraged Californians to seek direct admission to statehood, so avoiding the vexed intermediate stage of organized territorial government. When Congress convened, California had indeed formed a *de facto* civilian government and requested that the new Congress admit it to statehood. Taylor hoped that New Mexico would also leap-frog the territorial stage. These manoeuvrings infuriated Southern politicians: and not just Southern Democratic colleagues of Calhoun's. A prominent Southern Whig, Robert Toombs of Georgia, warned the House of Representatives in December 1849: 'if by your legislation you seek to drive us from the territories of California and New Mexico . . . and to abolish slavery in this District [of Columbia] . . . I am for disunion'.[6]

Battle was joined in 1850 by three groups. President Taylor (though a Southerner himself) and most Northern Whigs wanted a prompt, straightforward, and limited settlement of the practical questions involved in governing California and New Mexico. Senator Seward, for example, openly denied that slavery was relevant to those questions. To Seward, it was repulsive and moribund as an institution; California and

---

[4] Don E. Fehrenbacher, *The Dred Scott Case. Its Significance in American Law and Politics* (New York, 1978), pp. 147–57; William J. Cooper, Jr, *The South and the Politics of Slavery, 1828–1856* (Baton Rouge, 1978), pp. 269–72, 287–90; Ulrich B. Phillips (ed.), *The Correspondence of Robert Toombs, Alexander H. Stephens, and Howell Cobb* (Washington, D.C., 1911), II, pp. 152–76. Politicians have to deal with real problems as well as lead and stage-manage their parties. There is a tendency in some recent accounts to give party management pride of place in explaining political decision-making. Such an emphasis – a vital corrective to some political history – can be carried too far: see Cooper, *The South and the Politics of Slavery* and Michael F. Holt, *The Political Crisis of the 1850s* (New York, 1978), ch. 4.

[5] Fehrenbacher, *Dred Scott Case*, p. 157.

[6] My account of the Compromise is based on: Cooper, *The South and the Politics of Slavery*, pp. 275–84; Potter, *Impending Crisis*, ch. 5: quotation on p. 94; Hamilton, *Prologue to Conflict*; Fehrenbacher, *Dred Scott Case*, pp. 159–77.

New Mexico should be admitted as free states.[7] Southern Democrats and some Southern Whigs, however, demanded some real opportunity for slavery to extend into at least parts of the Mexican Cession and wanted some guarantees on federal policy with respect to slavery in the District of Columbia or to the rendition of fugitive slaves. Between these two groups stood most Northern Democrats − willing to see slavery extend where settlers welcomed it − and many Southern Whigs, worried about but not militant over Southern rights. Eventually, after prolonged wrangling in Congress, Northern Democrats and Southern Whigs helped produce a settlement far wider than most Northern Whigs expected, yet not quite as indulgent to slavery as Southern Democrats demanded.

The Compromise of 1850 comprised five acts passed by the end of September. The government of the Mexican Cession was arranged: California entered the Union as a free state; but New Mexico and Utah were organized as territories to become states 'with or without slavery, as their constitution may prescribe at the time of their admission'. The Compromise line of 36°30' established in 1820 was disregarded, for all Utah and small parts of New Mexico were north of that line and so Utah at least should have been closed to slavery. The acts passed in 1850 also placated Texas, which dropped its claims upon New Mexico, and which received a generous federal settlement of its debts: debts originally contracted when it had been an independent republic during the years 1836−45. Arrangements made for the Texas debt may have furnished scope for illicitly inducing some congressmen to support the Compromise measures. Two further acts directly affected slavery's position in the nation. Slave trading in the District of Columbia was abolished. But this was balanced by a Fugitive Slave Act creating procedures by which runaway slaves in the North could be recaptured by their owners. This act was furiously opposed in the North in the 1850s, largely because it brazenly disregarded the civil rights of any blacks accused of being runaway slaves. During the 1850s, of an estimated 8,000−15,000 fugitive slaves, only 157 were returned to their masters under the aegis of the act. While many Southern politicians in 1850 regarded the Fugitive Slave Act as a test of Northern goodwill, this draconian enactment merely exasperated Northern state legislatures in the 1850s and yielded meagre benefits to Southern slave-owners.[8]

Yet, if the Fugitive Slave Act turned out to be so repugnant to Northern civil libertarians; if the raw and raucous slave state of Texas did so well from the settlement; if Utah and New Mexico were opened to slavery despite the Compromise line of 1820 and strenuous Northern efforts since 1846 to impose the Wilmot Proviso; if, in other words, so much was

---

[7] *Appendix to the Congressional Globe*, 31:1, pp. 261–2.
[8] Stanley W. Campbell, *The Slave Catchers: Enforcement of the Fugitive Slave Law, 1850–1860* (New York, 1972 edn), pp. 136–7, 207; Norman L. Rosenberg, 'Personal Liberty Laws and Sectional Crisis, 1850–61', *Civil War History* XVII (1971), 25–44.

yielded to the South, why were the Compromise measures passed and subsequently acceded to by the North? And they *were* indeed accepted by the North. In 1850 the Northern Democrats did well in the mid-term congressional elections. By 1851 the Free Soilers — the men who violently opposed any further extension of slavery — were strongly organized only in Massachusetts and Ohio and won respectable electoral backing also only· in Wisconsin and in the New England states of Vermont, New Hampshire, and Maine; and their share of the presidential vote fell from 10.1 per cent in 1848 to 4.9 per cent in 1852.[9] Indeed, in 1852 both parties nationally supported the Compromise.

Perhaps the main reason for Northern concessions was the sheer force of Southern pressure. According to one Northern Democratic senator, Southern politicians 'pounded on the North until it became insufferable'. A leading Northern Whig, Senator Daniel Webster, noted in October 1850: 'We have gone through the most important crisis which has occurred since the foundation of this government, and whatever party may prevail, hereafter, the Union stands firm. Faction, disunion, and love of mischief, are put under, at least for the present, and I hope for a long time'.[10] Disunion sentiment made remarkable strides in the South in 1849–50. Of course, rhetorical demands for the full recognition of Southern rights had been a stock element in Southern politics since the mid 1830s; abolitionism had made Southern congressmen especially prickly about their constituencies' place in the Union. But ideas of state secession and a possible Southern confederation had been slow to germinate. Between October 1849 and February 1850, however, many slave state legislatures considered the desirability of holding a Southern convention to thrash out a common response to the threatened curtailment of alleged Southern rights. Although most Southern Whigs probably opposed such a step, and worked actively to quash the scheme in Maryland, Kentucky, Florida, and Louisiana, the sense of Southern rights endangered was quickened by this call. Even so, a Southern convention convoked at Nashville in June 1850 failed to represent the entire section and failed to formulate a set of 'Southern' demands. It contained no delegates from the following states of marked Whig strength or influence: Kentucky, Missouri, Louisiana, Delaware, Maryland, and North Carolina. And it adjourned to await congressional developments. On reconvening in November it was even less representative of Southern opinion; its assertion of the constitutional right of states to secede and its rejection of the congressional settlement were scarcely noticed.[11] Yet earlier, in the summer of 1850, the pressure for a

[9] The best source for all election figures is: *Congressional Quarterly's Guide to U.S. Elections* (Washington, D.C., 1975).

[10] Robert W. Johannsen, *Stephen A. Douglas* (New York, 1973), p. 283; *The Writings and Speeches of Daniel Webster* (*National Edition*: Boston, 1903), XVI, 568.

[11] Arthur C. Cole, *The Whig Party in the South* (Gloucester, Mass., 1962 reprint of 1914 edn), pp. 148–51, 157–62, 170–2, 181.

convention and the revolutionary steps openly pondered in the convention added pointedly to the national crisis.

The cry of 'Southern rights endangered' was raised in 1849–50 with particular spirit across the Deep South, the very region that started the rebellion of 1860–1. Politicians in the Deep South were specially sensitive to the implications of the Wilmot Proviso; they bitterly resented any attempt to stop the future extension of slavery into new territories. Some leaders in the Deep South fondly expected that the USA would extend its sway into the Caribbean, with Cuba as a prime target. Many leaders had participated in or vigorously supported the Mexican War of 1846–8: they anticipated material gains for Southerners and slaveowners from those martial and political endeavours.[12] The future of the Deep South and its white people seemed to depend upon opportunities for expansion to the West.

The importance of the West to Southern settlers was not entirely fanciful. For example, the south-western state of Arkansas had the fastest growing population of any slave state in the 1840s. This trend continued: between 1850 and 1860 the combined population of the south-western slave states of Arkansas and Texas rose from 422,000 to 1,041,000, and the number of slaves included in those totals increased from 105,000 in 1850 to 294,000 in 1860. Yet slaveowners and their human chattels did not surge into the two territories opened to them in 1850. Utah was a largely inhospitable region whose most enthusiastic settlers in the 1850s were the troublesome Mormons; New Mexico's population rose from 61,500 in 1850 to only 93,500 in 1860 and, despite Southern claims and Northern fears, none of them were slaves.[13] Although Utah and New Mexico proved quite fruitless for settlement by Southern slaveowners in the 1850s, this subsequent development should not, however, obscure the rational expectation of 1850. Slaveowners and slavery *had* moved westwards in the 1840s; Arkansas and Texas *would* grow appreciably in the 1850s; the *general* fact of westward extension for the South was firmly established in those two decades, even though Utah and New Mexico in particular were not settled by slaveowners. Moreover, Southern politicians generally wished to admit further slave states, in order to keep up their representation in the Senate. New Mexico territory, though devoid of slaves, strongly supported slavery;[14] if it had been raised to statehood before the Civil War, it would have joined the pro-slavery political camp. Opportunities for future western settlement and the balance of sectional power in the Senate both seemed threatened by Northern opposition to slavery extension. Hence the widespread,

[12] Avery O. Craven, *The Coming of the Civil War* (Chicago, 1957 edn), pp. 231–69; Clement Eaton, *Jefferson Davis* (New York, 1977), pp. 74–5, 80; Robert E. May, *The Southern Dream of a Caribbean Empire, 1854–1861* (Baton Rouge, 1973), pp. 16–19.

[13] *Population of the United States in 1860; Compiled from the Original Returns of the Eighth Census* (Washington, D.C., 1864), pp. 599, 604.

[14] Fehrenbacher, *Dred Scott Case*, pp. 176–7.

extreme, raucous, and bullying Southern pressure, notably powerful in the Deep South, for concessions in 1850.

Although sectional pressure scared some Northerners into yielding to the South in 1850, sectional animosities remained very strong. Section rather than party much influenced crucial congressional decisions. For example, Southern senators who actually voted joined together, irrespective of party, on three of the five crucial bills making up the Compromise. No Southern senator voted against the New Mexico bill or the Fugitive Slave bill; and a fair number of Southern Whigs voted with a rather larger number of Southern Democrats for each bill. Southern senators were more divided over the bill to end slave trading in the District of Columbia, but an easy majority of Southern Whigs opposed that bill, as did the overwhelming majority of Southern Democrats. Similarly, Northern senators voted together on three bills. All Northern Democrats and Northern Whigs who voted on the California statehood bill, and on the bill banning the slave trade in the District of Columbia, favoured those measures. The majority of Northern Whigs and the overwhelming majority of Northern Democrats actually voting supported the Texas boundaries and debts bill.[15] Yet clearly sectional loyalties were not the only force at work. In the two houses together 61 members (or 21 per cent of the total) supported at least four of the five measures and opposed none of them: this central group of compromisers consisted of 38 Northern Democrats, 11 Southern Whigs, 6 Southern Democrats, and 6 Northern Whigs.[16] A considerable body of Northern politicians − 44 of them − clearly felt that the South had to be placated in 1850. They were probably influenced by four considerations.

First, something had to be done about the government of the Mexican Cession. A few congressmen may have been induced to support the Compromise by back-room trading in Texas bonds, but there was also a major practical problem crying out for legislative solution. The leading compromisers in 1850 − initially Senators Clay and Webster and subsequently Senator Douglas − often prided themselves on their pragmatism. Secondly, the highly protracted debate in the Senate − proceeding from January to September and full of emotion, grand set-piece speeches and dramatic rhetoric − perhaps swung members of the House of Representatives towards compromise. The House, after all, was very inexperienced − over half its members were new to Congress − and must have been impressed at least in part by the sheer weight of Senatorial oratory.[17] Thirdly, the Northern leaders of compromise gustily exploited emotional nationalism to further their case. Just as the Northern argument against secession in 1861 rested heavily on an intense commitment to the Union, so in 1850 the Northern compromisers' enthusiasm for the

---

[15] These figures are derived from the full roll-call lists in Hamilton, *Prologue to Conflict*, pp. 191–2.

[16] Fehrenbacher, *Dred Scott Case*, pp. 162–3.

[17] *Ibid.*, p. 162.

Union was their trump card. Northerners opposing concessions to the South pointed out that such nationalism was vacuous if it placed loyalty to the Union above every consideration for the morality of slavery. But for many Northerners in 1850 the Union was cheap at the price of conceding the Fugitive Slave Act and of allowing slavery into New Mexico and Utah. Thus the Fugitive Slave Act passed the Senate by 27 votes (24 of them Southern) to 12 votes (all Northern), while no fewer than 21 senators were absent or abstained from the vote; 15 of those were Northerners. Some of these Northern absentees would probably have endorsed the Fugitive Slave Act. But one cannot help suspect that many senators simply dodged the issue for the sake of a settlement. On other key votes as well, absenteeism and abstention were major features of congressional voting behaviour in late 1850. The positive appeal of Unionism was perhaps reinforced at the end of the congressional session by weariness, frustration, and a desire to reassure the South.[18]

But for many Northern Democrats the Compromise was not simply a tame and tired surrender. They believed or came to believe − and Senator Douglas acted the part of high priest in this new faith − that the dispute over slavery extension had been resolved in 1850. This was the fourth reason for Northern support of the Compromise. From August 1846 to March 1849 the House of Representatives had insisted upon the Wilmot Proviso's prohibition of any further extension of slavery. In 1850, however, the House's hostility to slavery extension was broken. Northern Democrats claimed that the doctrine of popular sovereignty was vindicated, since the people of New Mexico and Utah could decide for themselves whether or not they wanted slavery. Yet the wording of the relevant act declared that New Mexico and Utah would be admitted as states 'with or without slavery, as their constitution may prescribe at the time of their admission'. If Northern Democrats asserted that this phrasing implied popular sovereignty, many Southern Democrats argued that *only* when a territory applied for statehood could it ban slavery: until that time, the people in the territory had no control over slavery. As far as New Mexico and Utah went, the precise meaning of the act was not politically relevant. But when the same phrase was applied in 1854 to the territories of Kansas and Nebraska it provoked a semantic dispute over constitutional rights which by 1858 threatened to tear the Democratic party to pieces. In 1850, however, this very uncertainty over the meaning of the legislation probably eased the passage of the Compromise acts. If the Democrats seem in retrospect to have prospered in 1850−2 only to pay later in 1854−8, they could reasonably claim to have avoided the opposite extremes of the Wilmot Proviso and Calhoun's radicalism in the political circumstances of 1850. A compelling reason for Northern

---

[18] Johannsen, *Stephen A. Douglas*, pp. 278–80, 301–2; Robert F. Dalzell, Jr, *Daniel Webster and the Trial of American Nationalism, 1843–1852* (Boston, 1973), pp. 175–95; Hamilton, *Prologue to Conflict*, pp. 140–3, 192, 200.

acceptance of the Compromise of 1850 was that it actually looked like a compromise settlement at the time.

Such was especially the case when one considers the Deep South's response to the five acts. Virtually no politician from the Deep South actively supported the Compromise as a legislative package in 1850.[19] After the measures' eventual passage, various efforts were made in the Deep South to condemn and reject the Compromise. In November 1850 Jefferson Davis, a senator from Mississippi, called for the summoning of a state convention to consider Mississippi's response to the legislation. Simultaneously, he urged that a convention of the slave states should draw up demands to present to the free states, for the guarantee of Southern rights and Southern equality in the Union. If these guarantees were not provided, the South should peacefully secede. This call for concerted Southern action won little favour. But in Mississippi, Alabama, South Carolina, and Georgia various separatist proposals were advanced in 1851. By May 1851 the secessionist cause was most powerful in Calhoun's home state of South Carolina. So Senator Davis changed his tack, advised South Carolina not to secede, but publicly declared that, if South Carolina did leave the Union and were attacked by the federal government, then Mississippi should go to South Carolina's aid. Such separatist stirrings drove Union-minded Southern Democrats and the great majority of Southern Whigs into Unionist coalitions which, by the end of summer, had trounced the secessionists of Georgia and Alabama. In September 1851 Mississippi's election for delegates to a state convention to discuss the Compromise yielded 28,402 votes to Unionist delegates and 21,242 votes to their opponents; and Jefferson Davis was subsequently defeated as a States Right Democratic candidate for Mississippi's governorship. At the end of 1851 only South Carolina opposed the Compromise.[20] But even South Carolinians refused to break up the Union on this matter. As an anti-slavery jurist teaching in South Carolina wrote in May 1851: 'I believe I can say Secession is dead — at least, dying; but I cannot say what labour and anxiety it has cost us, and will long cost us'.[21]

This, surely, was why the Compromise looked like a compromise in 1850–1: leaders of the Deep South were opposed to it, as a general settlement, in Congress; some of them worked to have it rejected by their various states in 1851; but no state in the Deep South felt the South's political or social or constitutional position so threatened in 1851 that secession would be justified or desirable.

If the Deep South was less than enthusiastic about the Compromise measures, so the Free Soilers, especially vociferous in Massachusetts, were equally unimpressed. In February 1850 Charles Sumner (elected to the

---

[19] Fehrenbacher, *Dred Scott Case*, p. 163.
[20] Eaton, *Jefferson Davis*, pp. 76–9; Craven, *Coming of the Civil War*, pp. 264–9.
[21] Frank Freidel, *Francis Lieber. Nineteenth-Century Liberal* (Baton Rouge, 1947), p. 256.

US Senate in the following year) privately urged Free Soilers not to 'sacrifice one jot or tittle of our principles' to make excessively generous concessions to the South: even if the Union were at stake.[22] The Free Soilers indeed continued to oppose the Compromise. If their popular support was very limited (they captured only 9 of the 142 congressional districts in the free states at the mid-term elections of 1850–1), their very presence and persistence underscored the 'moderate' character of the Compromise. During the summer of 1852, with the presidential election campaign in full swing, Sumner moved that the Senate repeal the Fugitive Slave Act. The timing was unpropitious, for both parties publicly adhered to sectional conciliation; even so, although a number of Northern Senators disliked the act, only three voted with Sumner for repeal, and they were two Free Soilers and a free soil Whig.[23]

Between secessionism and free soil the legislation of 1850 offered a path described by one Northern Democratic senator: 'The Ultra pro-slavery man is intolerable. The Ultra Free-Soil man is still worse. It should be our effort to keep the middle course between two extremes'.[24] By 1852 the settlement was widely applauded or endorsed for this reason. In the congressional elections held in 1850–1 the Democrats captured 79 out of 142 House seats in the free states and, although not all Northern Democrats were eager Compromisers, the majority of them sustained the settlement. And in the presidential election of 1852 the Democrats kept up their momentum by winning 50.3 per cent of the national vote; they did so on a platform that supported the Compromise measures and that promised to avoid further agitation over slavery.[25] So, too, in 1852 the defeated Whigs endorsed the Compromise, though they went further than their opponents by declaring it a *final* settlement of slavery issues.

Perhaps, then, majority opinion supported Douglas's assessment of the settlement:

> The measures are right in themselves, and collectively constitute one grand scheme of conciliation and adjustment . . . . The North has not surrendered to the South, nor has the South made any humiliating concession to the North. Each section has maintained its honor and its rights, and both have met on the common ground of justice and compromise.[26]

An adjustment made with difficulty upon the common ground of compromise fairly well described the acts of 1850. Of course, many Northerners disagreed that the Fugitive Slave Act maintained their section's honour and rights. Objections to that act were expressed immediately after the settlement and with continuing vigour in the

[22] David Donald, *Charles Sumner and the Coming of the Civil War* (New York, 1961), p. 184.
[23] *Guide to U.S. Elections*, pp. 591–4; Donald, *Charles Sumner*, pp. 224–37.
[24] Johannsen, *Stephen A. Douglas*, p. 283.
[25] *Guide to U.S. Elections*, pp. 591–4, 269.
[26] Johannsen, *Stephen A. Douglas*, pp. 296–7.

1850s: by the end of the decade the act was fully enforced in very few states of the North. But the Fugitive Slave Act never became the political rallying point that, say, the Wilmot Proviso had once been: there were, after all, various ways in which individual states circumvented the harsh provisions of the federal act. Even so, looking to the future, there were three clear dangers inherent in the settlement and its reception.

First, support for the measures in the Deep South was conditional upon Northern good behaviour. Indeed, the Compromise's success depended upon a corollary attached to it in Georgia. Congress in 1850 rejected the Wilmot Proviso, so removing a stigma − upon their society and their rights − bitterly resented since 1846 by many Southerners. Yet for Unionism to succeed in the Deep South something more than the rejection of the Wilmot Proviso was required. Union-minded politicians in Georgia had been forced in the famous Georgia platform of December 1850 to qualify their commitment to the Union: Georgians should accept the settlement if the North enforced the Fugitive Slave Act; but if Southern rights were infringed, then secession might well be a legitimate response. This vital corollary − demanding much of the North and conceding much to secessionist thinking − was widely embraced in the Deep South. It presented dangerous hostages to fortune.[27] Secondly, Douglas and other Northern Democrats believed that the territorial bills reflected their own version of popular sovereignty, that New Mexico, like California, would reject slavery, and that future territorial organization would be free of the twin extremes of the Wilmot Proviso and Calhoun's doctrine.[28] In fact the wording of the territorial bills proved to be a Delphic precedent: it could be and would be interpreted either way to buttress Douglas's popular sovereignty or Calhoun's doctrine.

Finally, Douglas and many of his Democratic colleagues (and the Democrats were the national majority between 1850 and 1854) were hopelessly deluded about the future path American white society would take. Armed with the doctrine of popular sovereignty, Douglas sincerely believed that he could press ahead with the development of the West while avoiding controversy over slavery: indeed the two things would feed one another, for as the West grew, so it would more thoroughly assuage the sectional animosities of North and South. As he said in January 1852, 'The North and South may quarrel and wrangle about a question which should never enter the halls of Congress; but the Great West will say to the South, You must not leave us; and to the North, You must faithfully observe the constitution − with all its compromises'.[29] To many politicians this idea might have been a worthy, charming, but empty fancy. Within two years the restless Douglas was busy translating it into practical policy; and a new sectional crisis began.

[27] Ulrich B. Phillips, *Georgia and State Rights* (Antioch, 1968 reprint of 1901 edn), pp. 163–7.
[28] Johannsen, *Stephen A. Douglas*, p. 301.
[29] *Ibid.*, p. 357.

7 Kansas and the Democratic Party, 1854–1858

It would be foolish to believe that elections themselves settle very much in politics. It would be equally foolish to believe that we can ever truly understand why voters respond in elections in the various ways that they do. But election campaigns − despite their general tendency to encourage vagueness, generalities, and appeals to the soft centre of floating voters − do reveal something about the public mood at a given time. The presidential election of 1852 revealed a widespread desire for an end to − or a patching up of − heated sectional disputes. Although the Democrats did not agree with the Whigs that the Compromise measures constituted a final settlement of sectional grievances, both major parties endorsed those measures of 1850. Northern voters were offered a fairly radical alternative to Whigs and Democrats; but the Free Soilers' hostility to any further extension of slavery won them only 4.9 per cent of the presidential vote, a sharp drop from the Free Soilers' 10 per cent in 1848. When Senator Charles Sumner of Massachusetts attempted in August 1852 to repeal the hated Fugitive Slave Act, he secured only three other senators' support. With provocation towards none, the national parties in 1852 struggled to keep their various wings together and their assorted extremists isolated. If ever American public opinion seemed to yearn for the quiet centre it was surely in 1852.

Yet when the mid-term congressional elections occurred in 1854, party politics had been blown apart: political rhetoric was accusatory and menacing and the political map had been splashed with new colours. This upheaval of 1854 resulted in large measure from the Democrats' efforts to organize the new territories of Kansas and Nebraska. It involved: the formation of state Republican parties in the Midwest in the spring and summer of 1854; the election of 117 anti-Nebraska congressmen in the autumn of 1854, with 42 of those Congressmen being *primarily* devoted to stopping slavery's further extension;[1] the consolidation of a purely Northern Republican party during 1855; and the establishment of a powerful and well-organized Republican movement by February 1856. Whereas in 1852 both national parties tried to contain

---

[1] The figures are not definitive because party affiliations in 1854–5 were extremely complex. I have taken these figures from James A. Rawley, *Race and Politics. 'Bleeding Kansas' and the Coming of the Civil War* (Philadelphia, 1969), p. 111.

America in 1860

sectional rivalries as best they could, by 1856 the Republicans had no Southern base and pressed explicitly, and as their main plank, for a policy seen in the South as sectionally selfish and sectionally aggressive. For in 1856 the Republicans argued that the North's liberties and rights and future material prospects in the western territories were excessively and wrongly threatened by the Slave Power's insistence on slavery extension. A congressional ban on any future extension of slavery was the central and overwhelmingly most important demand put by the Republicans in 1856. In the presidential election of 1856 the Republicans won 45.2 per cent of the *Northern* vote and became the North's leading party; and in the congressional elections of 1858 they consolidated their hold and became undisputedly the *majority* party in the free states, so completing a revolution in party politics. This party transformation was – by historical standards – thorough and swift. Perhaps, therefore, the peace of 1850–2 passed merely as an understanding between irreconcilable forces.

Yet, ironically, the new sectional crisis was precipitated not by the discontented radicals of 1850–2 but by the energetic Western Democratic adjusters of 1850, the shapers and fixers of Compromise.

The Kansas – Nebraska Act, 1854

Three important groups of politicians had irreconcilable aims in 1850–2. First, many Northern Whigs abided only grudgingly by the settlement of 1850. Led by Senator Seward of New York, these anti-slavery Whigs not only opposed any further extension of slavery; they devoutly wished for some future end to slavery in America. Seward was no crude or explicit abolitionist, but he argued in the debates of 1850 that the South must face the cold fact of emancipation, even if emancipation would not come for perhaps another 10 or 50 years.[2] In the light of history, Seward's position in 1850 was undoubtedly wise; men of his own time, however, could readily accuse him of folly. For one thing, few Southern politicians of weight could have conceded in 1850 that slavery should end. Ordinary Southern whites would not accept that their property-rights and notions of racial superiority should be surrendered, modified, or even impaired. The growing body of middle-class Southern professionals – the increasingly better educated clergymen, scientists, creative writers, and intellectuals – all defended, justified, and praised slavery.[3] And the larger planters – with cotton prices again booming after the economic depression of the early 1840s – were highly satisfied with their system of

---

[2] Glyndon G. Van Deusen, *William Henry Seward* (New York, 1967), pp. 103–4, 119–25, 140; William R. Brock, *Parties and Political Conscience. American Dilemmas, 1840–1850* (Millwood, N.Y., 1979), pp. 300–10.

[3] Drew Gilpin Faust, *A Sacred Circle. The Dilemma of the Intellectual in the Old South, 1840–1860* (Baltimore, 1977), pp. 51–9, 87–111, 121–6; Donald G. Mathews, *Religion in the Old South* (Chicago, 1977), pp. xv – xvii, 81–94.

labour. This Southern consensus on slavery was amply demonstrated in 1849, when a very mild emancipation scheme in a border slave state (Kentucky) was overwhelmingly rejected by the voters.[4] Southern leaders could not survive politically by suggesting schemes of emancipation.

One delusion entertained by Seward and most other Northern anti-slavery men was that the South's lower-class whites would express their resentments against the planting grandees by opposing slavery. The entire history of the South affords meagre evidence for class feelings being thus transformed into racial tolerance. But many Northern Whigs believed − as Liberty party men had done before them − that a North-ern anti-slavery party need not be devoid of electoral support in the South. For this reason Senator Seward was reluctant to abandon the Whig national organization. In 1852 he worked within the existing party to further his own ends. During the years 1851–3 he and one of his closest Whig colleagues (Greeley, editor of the *New York Tribune*) pressed traditional party ideas (a restrained foreign policy, protective tariffs, more federal promotion of economic development) in order to maintain Whig unity and increase Whig support. Seward's long-term strategy was presumably to move this national Whig party − with its solid following in the poorer regions of the Upper South − to an increasingly anti-slave-power position. Only very reluctantly therefore, in September 1855, did Seward agree to merge the New York Whigs with the new, purely Northern, Republican party. So Seward, for all his distaste for the legisla-tion enacted in 1850, was not an enthusiastic engineer of new party formations. Nor did he, when the new Congress convened in December 1853, introduce disruptive legislation.[5]

The second important group of malcontents were the separatist Southern Democrats. The separatists' history is still somewhat murky − how intent upon secession, how numerous, and how cohesive they were as a group is difficult to say. In some states of the Deep South − in South Carolina notably (everyone in the 1850s recognized South Carolina as a hot-bed of anti-national sentiment), but also in Georgia, Mississippi, and Alabama − strong efforts were made to pro-mote secession in 1850–1. Even if secession was rejected, the idea of secession was widely discussed as a practical option for the first time throughout the Deep South. By 1852 the separatists of the previous year were back in the Democratic fold. But what did they want? And how long would they stay? Union-minded Southern Democrats − and other Southerners who refused to cry 'secession' every time some theoretical right of the South was infringed − were deeply suspicious of those whom

---

[4] Brock, *Parties and Political Conscience*, pp. 273–4.
[5] Eric Foner, *Free Soil, Free Labor, Free Men. The Ideology of the Republican Party before the Civil War* (New York, 1970), ch. 2; Van Deusen, *William Henry Seward*, pp. 147–9, 154–9, 162–3; Horace Greeley, 'Why I am a Whig', *Whig Almanac and Statistical Register for 1852* (n.p., n.d.), pp. 6–12.

they had fought so earnestly in 1851. The separatists themselves were extremely proud, hypersensitive to Northern rebukes or implied rebukes to slavery, and ever watchful. They kept other Southern politicians up to an ever higher mark in the defence of Southern rights. They were not, however, directly responsible for disrupting the old party system.[6]

Separatist Southern Democrats exerted their influence in various ways. They were conciliated by President Franklin Pierce and one of their number – Jefferson Davis – was brought into Pierce's cabinet. They perhaps induced Pierce to enforce the Fugitive Slave Act in controversial cases, as, notably, in that of Anthony Burns in May 1854. Some of them induced Pierce to appoint pro-slavery expansionists to the overseas missions in Paris and Madrid; from those representatives, and from the minister in London, came in October 1854 an extraordinary attempt to persuade or force Spain to sell Cuba to the USA.[7] They encouraged piratical, 'filibustering' expeditions in Central America, by which various Southerners or men of Southern sympathies sought to promote American influence in such places as Nicaragua. Some of them pressed for the building of a transcontinental railway to the Pacific by a Southern route. Jefferson Davis as Secretary of War actively worked to that end; the Pierce administration in 1853 (through the Gadsden Purchase) acquired from Mexico a strip of land essential for that purpose; and the strongest organ of Southern Rights opinion – *De Bow's Review* – eagerly argued for the fullest possible development of Southern commerce and communications, including those to the far West. Finally, some extreme separatists mounted an ever wider campaign for the re-opening of the African slave trade, which, by the late 1850s, provided an embarrassing sub-theme in Southern state politics. In 1853–4, however, the separatists', and many other Southerners', sights seemed to be set upon American expansion into the Caribbean region. Yet the break-up of the party system was precipitated not by overseas affairs but by territorial policy.

Curiously, the new sectional crisis was created by those who had gained most politically from the Compromise of 1850, the Mid-western Democrats under Senator Douglas. Between 14 December 1853 and 23 January 1854 Douglas, as chairman of the Senate Committee on the Territories, drafted a bill to organize two new western territories. In its final version, when it came before the Senate, the Kansas–Nebraska bill opened two territories north of 36°30' to slavery; it declared that the two territories would become slave or free states as their constitutions

---

[6] William J. Cooper, Jr, *The South and the Politics of Slavery, 1828–1856* (Baton Rouge, 1978), pp. 103–18, 287–99, 304–10, 317–21, 331–2; Ulrich B. Phillips (ed.), *The Correspondence of Robert Toombs, Alexander H. Stephens, and Howell Cobb* (Washington, D.C., 1911), II, 284–7.

[7] Stanley W. Campbell, *The Slave Catchers: Enforcement of the Fugitive Slave Law, 1850–1860* (New York, 1972 edn), pp. 102–6, 24–31; Clement Eaton, *Jefferson Davis* (New York, 1977), p. 101.

provided when they applied for admission to statehood.[8] From the day of its introduction – 23 January 1854 – until 1858, the bill's stipulations concerning slavery extension were never far from the forefront of public debate. For what reasons was the Kansas–Nebraska bill – arguably the most important act of the 1850s – introduced?

In the first place, the bill seemed to meet a number of party needs. President Pierce was an ineffective party leader and presented no obvious programme to the overwhelmingly Democratic Congress. Douglas had a golden opportunity to stake his claim to party leadership. But Douglas was also worried at the state of the Democratic party. Pierce had so handled patronage appointments that the Democrats of New York fought the state elections of November 1853 as two distinct factions. Essentially, this internecine squabble had been provoked by the pro-compromise Democrats' anger at the preferment accorded the free soil Democrats and those willing to accommodate them; Douglas – and others – wanted to stop such factionalism spreading. He thought he could best achieve that end by rallying the former pro-Compromise Democrats with a further dose of popular sovereignty; he might also expose, isolate, and drive from the party the free soil extremists. This concern for Democratic party affairs perhaps explains Douglas's special rage against Senators Sumner and Chase who, as Free Soilers and not free soil Democrats, issued 'The Appeal of the Independent Democrats in Congress to the People of the United States'. The appeal – published on 24 January – sweepingly denounced the Kansas–Nebraska bill and attempted to convert what Douglas intended to be a squeeze on party dissidents into a moral exodus. Douglas, in trying to remove responsibility for slavery from Congress, quickly lost control of legislative events. From the Southern side, he was pressed to state very explicitly that the Missouri Compromise dividing line of 36°30' was now void and inoperative. From the free soil side, he was denounced for a further sell-out to the Slave Power. Why was Douglas prepared to go so far in endangering the unity of the party which he hoped to lead?

Douglas's second reason for introducing the Kansas–Nebraska bill stemmed from his broad commitment to Western development:

> It is to be hoped that the necessity and importance of the measure are manifest to the whole country, and that so far as the slavery question is concerned, all will be willing to sanction and affirm the principle established by the Compromise measures of 1850.[9]

Douglas had long pressed for the opening of this region to white settlement. In 1844 he introduced a bill for organizing Nebraska Territory; in 1852–3 he pushed hard for a Pacific railway to follow the

[8] The following account relies heavily on: Robert W. Johannsen, *Stephen A. Douglas* (New York, 1973), pp. 386–434; Potter, *Impending Crisis*, ch. 7.
[9] Robert W. Johannsen (ed.), *The Letters of Stephen A. Douglas* (Urbana, Ill., 1961), p. 271.

central route and for the organization of Nebraska Territory.[10] He argued that one way of securing the central route for the Pacific railway would be by stimulating settlement in new territories along that route. Moreover, strong demands for the opening up of this region came from the western and Democratic states of Iowa and Missouri. Urgency was given to this work by Jefferson Davis's active promotion of a Southern route in 1853: the Gadsden Purchase signed on 30 December 1853 cleared the path for a Southern route and in his report as Secretary of War in December 1853 Davis argued for the Pacific railway along such a route.[11] So, Douglas's reasons for urging 'the necessity and importance' of the Kansas–Nebraska bill were: to build up the West as a countervailing bloc; to strengthen the western Democrats by creating new territories (and thus more political patronage) and then to shape the politics of these embryonic states; and to encourage settlement, economic growth, and railway building for the whole region (and for personal profits). The motives of Douglas, the chairman of the Senate's Committee on the Territories, and other western Democrats were thus complex, but unconnected with a concern for extending slavery westwards.

Yet this idea that the initial plunge into a further round of slavery extension largely resulted from Western preoccupations has been questioned. Why, it has been asked, did interest in the Pacific railway and the great cause of Western development wane so rapidly after the passage of the Kansas–Nebraska act?[12] The simple answer is that Douglas did in fact continue to struggle for the Western cause: in February 1855 the Senate passed a railway measure of a sort and pressed for the construction of a telegraph line to the Pacific; and the arguments over a federally chartered and aided railway to the Pacific flowed on for the rest of the decade.[13] But Douglas in 1854 – as had Polk in 1845 – underestimated the hostility that a policy permitting, even encouraging, slavery extension would provoke in the North. The initially primary object of Western development became subsidiary because *who settled* in the new territories – slaveowners or free men? – became the point of fierce controversy. By the time the Kansas–Nebraska bill passed the Congress, on 22 May 1854, it was the central issue in all debate about the West.

Douglas allowed his broad concern for Western development to be diluted by legislative provisions for slavery extension partly because of his genuine feel for the requirements of party and national balance, partly because he lacked strong moral susceptibilities over slavery, partly

---

[10] Johannsen, *Stephen A. Douglas*, pp. 390–8.

[11] Eaton, *Jefferson Davis*, p. 82.

[12] Don. E. Fehrenbacher, *The Dred Scott Case. Its Significance in American Law and Politics* (New York, 1978), p. 179.

[13] Johannsen, *Stephen A. Douglas*, p. 437; Robert R. Russel, *Critical Studies in Antebellum Sectionalism. Essays in American Political and Economic History* (Westport, Conn., 1972), ch. 6.

because he believed that slavery would extend very little into the new territories, and also because he had to meet the political needs of a Democratic senator from Missouri. This senator, David R. Atchison, was important in the Senate because of his position — as its presiding officer — rather than his intellect. He was eager to open up Kansas to settlement and intent upon introducing slavery into the new territory. His stake in slavery extension resulted partly from the balance of forces in his own state's politics: he led the pro-slavery wing of Missouri's Democrats. It resulted also from the simple facts of geography. The areas most suitable for settlement in Kansas lay directly across the border from one of Missouri's strongest slave-owning regions. Six counties stretching alongside the most vital area of Kansas held, in 1850, 17,357 slaves and 56,726 free people: slaves provided 23 per cent of the population in those border counties, against only 13 per cent of Missouri's total population.[14] Slave owners in western Missouri wanted no haven of freedom immediately across their border. And so Atchison insisted that the Kansas–Nebraska bill specifically open the new territories to slavery. In turn, Douglas, who never believed that slavery would take root in Kansas and Nebraska, was prepared, under pressure, to push his doctrine of popular sovereignty to the very extreme point of theoretically opening all new territories to slavery.

Here then was the Mid-western Democrats' policy. To squeeze out the free soilers, they would enforce popular sovereignty as true party doctrine; to activate the Democrats' huge congressional majorities, they would press for a full and large programme of Western development; to outmanoeuvre the South-western Democrats intent upon a Southern route for the Pacific railway, they would promote settlement and economic growth along the line of a central route; to prevent the Administration's merely waiting upon achievements in foreign affairs, they would commit Pierce, within seven weeks of the convening of the 33rd Congress, to a strong, if not audacious, territorial policy.

This western strategy held two potential advantages to the Democrats nationally. Ensconced in power at Washington, they were splendidly placed to establish Democratic administrations in new territories and so, in the near future, in further states. Secondly, by offering some chance, however theoretical, for slavery to expand, they would prove to the South that the Southern Unionists of 1850–1 were right: the South would be treated fairly in the Union. This point was important to moderate Southern Democrats and various Whigs who had co-operated with them in 1850–1. They believed that the doctrine of popular sovereignty as defined in the Kansas–Nebraska act offered the prospect of real sectional stability.[15]

[14] Allan Nevins, *Ordeal of the Union* (New York, 1947), II, 302–3; Rawley, *Race and Politics*, p.80.
[15] Phillips (ed.), *Correspondence of Toombs, Stephens, Cobb*, pp. 342–3, 346.

Instead, within two years of the act's passage, the North had produced an entirely sectional party and Kansas was on the verge of civil war. The Democratic leadership made numerous and glaring miscalculations.

Although Douglas believed that Kansas and Nebraska would eventually become free states, he gravely underestimated the effect that opening them up to slavery would have on Northern opinion. After all, if they would eventually be free states, why should slaveowners be allowed even a theoretical chance of settling in them? As Senator Benjamin Wade said in July 1856:

> When the American people so far forget what is due to Republicanism, equality, justice and right, as to say that slavery is equally entitled with freedom to encouragement, then liberty is no more. The principles of the fathers are overthrown, and there is nothing left worth preserving . . . . We intend, above all other things, that you shall not have another inch of territory anywhere for slavery, and especially not Kansas, which you have attempted to steal.[16]

The central provision of the Kansas–Nebraska act was shocking and absurd to many Northerners, since it effected a revolution in territorial policy. From 1790 to 1850 the federal government had two policies for the western territories. In the North-West Territory, slavery was banned; south of the Ohio river, settlers were free to introduce slaves. This dual policy was formally extended further west in 1820. In 1848 the federal government admitted Oregon, in 1849 Minnesota, and in 1853 Washington Territories with *prohibitions on slavery* (Washington was merely lopped off from Oregon). Yet in 1854 the Democratic leadership swept aside the line of 1820 and insisted that all territories were henceforth open to slavery.[17]

Douglas believed that the doctrine of popular sovereignty would provide a *modus vivendi* for Northern and Southern interests. Yet the wording of the Kansas–Nebraska act delayed the operation of popular sovereignty in the territories until the time when the territories applied for admission to statehood. Douglas and other Northern Democrats evaded this point and insisted that the settlers could control their own territorial affairs. Their Northern opponents repeatedly quizzed them on the precise meaning of popular sovereignty. After all, territorial laws could not be established when a territory was opened to settlement, for legislatures would not be created and elected immediately. For example, Kansas was formally opened to settlers on 30 May 1854; but no elections

---

[16] *Appendix to Congressional Globe*, 34th Congress, 1st Session (Washington, D.C., 1856), pp. 752–3.
[17] Richard H. Sewell, *Ballots for Freedom: Antislavery Politics in the United States, 1837–1860* (New York, 1976), pp. 254–65; Fehrenbacher, *Dred Scott Case*, pp. 86–7, 115–17, 182–4.

to the territorial legislature occurred until 30 March 1855; and the territorial legislature did not meet until 2 July 1855.[18] During a period of 13 months, therefore, no anti-slavery laws *could* have been passed and many slaves could be and were brought into the territory. But, once elected and convened, could a territorial legislature then ban slavery? According to Northern Democrats' vague pronouncements, yes. But the Kansas–Nebraska act said not. And in March 1857, in the Dred Scott decision, the Supreme Court concurred: no territorial legislature could deprive a slaveowner of his right to own slave property by excluding slavery from federal territories; only when a territory drew up its constitution as a putative state was a complete ban upon slavery permissible. The Dred Scott decision merely gave a new twist to the argument over popular sovereignty, but it clearly revealed how radical the legal effects of the Kansas–Nebraska act were. In truth, the act imposed 'the Wilmot Proviso in reverse': all new territories would be open to slavery.[19]

Not surprisingly, therefore, the bill did rather more damage to the Northern Democratic party than merely squeeze out a few free soilers. In the House of Representatives about half the Northern Democrats opposed the bill or abstained or avoided the vote. During 1854 about one in five or one in four party supporters left the Democrats and joined their various opponents. Not all these aggrieved Democrats disavowed the party because of slavery extension: indeed perhaps not even a majority did so. But among Northern Democratic congressmen and other men of influence the new territorial policy provoked party rebellion. A new outburst of anti-Southernism swept through Northern congressional ranks in the spring of 1854 and was channelled by them out into the country at large. As a consequence, in the mid-term congressional elections of 1854, the Democrats suffered one of the greatest reverses in American electoral history. The losses were virtually all in the North; and they flowed partially at least from a policy initiated by the best and the brightest of Northern Democrats.

Part of the trouble lay in Douglas's further misunderstanding of Northern public opinion. Douglas was vastly energetic, fairly pragmatic, and, above all, very much attuned to the needs and aspirations and opinions of his own region. Yet in 1853–4 he underestimated the force of feeling against slavery extension. It was relatively easy to dismiss the handful of out-and-out Free Soilers in Congress. But, when Senator Sumner had written in December 1853, 'This Congress is the worst – or rather promises to be the worst – since the Constitution was adopted', he had prophesied reasonably accurately.[20] For the re-opening of the slavery extension question was readily perceived in the North as an astonishing challenge laid down by a Democratic congressional majority

[18] Events in Kansas are described in Rawley, *Race and Politics*.

[19] Fehrenbacher, *Dred Scott Case*, p. 180.

[20] David Donald, *Charles Sumner and the Coming of the Civil War* (New York, 1961), p. 249.

controlled by the Slave Power; Douglas, the only Northerner to chair a Senate committee, was simply doing the South's work for it. The question immediately arose: was the Democratic party worth sustaining if all it could do with its thumping congressional majorities was re-open the most controversial question of the era?

In the North as a whole in 1852–4 considerable disaffection with existing parties had already been revealed in apathetic turn-out in elections, the somewhat strained Whig–Democratic consensus in the presidential election of 1852, and numerous local and state efforts to form new political groupings. The Kansas–Nebraska act, far from injecting new purpose and vigour into the existing national parties, drove many Northerners – Free Soilers, free soil Democrats, and former Whigs – into new party combinations. The extent and power of Northern anti-party and anti-Southern feelings in 1852–4 were vital factors omitted from Douglas's calculations.

Despite these miscalculations and despite heavy losses in the congressional elections of 1854, Douglas stuck to his formula of popular sovereignty. And so, to a very large extent, national policy was shaped by events in Kansas from June 1854, when formal settlement began, to August 1858, when popular sovereignty there at last came into effect.

Kansas and the Northern Democrats, 1854–8

The events of 1854 completed a decade of change in the Northern Democratic party. Disquiet in 1845 over Texas annexation was followed in 1848 by a brief schism in some states over the Wilmot Proviso; in 1854 restive free soilers finally left the party. These various internal party disputes arose from a complicated interaction between growing anti-slavery and anti-Southern feeling and more local, specific, and shifting factional rivalries. Looked at over the long term, these disputes seem to manifest a steady deterioration in the Northern Democrats' ability and willingness to accommodate Southern political needs. Northerners' anxiety in 1845 led to temporary revolt in 1848, only to be followed by a dramatic flight from the party in 1854. Moreover, the continuing debate over Kansas provoked yet another burst of anti-Southernism in 1857–8, this time led by Senator Douglas himself. And the outcome of that explosive debate was Southern rejection of Douglas in 1860 as the party's presidential nominee and a split in the national Democratic party. Yet while such a central line of steady deterioration may be drawn conveniently and with good reason, it would oversimplify a tortuous process of change. For, certainly in the major crisis of party break-down in 1854, more forces were at work eroding the two-party system in the North than anti-Southernism and anti-slavery. One reason for Northern Democratic electoral weakness in and after 1854 was the increasing militancy of nativists and the Democrats' loss of support from party members who believed in the mid 1850s that nativists had now to make their stand.

Since the 1830s the Democrats had been the political home of Irish and German Catholic immigrants to America. The Democrats tended to side with these immigrants in their often harsh struggles to obtain religious toleration and the suffrage. Immigrants' ethnic consciousness and solidarity resulted in part from nativists' (and usually Whigs') efforts to restrict their access to the vote. In the years 1845–54, when 2,939,000 immigrants entered the country, the political connection between the Democrats and the Irish and Catholics became firmer and clearer. In 1852 the Whigs made some effort to woo the foreign vote and succeeded only in angering nativist opinion, with the consequence that a strong undercurrent of nativism was ready to surface by 1853; in 1854 it did so. Nativist Whigs were keen to establish a forceful and populist anti-immigrant, anti-Catholic, anti-drink party and, with party ties cut by disputes over slavery extension, many nativist Democrats were prepared to join them in the American or Know-Nothing party.[21]

These losses – to the causes of free soil and nativism – left the Northern Democrats in an apparently hopeless position. In various state and congressional elections held in all 16 free states from the autumn of 1854 to the spring of 1855, the Democrats won 47 per cent or more of the vote in only four: Illinois, Iowa, Michigan, and California (with the Democrats' total in the last-named state divided between two factions). From this situation the Northern Democrats never really recovered. In the presidential election of 1856 they won 47 per cent or more of the vote in only four states (Pennsylvania, Indiana, California, and New Jersey). Yet Democratic hopes were kept alive in the North both by divisions among free soilers and nativists *and* by their positive commitments.

The new alignment of political forces was indeed confusing. In the congressional elections of 1854 – and, in some Northern constituencies, 1855 – different party systems emerged in the different major regions of the North. In Ohio, Michigan, Indiana, Illinois, Iowa, and Wisconsin the congressional contests of 1854 were, with only one or two exceptions, straight fights between Republicans and Democrats. The Republicans won 41 seats to the Democrats' 9 in the Midwest. Even so, this neat pattern did not hold up for all elections; in the presidential election of 1856 the Know-Nothing party emerged as an independent organization in the most important of those states: Ohio, Indiana, and Illinois. For the rest of the North the situation was far more confused in 1854–5. In New York, New Jersey, and Pennsylvania straight Whigs gained 37 seats, Whigs in open alliance with Know-Nothings gained 11 seats, and various kinds of Democrats gained 14 seats (though one of them was a Free Soil

---

[21] Michael F. Holt, *The Political Crisis of the 1850s* (New York, 1978), pp. 139–71; Ronald P. Formisano, *The Birth of Mass Political Parties: Michigan 1827–1861* (Princeton, 1971), pp. 81–101, 195–205, 217–38; Potter, *Impending Crisis*, ch. 10. The nativist backlash of the mid 1850s was sometimes very violent: for example, in the local and presidential elections held in Baltimore in October–November 1856 at least 14 people were killed and over 300 injured in election riots. William J. Evitts, *A Matter of Allegiances. Maryland from 1850 to 1861* (Baltimore, 1974), p. 98.

Democrat). In New England, the Know-Nothings swept the board in Massachusetts, Connecticut, New Hampshire, and Rhode Island, capturing all the seats in each state − a tally of 20. In Maine, however, the Republicans won five out of six seats and in Vermont Whig candidates took all three seats.[22] Defeated everywhere in the North, the Democrats could at least console themselves with the thought that their opponents would find little common cause: nativists in most of New England, Old Whigs in most of the Middle Atlantic seaboard area, and Republicans in the Midwest might soon be at each other's throats. And indeed these parties in the House of Representatives took two months to elect a Speaker when the new Congress first met in December 1855.

But what − apart from a divided opposition − persuaded a substantial body of politicians and voters that the Democratic party was worth sustaining in the North after 1854? First, the Democrats maintained a strong ethnic appeal. In Congress and in many states they opposed attempts to extend the period of residence required before immigrants could become naturalized US citizens. During the winter of 1854–5 Senator Douglas in Illinois was eager to raise the level of the Democrats' appeal by stressing their repugnance at nativism. And Democrats generally opposed another manifestation of puritan moralism in 1854–6, the temperance movement. Prohibition was widely interpreted as an interference with the habits and values of the Irish and German urban poor. Democratic opposition to temperance legislation thus drew upon both their party's traditional hostility to moral regulation by state governments, and their political connections with the immigrant masses. Throughout the 1850s the Democrats retained a strong Catholic base: one which probably became increasingly important to the party as the Irish immigrants of 1845–54 secured the vote. Although Democrats were not above making local alliances with Know-Nothings, in general they fought off nativist prejudice with creditable energy.[23]

Secondly, the Northern Democrats appealed powerfully to Unionist sentiment. The very cause for which the Republican administration went to war in 1861 − the preservation of the Union − was the central theme of Democratic rhetoric. Douglas envisaged a greatly expanded West to act as a stabilizing counter-part to North–South antagonism. James Buchanan, as American minister in London, in 1854 pushed for the acquisition of Cuba as a legitimate concession to Southern interests. In the presidential election of 1856 Northern Democrats rallied behind

[22] *Congressional Quarterly's Guide to U.S. Elections* (Washington, D.C., 1975), pp. 598–600.
[23] Bruce Collins, 'The Ideology of the ante-bellum Northern Democrats', *Journal of American Studies*, XI (1977), pp. 103–21; *Congressional Globe*, 34th Congress, 1st Session (Washington, D.C., 1856), pp. 730–1, 979; *Appendix to the Congressional Globe*, 34:1, pp. 1087–9, 1227–8; Johannsen, *Letters of Stephen A. Douglas*, pp. 331, 333–4; Formisano, *Birth of Mass Political Parties*, pp. 298–310; Michael F. Holt, *Forging a Majority. The Formation of the Republican Party in Pittsburgh 1848–1860* (New Haven, 1969), pp. 110–13, 119–21, 165–7, 215–18, 258–61, 282, 287–8.

Buchanan as the candidate most capable of preserving the Union; they warned that a Republican victory would create tumult in the South and they claimed that only they could reconcile Northern moderates and the majority of Southerners. Even Martin van Buren, who had accepted the Free Soilers' presidential nomination in 1848, was satisfied with Buchanan as the best guarantor of Union and national balance.[24]

Unionism was not meant to be a policy of self-congratulatory inertia. The Union as Democrats conceived it was highly pluralistic. Democrats believed in a fédéral government active in foreign affairs but generally quiescent in internal matters; they argued that, just as state governments should tolerate cultural diversity and not regulate moral conduct, so the Union could continue to exist only if it permitted wide divergence in 'domestic institutions'. This sense of pluralism led straight to the doctrine of popular sovereignty, described by Douglas as 'that great fundamental principle of Democracy and free institutions which lies at the basis of our creed, and gives every political community the right to govern itself in obedience to the Constitution of the country'.[25] This contention was accurate: the difficulties of establishing national moral precepts for political life (let alone for social legislation and relations) were revealed when the South again went its own way in racial matters once post-war Reconstruction had ended. But in the 1840s and 1850s Democrats were trapped by the consequences of such pluralism when they pushed into practice their third major policy, territorial expansion.

Further expansion was rarely far from Democrats' minds. In December 1853 the Gadsden Purchase was negotiated. In October 1854 a clumsy declaration was made by the American ministers in London, Paris, and Madrid that the USA wished to acquire, by force if necessary, Cuba from Spain. Embarrassments in Kansas then quieted expansionist fever for a few years. But in 1858–60 Douglas made a strong bid for the party's national leadership by emphasizing his enthusiasm for the acquisition of Cuba. And, in the depths of the secession crisis of 1860–1, Northern Democrats tried to reassure Southerners by suggesting that further territories could be readily secured in order to satisfy Southerners' appetite for new areas for slavery.[26] Expansion clearly depended upon indifference to the morality of slavery.

The fourth reason for Northern Democratic resilience was, therefore, racism. Both Republicans and Northern Democrats exploited racism for

[24] Potter, *Impending Crisis*, pp. 261–2; *Appendix to Congressional Globe* 36:1, pp. 1228–9; a Democratic campaign pamphlet of 1856 summarized the point in its title, *The Fearful Issue to be Decided in November Next! Shall the Constitution and the Union Stand or Fall? Fremont, the Sectional Candidate of the Advocates of Dissolution! Buchanan, the Candidate of Those who advocate One Country! One Union! One Constitution! and One Destiny!* (n.p., n.d.); *Letters and Literary Memorials of Samuel J. Tilden*, ed. by John Bigelow (New York, 1908), I, 119–21.

[25] Johannsen, *Stephen A. Douglas*, p. 421.

[26] Johannsen, *Stephen A. Douglas*, pp. 147, 528–9, 683–4, 692–3, 753; Senator George E. Pugh of Ohio, *Appendix to the Congressional Globe* 36th Congress, 1st Session (Washington, D.C., 1861), pp. 30–1.

electoral purposes in the middle and late 1850s: the Republicans accused Democrats of introducing blacks into the western territories, while the Democrats asserted that the Republicans were amalgamationists and abolitionists, whose victories in Northern states would lure thousands of Southern blacks – free men and fugitive slaves – to an imagined Northern promised land. In practice, however, significant numbers of Republicans – perhaps half, perhaps more – objected to the more flagrant forms of racial discrimination practised in the ante-bellum North. But when the Republicans took a stand against the comprehensive racial burdens placed upon blacks in the Dred Scott decision of 1857 – which denied vital federal rights to free blacks – they won no electoral gains for their stand. Instead, the racist implications of the Dred Scott decision probably helped revive the Democrats' fortunes in the North in 1857.[27]

Yet the Democrats' general willingness to tolerate slavery, to wink at blatant cases of racial discrimination against Northern free blacks, and to spread alarm at the allegedly amalgamationist consequences of Republican proposals, did not mean that the Democrats monopolized Northern racist rhetoric. Republicans could always counter-charge that the 'African' or 'Congo' Democracy, as they labelled their opponents, would be responsible if the obnoxious blacks were introduced as slaves into the western federal territories in the 1850s. The anti-slavery groups in Kansas who won Republican support in Washington, and Republican encouragement throughout the North, intended, if they gained control of Kansas Territory, to exclude not only slaves but free blacks from their inviting prairies.[28]

This chink in the Democrats' racist armour partly explains their political slippage in the North in 1854 and thereafter. The Republicans were able to argue that Douglas's Kansas policy not only opened the new territories to slavery – objectionable in itself – but in doing that reduced opportunities for Northern whites to settle in those fresh lands and enhanced the economic advantages and political power of the slavocracy. Sectional jealousy and resentment against further gains culled from the federal government by an aggressive Slave Power much reinforced the Republicans' case. Douglas, the leading Midwestern Democrat of the decade, had become, according to Senator Sumner, 'the squire of Slavery, its very Sancho Panza, ready to do all its humiliating offices'.[29] Northerners grew ever more frustrated in the 1850s as federal policy seemed to be subordinated to Southern requirements; and slavery in Kansas and Nebraska was a pill that a majority of Northerners refused to swallow.

[27] Foner, *Free Soil, Free Labor, Free Men*, pp. 261–7, 281–300; Michael J. McManus, 'Wisconsin Republicans and Negro Suffrage: Attitudes and Behavior, 1857', *Civil War History*, xxv (1979), 36–54; Fehrenbacher, *Dred Scott Case*, pp. 417–23, 428–43, 561–7.

[28] Northern racism generally is treated in: Eugene H. Berwanger, *The Frontier Against Slavery* (Urbana, 1967); Leon F. Litwack, *North of Slavery* (Chicago, 1961).

[29] Johannsen, *Stephen A. Douglas*, p. 502.

The battle for Kansas went through various phases. Between January and May 1854 the organization of Kansas and Nebraska was a congressional question, provoking immediate opposition within Congress and, subsequently, considerable opposition in the North at large. From the summer of 1854 until December 1857 events in Kansas territory were usually at the centre of national attention. Although Congress in 1855–7 continued to discuss those events, congressional deliberation upon Kansas did not once more become the central element in the controversy until December 1857. During the debates which continued until April 1858, the Northern Democrats split. This division continued into the congressional elections of October–November 1858 and poisoned relations within the party nationally in 1859–60. Effectively, however, the situation in Kansas itself ceased to cause alarm after August 1858, when the pro-slavery forces in the territory were routed.

From June 1854 to August 1858 the struggle in Kansas concerned popular sovereignty in every meaning of the term. At the most basic level, properly conducted and legitimate elections were hardly held in Kansas. Elections for a territorial delegates to Congress in November 1854 and for a territorial legislature in March 1855 were marred by frauds, as were the later elections for the territorial legislature in October 1857. These frauds were perpetuated by pro-slavery Missourians who rushed across their border to protect an important flank from possible anti-slavery influence. Not only were these men the very worst exemplars of frontier manners – uncouth, unkempt, quick to swagger, swear, and drink – they were also armed and ready to intimidate all who opposed them. Election judges in Kansas in March 1855 were threatened and displaced and sometimes tarred and feathered by these unruly Missourians.[30] Worse still, they were encouraged and led by Senator Atchison, who once boasted: 'There are eleven hundred coming over from Platte County to vote, and if that ain't enough we can send five thousand – enough to Kill every God-damned abolitionist in the Territory'.[31] Such was the unedifying example of the presiding officer of the United States Senate.

After the elections of March 1855 the heavily pro-slavery legislature ignored all other groups' sensibilities. Democratic government depends not merely upon rule by legislative majorities but also upon respect for a whole range of rights and assumptions. In the summer of 1855 the territorial legislature passed very harsh pro-slavery laws at a time when it was entirely unrepresentative of the increasingly anti-slavery settlers in Kansas. In disgust, these free soilers set up their own territorial government at Topeka. For nearly a year – until September 1856 – civil war in Kansas appeared imminent. It almost exploded in December 1855 in the so-called 'Wakarusa War'. It again threatened in May 1856 when 700 pro-slavery men sacked the free-soil town of Lawrence, when John

[30] Rawley, *Race and Politics*, pp. 82–179.
[31] Nevins, *Ordeal of the Union*, II, p. 385.

Brown retaliated by murdering five pro-slavery people at Pottawatomie Creek, and when the vehemently anti-slavery senator, Charles Sumner, was caned unconscious in the US Senate chamber by a Southern congressman. But through all these troubles in 1855–6, when about 200 people were killed in Kansas, antagonism between pro-slavery and free soil settlers never quite provoked organized warfare.[32] Further afield, however, election frauds, pro-slavery laws, and sporadic violence in Kansas all fanned the Republicans' attack on slavery extension and the Slave Power.

Americans have always been ambiguous in their attitudes to the frontier. Many have regarded frontier communities as the forcing-houses of democracy, places of endeavour, struggling orderliness, and fair, if occasionally rough, play. Others have looked upon them as crude, lawless, and intolerant societies. In 1855–6 the Republicans depicted Kansas as a paradise being lost to rapacious slavery men, an area set aside since 1820 for settlement by free whites being seized by ruffians indifferent to human liberty. This Republican description of events in Kansas was much embellished and assiduously broadcast for propaganda and political purposes in the North. The free soilers' Topeka government was no paragon of toleration, but rigorously excluded *all* blacks, slave and free, from the territory; most free soil settlers came from the Midwest and resembled their fellow settlers from Missouri and the upper South rather than New England moralists; and a majority of all whites in Kansas were probably Democrats, not Republicans, as late as 1857.[33] Yet clearly the contrast drawn by Republicans between the promise of freedom in Kansas and the fraud, violence, and gross misgovernment in the territory undermined the doctrine of popular sovereignty.

This failure to provide the basic working arrangements necessary to the operation of popular sovereignty was not entirely the fault of the settlers themselves. Although Democrats asserted that *Congress* should not – perhaps could not – interfere in territorial government over slavery, they did not deny *presidential* authority in certain territorial matters. Yet President Pierce was totally unwilling or unable to take firm measures to guarantee proper elections and orderly government. Indeed, from October 1854 to December 1857 three of Kansas's four governors were dismissed or resigned because of their frustrated efforts to do justice to the free soilers. In December 1855 Pierce publicly declined to intervene in the affairs of Kansas; a year later he failed to support Governor John W. Geary's efforts to bridle the excesses of the pro-slavery politicians in their 'felon legislature'.[34] This complete failure of presidential policy was amply recognized by the Democrats themselves; they ditched Pierce as

[32] Rawley, *Race and Politics*, pp. 87–97, 130–4, 160.
[33] Nevins, *Ordeal of the Union*, II, pp. 381–83; 'Covode Report', *House Reports*, 36 Congress, 1 Session, No. 648 (Washington, D.C., 1860), p. 115.
[34] Rawley, *Race and Politics*, pp. 177–9.

their presidential candidate in 1856. Yet Northern Democrats continued in 1856 to defend the pro-slavery territorial legislature. One senator argued that slavery had been partially allowed or very nearly adopted in much of the Old North-West. Yet all his examples came from before 1820! Senator Douglas blamed all the trouble in Kansas upon societies that organized emigration from New England as a deliberate and provocative challenge to settlers from Missouri. Yet by the end of 1855 the Massachusetts Emigrant Aid Society — the leading one — had assisted only 1,240 settlers in Kansas; and the proportion of settlers who came from New England was very low.[35]

Northern Democrats lived a political lie between March 1854 and December 1857. They said that popular sovereignty would take care of sectional differences over slavery and that popular sovereignty was actually at work in Kansas. On both counts they were wrong. But their party continued to fight and to fight quite effectively in the North in 1856. Their cause was probably aided in 1856 by the Republicans' sectional character and political recklessness. Republicans insisted that slavery should never extend into any further territories *and* that Kansas should be admitted directly as a state under the rebellious free soilers' Topeka government. This latter insistence was a tactical mistake. Northern Democrats could repeat with considerable justification their claims to represent Unionism and safety in 1856. They succeeded in clawing their way back to a respectable showing in the presidential election: they won 41.5 percent of the free states' votes, compared with the Republicans' 45 per cent; and they captured 5 of 16 free states, just enough to secure the presidency. But could they resolve the Kansas question as their new president, James Buchanan, promised? Could they yet vindicate their doctrine of congressional non-intervention and popular sovereignty?

Events in Kansas throughout 1857 proved, as usual, extremely difficult to control. The pro-slavery official legislature decided to hold a convention to draw up a state constitution and apply to Congress for admission as a state. Elections for delegates to this convention at Lecompton occurred in June 1857. They were, not surprisingly, boycotted by free soil settlers who had their fill of pro-slavery election fraud and violence. The constitutional convention — legally elected but highly unrepresentative — proceeded, in November, to draft a pro-slavery constitution and arrange for it to be submitted to a referendum in Kansas on 21 December. This action created a storm among Northern Democrats, who, almost as soon as the details of the constitution were known, began to divide into Lecompton and anti-Lecompton camps. And so Kansas's affairs returned to the very centre of congressional politics.

Northern Democrats in 1854–7 staked their fortunes on the doctrine

---

[35] *Appendix to the Congressional Globe*, 34:1, pp. 606–19; Rawley, *Race and Politics*, p. 122; Nevins, *Ordeal of the Union*, II, pp. 381–3.

of popular sovereignty. They happily contested the Republicans' claim that Congress could and should decide whether or not territories would have slavery. In 1854 they had argued that this question of congressional non-intervention was a matter of political expedience: for the sake of sectional peace, Congress should retreat from territorial responsibilities. By 1856, however, Northern Democrats were coming to regard this question as one of constitutional interpretation: perhaps the federal courts should decide whether Congress indeed had the power to rule the territories. In March 1857 the Supreme Court, dominated by Democrats and comprising five Southerners and four Northerners, held, in a very confusing and complex set of judicial opinions, that neither Congress *nor* territorial legislatures could exclude slavery from a territory. This sweeping and revolutionary decision surely went too far for Northern Democrats. The Republicans' insistence on congressional intervention was ruled out; but so, too, was popular sovereignty. Senator Douglas, however, swiftly salvaged something from the judicial wreckage. In June 1857 he declared that, because slavery required elaborate and tough police regulations, territories could still effectively determine whether or not they wanted slavery by providing or not providing such police laws. Northern Democrats could therefore use the Dred Scott decision to denounce Republican proposals as unconstitutional while claiming that popular sovereignty could still operate, albeit at one remove. But Northern Democrats during 1854–7 also confronted another argument over popular sovereignty.

Northern Democrats held that a territorial legislature could decide whether or not to permit slavery in a territory. Southern Democrats disagreed; by 1854 they were arguing that *only* when a territory applied for admission to statehood could the people in a territory decide whether or not to have slavery in the putative state. In November 1856 Buchanan, as president-elect, endorsed that view, as did the Supreme Court in March 1857. In practical terms, however, this important distinction was apparently irrelevant to Kansas, where the officially recognized legislature favoured slavery anyway. But, suddenly, in November–December 1857 this distinction became dramatically central to congressional debate over the Lecompton constitution.

Everyone in the Democratic party agreed that territories could exercise complete freedom of choice over slavery when they applied for admission to statehood. But the Lecompton constitution totally failed to provide such freedom of choice. Technically, the referendum of 21 December gave the voters a choice between the constitution *with slavery* and the constitution *without slavery*. But the only thing covered by the clause 'without slavery' was the exclusion of *further* slaves from the state. All slaves already in Kansas, and their descendants, could remain in the state; and the right to hold these slaves was guaranteed in the constitution for at least seven years from the date of Kansas's admission to statehood. In the normal understanding of the term, the Lecompton constitution as submitted to the referendum failed entirely to meet the requirements of even the most pro-Southern interpretation of the doctrine of popular sovereignty. Although Douglas had tactical reasons of his own for wishing to distance himself from Buchanan's Administration, his immediate denunciation of the Lecompton constitution and the terms of its submission was perfectly logical, since the Lecompton constitution contravened the doctrine of popular sovereignty. On a whole range of matters – on transport development, banking laws, and state constitutional arrangements as well as on slavery – the people had to be given a choice: here was the simple core of the Democrats' notion of American pluralism. Yet on the Lecompton constitution no such choices were offered.

Despite this defect, Buchanan publicly approved the procedure adopted by the constitutional convention at Lecompton and, in February 1858, formally recommended to Congress that Kansas be admitted as a state with slavery. This was done despite the fact that free soilers had held their own referendum on 4 January 1858 and shown conclusively that a large majority opposed the Lecompton constitution. Buchanan, however, stuck to the legal procedures and tried to force Kansas's admission as a slave state. His intransigence and blatant failure to implement in Kansas the commonly accepted norms of popular sovereignty appalled about half the Northern Democratic members of the House of Representatives. They opposed Kansas's admission under the terms of the Lecompton constitution, and their opposition paid off. The Administration agreed in April to re-submit the whole Lecompton constitution to the voters of Kansas; and in August 1858 the free soilers in Kansas participated in an election with the pro-slavery men and defeated them soundly in yet another referendum. Kansas remained a territory; the pro-slavery faction there was crushed; only two slaves were held in Kansas by 1860; the battle for Kansas had been decided. Yet for Northern Democrats the consequences of that battle were grim.[36]

Between December 1857 and April 1858 Douglas and the anti-Lecompton Democrats joined the Republicans in opposing Buchanan's recommendation. After the Administration had backed down and agreed to re-submit the constitution to Kansas's electorate (under a face-saving formula) many Democratic dissidents agreed to patch up local compromises with their party colleagues. But some anti-Lecomptonites joined the Republicans and others remained independent of the Northern Democratic party organization. These defections and independent candidacies very greatly weakened the Democrats in the congressional elections of 1858. For example, in the crucial state of Pennsylvania – in

[36] This discussion is based primarily upon: Potter, *Impending Crisis*, ch. 12, Fehrenbacher, *Dred Scott Case*, chs. 7, 19. Some important speeches are usefully available in *A Political Text-Book for 1860* (New York, 1860: reprinted New York, 1969), pp. 79–143, 154–8.

which the Democrats secured a majority in 1856 – Democratic congressional candidates won 43.2 per cent of the votes in 1858, while anti-Lecomptonites won 3.3 per cent. And in New York, more accustomed to party in-fighting, the proportions were 40.8 per cent and 5.7 per cent respectively. Even where party unity could be maintained and where the state Democratic leaders were favourable to Buchanan, party losses were serious. In 1856 Pennsylvania and Indiana were the only free states to give Buchanan a majority of the presidential vote. In 1858 Pennsylvania gave Lecompton Democrats only 43.2 per cent of the congressional vote; Indiana, with a united, pro-Buchanan party leadership, gave Democratic congressional candidates 47.7 per cent of the total vote. The swing was not dramatic; but the margin of error for Northern Democrats after 1854 was razor-thin. The Democratic party was not destroyed in the North in 1858; it won over 46 per cent of the vote in elections for *state* offices in 11 of 17 free states between September 1858 and April 1859. But it was virtually incapable of gaining a majority anywhere. This inability was disastrous because the Democrats' opponents were drawing more forcefully in 1858 into a single Republican party.[37]

Worse still, the Kansas dispute left a legacy of party acrimony. The only Northern state where the Democrats fared well in the elections of 1858 was Illinois. There Douglas kept tight control over the state party and argued that the only true Democratic course of action was opposition to the Lecompton fraud and to the Buchanan Administration. Public disagreement with the cabinet's policies was matched by bitter private aspersions against their personalities. Although Douglas had won his own contest to ensure re-election to the Senate, he did so at the cost of deeply alienating the Administration and the leading senatorial Democrats. Southern Democrats in 1858 regarded him as a traitor to the party; the Democratic senators stripped him of his committee chairmanship in December 1858.[38]

The Kansas question between January 1854 and November 1858 thus weakened, demoralized, and divided the Northern Democrats. Many found the doctrine of popular sovereignty itself to be unacceptable in any form: they wanted slavery excluded from the western territories, and so they left the party in 1854. Others, prepared to defend the actions of the pro-slavery legislature in Kansas, were amazed at the Buchanan Administration's insistence on the admission of Kansas under the Lecompton constitution. Douglas in 1858 stuck to his earlier position and maintained that the territories themselves would have to decide – if not explicitly, then through the passage or non-passage of police laws – whether or not to introduce slavery. The Douglasites stayed in the party

[37] Bruce Collins, 'The Democrats' Electoral Fortunes During the Lecompton Crisis', *Civil War History*, XXIV (1978), pp. 314–31.

[38] Fehrenbacher, *Dred Scott Case*, pp. 467–8, 483–4, 496–501, 506–13; Phillips (ed.), *Correspondence of Toombs, Stephens, Cobb*, pp. 442–4.

in 1858; but they provoked a fierce factional clash in which the previously accommodating Douglas was regarded by the Southern Democrats as a dangerous and treacherous foe. Douglas, however, confident that he could weather this Southern storm, set out to rally the Northern Democrats to the traditional cause of Union, robust territorial expansion and a working relationship with slavery. By 1860 he was the undisputed master of the Northern Democracy. But after 1858 his reputation in the South was shabby, tarnished, indeed beyond redemption: in the words of Jefferson Davis, 'a little electioneering grog drinking demagogue'.[39]

Kansas and the Southern Democrats, 1854–8

Between January 1854 and November 1858 the Kansas dispute moved through various phases, starting as an argument over federal allowance of slavery north of the old Missouri line in the territories, degenerating to a point where civil war threatened on the distant prairies, and culminating in a mighty presidential push to conscript Kansas into the ranks of the slave states. By the end of 1858 the whole effort to foist slavery upon the new territory had failed abysmally and at grievous political cost to the national Democratic party. By over-reaching themselves in trying to lodge slavery in Kansas and Nebraska, the slave state Democrats had embarrassed and weakened their Northern allies, their last, best hope for preserving slavery securely in the Union. Yet did the Southern Democrats grasp the implications of their insistence on slavery extension in 1854–8? Or did they simply blunder on, blinded by the constricting requirements of Southern pro-slavery politics and by the proud, parochial introversion of Southern intellectual life?

It is often argued that the Southerners adopted an essentially passive rôle in 1854. Southern Democrats were not greatly interested in Kansas, but longed instead for Cuba or for American expansion into Central America. Politicians' equanimity was more than matched by indifference to Kansas among the general public. Only in 1855 were Southern politicians and public alike angered by events in Kansas. But the reasons given for this claim or indifference are conflicting. On one side, Southern indifference supposedly stemmed from the sheer irrelevance of Kansas. Of over 50 Southern members of both houses of Congress who spoke on the Kansas–Nebraska bill in 1854, only two expressed a firm belief that slavery would prevail in the new territories. Wounded pride and self-respect alone aroused Southern opinion in 1855 when Northerners seemed aggressively intent upon flooding Kansas with free soil immigrants.[40] Against this view it has been argued that politicians and public in the Deep South calmly believed that slavery would triumph in Kansas. Only in 1855 did revived party politics in the Deep South

[39] Eaton, *Jefferson Davis*, p. 110.
[40] Avery O. Craven, *The Coming of the Civil War* (Chicago, 1957 edn), pp. 348–60.

question this assured belief. The Know-Nothing party in 1855 campaigned hard on nativism. In the Deep South it insisted that the threatening incursion of free soil settlers into Kansas would be stopped if the internal pressure of foreign immigrants upon the North were removed; an end to heavy immigration would thus clear the path for Southern preponderance in Kansas.[41] So a passive South was activated either by indignation or by renewed party warfare. This view of the South as victim is not entirely persuasive.

In the first place, Southerners were far more self-conscious sectionalists in 1853–4 than they had been 10 years earlier. And their general, often vague anxiety about their place in the nation was well founded in reality. No new slave state had been admitted after Florida and Texas in 1845; since then, Iowa (1846), Wisconsin (1848), and California (1850) had become free states; and Minnesota and Oregon were territories on the threshold of statehood (they became states in 1858 and 1859 respectively) and untouched by slavery. Even if Kansas and Nebraska were not added to the ranks of slave states, their establishment as organized territories would have to be accompanied by a major constitutional concession to the South. As one newspaper asserted in March 1854:

> All agree that slavery cannot exist in the territories of Kansas and Nebraska . . . . The South advocates the repeal of the Missouri restriction . . . solely for the reason that it would indicate the equality and sovereignty of the States. The single aim of the Nebraska bill is to establish the principle of *Federal non-intervention* in regard to slavery.

At the most general level, Southern rights would have to be respected: this point was emphasized throughout the congressional debates on Kansas. Among the extremists, Congressman Preston Brooks of South Carolina argued in March 1856:

> The admission of Kansas into the Union as a slave state is now a point of honor with the South. . . . It is my deliberate conviction that the fate of the South is to be decided with the Kansas issue. If Kansas becomes a hireling State, slave property will decline to half its present value in Missouri as soon as the fact is determined. Then abolitionism will become the prevailing sentiment. So with Arkansas; so with upper Texas.

Beyond symbolic respect for Southern political rights in the Union, the fate of slavery in Kansas appeared to Southern extremists full of grave implications for slavery generally in the Western slave states.[42]

[41] J. Mills Thornton, III, *Politics and Power in a Slave Society. Alabama, 1800–1860* (Baton Rouge, 1978), pp. 349–58. The Southern Know-Nothings' general case was that foreign immigrants were opposed to slavery: Senator Adams of Mississippi, *Congressional Globe*, 34:1, p. 1413.

[42] Craven, *Coming of Civil War*, p. 352; Nevins, *Ordeal of the Union*, II, p. 427.

Once given theoretical and symbolic importance, Kansas thus became a pressing concern to Southern politicians. Freedom in Kansas would become the entering wedge of abolitionism to the South-West. But Kansas concerned Southern politicians in 1854 rather than later because it was intertwined with, not separate from, the Southern drive for expansion into the Caribbean. President Pierce in March 1854 urged that the USA acquire Cuba from Spain; and various pro-slavery expeditions into Central America received some Southerners' support in 1854 and later. The quest for Cuba came not from rabid Southern Rights Democrats (indeed, dedicated secessionists opposed expansion in the 1850s as a mere sop and palliative to the South), but from Union-minded Southern Democrats and various Whigs who had worked with them in 1850–1 to quell secession. These Unionists strove to prove to Southerners that the Union worked; just as expansion into the Caribbean would meet, in their view, real needs in the South, so they aimed to show that Southern rights in the new territories would be respected by the North.

Moderate Southern Democrats in particular used the principle of congressional non-intervention as stated in 1850 to vindicate their actions of 1850–1 against the extremists. But this insistence on congressional non-intervention in 1854 had other purposes. Southern Democrats in rallying their own moderates would put any feeble-spirited, free soil Northern Democrats to a severe test and, they hoped, drive them from the national party. In thus cleaning out their own stable, the Southern Democrats hoped to embarrass the Southern Whigs by exposing the Northern Whigs as thoroughly committed to free soil and completely unreliable as friends to the South. If the Southern Democrats lost some Northern free soilers, the Southern Whigs would lose virtually their entire Northern base. While vindicating their Unionism and isolating the State Rights extremists, the Southern Democratic moderates would attract a substantial addition of Southern Whig defectors. Party differences in the South thus positively encouraged active Southern participation in framing the Kansas–Nebraska bill during the winter of 1853–4.[43]

But there is a further reason for being sceptical about supposed Southern indifference to the Kansas–Nebraska bill. By 1854 sectional rhetoric permeated press, pulpit, politics, and everyday discourse. Jefferson Davis ascribed his own fastidious Southernism to 'the denunciation heaped upon us by the press of the North, and the attempts to degrade us in the eyes of Christendom − to arraign the character of our people and the character of our fathers from whom our institutions are derived'. By 1854 the Liberty party's attack on the Slave Power as obtrusively dominant in the nation as well as in the South was widely parrotted by Northern publicists. Increasingly, the South was depicted

[43] Robert E. May, *The Southern Dream of a Caribbean Empire 1854–1861* (Baton Rouge, 1973), pp. 59–60, 67, 190–205, 235–6, 239–41; Cooper, *The South and the Politics of Slavery*, pp. 346–59.

as a road-block to Northern progress. In reply, an aggressive generation of Southern publicists took up the Southern cause. Led by J.D.B. De Bow, they urged that Southerners co-operate to develop their own manufacturing, railway building, commerce, and shipping, to create their own culture and education, and even to formulate their own Magna Carta of Southern political rights. Often these publicists were alienated from the political establishment, disgusted at the lack of tough-grained sectional consciousness in the South and despondent at the possibility of ever triggering off their region's economic transformation. But their writings, when backed up by the political activities of State Rights extremists, did not permit Unionist Southern Democrats to rest content with the work done in 1850–2.[44]

By their insistence in 1853–4 that slavery be given its head in the new territories, Union-minded Southern Democrats set the pattern of political debate for the following four years. In 1855, 1856, and 1857 Southern Democrats and their Know-Nothing opponents competed against each other's claims to be the more effective defenders and extenders of slavery. This party competition undoubtedly stiffened the Unionists' resolve to press the pro-slavery cause in Kansas. Very few settlers went from the South to Kansas; very little financial aid flowed in that direction; very few slaves were taken into that region of risk and hazard. Even so, sensible, moderate Southern politicians turned Kansas into a matter of apparent life and death to the South. By early 1857 they had enmeshed themselves in an extraordinary contention that the proper safeguarding of Southerners' constitutional rights as Americans, and their property rights as slaveowners, hinged upon the fate of slavery in a territory attractive for settlement to, and known intimately by, hardly any Southerner beyond the border states. They had further persuaded themselves – or pretended to believe – that Kansas should and would become a slave state. When Buchanan's new governor of Kansas Territory tried to persuade free soil settlers to participate in the election of delegates to a constitutional convention in June 1857, a real dog-fight started in the Deep South. Some hot-heads spoke of Governor Robert J. Walker (the great Texas annexationist of 1844) and the president as traitors; some Democratic meetings repudiated the governor's policy; weak and disorganized opposition groups – former Whigs and Know-Nothings – challenged Democratic credentials to represent Southern interests. Thus cornered, moderate Southern Democrats had to push further into the Kansas quagmire.[45]

The Lecompton constitution, with its spurious appearance of choice and its rugged, blunt enthusiasm for slavery, was not necessarily

[44] Eaton, *Jefferson Davis*, p. 80; Craven, *Coming of Civil War*, pp. 273–83, 292–5, 302, 340–4; Faust, *A Sacred Circle*, pp. 17–55, 87–111, 132–43.
[45] Cooper, *The South and the Politics of Slavery*, pp. 366–74; Holt, *Political Crisis of the 1850s*, 245–8.

welcomed by all Southern Democrats. The leading Southern Democrat in Buchanan's Cabinet, Howell Cobb, had wanted Kansas to become a slave state by indirection rather than blatant seizure: the constitution, he argued in October 1857, should not mention slavery, but Kansas should become a state under the care of the pro-slavery territorial legislature and with its pro-slavery laws intact.[46] Perhaps Cobb, and others, assumed that the majority of settlers, apparently Democrats, would naturally approve slavery almost unquestioningly. Such an assumption was understandable given Cobb's general thinking; he was intelligent enough to realize that Kansas would hardly remain a slave state for very long; but he needed and expected a clear and full recognition of the South's equal rights in the territories and the psychological boost to the South of an additional slave state. Yet although the precise form of the Lecompton constitution was not the one most desired by all Southern Democrats, the attempt to make Kansas a slave state had their energetic and united backing.

Not surprisingly, therefore, the failure in 1858 of both the Lecompton formula and the Buchanan Administration's efforts to push it into effect sparked off further debate in the South. The State Rights faction was especially angry at the compromise scheme which referred the constitution once more to the voters of Kansas. Some extremists had earlier urged that secession would be perfectly justified if Kansas were not admitted under the Lecompton constitution.[47] Although this threat was not followed up in 1858, the Administration's failure to make Kansas a slave state clearly strengthened the separatists in the Southern Democratic camp.

Many separatists tried to exploit this mood of frustration with the federal government by pressing for the re-opening of the African slave trade. From 1853–4 this idea gained currency in various newspapers in Charleston and, in November 1856, the proposal was aired also by the Governor of South Carolina. Within the next few years an increasing number of State Rights Democrats, many of them state office-holders, pressed in South Carolina, Georgia, and Mississippi for the lifting of the federal ban on the African slave trade. Some of them did so on the limited constitutional grounds that the federal government should not constrict state rights; *states* should be free to decide for themselves whether or not they wanted African slave-trading. Others obviously used the issue as yet another stick with which to beat the federal government.

Although the agitation for the re-opening of the external slave trade grew appreciably in 1858–9, it never won the support of a majority of state legislators in any one state of the Deep South. In Louisiana in March 1858 a scheme to import African 'apprentices' for periods from 15 to 50 years failed to win legislative approval. In November 1858 Georgia's legislature narrowly defeated motions to remove the prohibition of the

---

[46] Phillips (ed.), *Correspondence of Toombs, Stephens, Cobb*, p. 424.
[47] *Ibid.*, p. 431.

African slave trade from the state constitution. In July 1859 Mississippi's state Democratic convention took no concerted action on the question, but left individual party members to decide the matter for themselves. Finally in South Carolina, during 1857–9, the representatives of up-country districts, and of Charleston, defeated efforts made by the representatives of the heavily slave-owning low-country to re-open the trade. And in October 1858 South Carolina's legislature elected to the United States Senate James Chesnut who opposed such an abrupt return to the eighteenth century.

Opposition in the Deep South to the re-opening of the trade centred on three objections. In the first place, many committed secessionists contended that this question was trivial in relation to the larger cause of pushing the South from the Union. Why waste time on peripheral matters when the general good of the South itself was at stake? Secondly, some Southern Democrats bluntly questioned the value of re-opening the African slave-trade. Senator Albert G. Brown of Mississippi saw no need for vast imports which would little benefit the yeomen farmers he represented. But, thirdly and more importantly, many Southern Democrats − even those of separatist leanings − urged that the issue would do more to weaken and disrupt the national Democratic party than it was worth. So, rather ironically, the separatist cause was neatly detached from the boldest and widest-ranging defence of the morality of slavery. Even the most assertive Southern patriots admitted that the African slave-trade was intolerable: to that extent they bowed to Northern, and world, opinion.[48]

Tough-minded Southern Democrats in the late 1850s raised another issue which won far more general Southern support. A demand for a slave code in the federal territories arose directly from the events of 1854–8, giving a new twist to the familiar process of defining Congress's responsibilities in the territories. In 1837 Calhoun had insisted that the federal government had no power to intervene against slavery in the territories, but indeed had the responsibility for safeguarding slavery there. In 1849 Jefferson Davis claimed that the federal government was obliged to offer positive protection to slaveowners in territories south of 36°30'.[49] From 1854 to 1858 this point receded from view because the central Southern contention about Kansas was that the legitimate territorial government wanted − and would therefore protect − slavery. But the final defeat of the Lecompton scheme in August 1858, preceded as it was by the coming to power of a free soil legislature in Kansas in October 1857, produced novel implications for Douglas's doctrine of popular sovereignty in the summer of 1858. If, as Douglas contended, the territorial legislature could reasonably refuse to provide police protection for slavery, then, to

[48] Ronald T. Takaki, *A Pro-Slavery Crusade. The Agitation to Reopen the African Slave Trade* (New York, 1971), pp. 1, 5–6, 11–14, 78–81, 166–98, 231–3.
[49] Fehrenbacher, *Dred Scott Case*, pp. 122–4, 165.

an increasingly large body of Southern Democrats after 1858, the federal government itself would have to sustain slaveowners in the full enjoyment of their constitutional rights to property in the federal territories. Douglas, after all, argued that even though slavery was, by the terms of the Dred Scott decision of 1857, admissable automatically into all federal territories, the territorial majority could still exercise effective sovereignty by refusing to provide adequate police measures for the full control of slaves. The new political context – with the 'loss' of Kansas – meant that slavery was by late 1858 just as vulnerable as it had been before 1854 in the territories. So, Southern Democrats began demanding a federal slave code for the territories; this was a logical extension of the Dred Scott decision but it entailed a very obtrusive extension of federal power.

The demand for a federal slave code was also a radical one. In 1848 an obscure political orator from Alabama, William L. Yancey, had walked out of the Democratic national convention when it scoffed at his proposal for such a code. By 1858–9 Yancey had become one of the leading politicians in his state. How far various Southern Democrats began accepting the need for a federal slave code in 1858–9 in order to contain such committed secessionists of long standing as Yancey is impossible to determine. Some Southern Democrats may have moved sideways to radicalism to avert the triumph of extreme separatism. Others may simply have used the slave code issue as a party test, in order to deny Douglas the presidential nomination in 1860. Knowing that Douglas would oppose the idea of a code, they may have baited him to do so openly. During a fateful exchange in the Senate on 23 February 1859, Senators Brown and Davis of Mississippi thus goaded Douglas into rejecting a code. Whether Brown intended to carry out his threat that non-passage of a federal slave code should be answered by Southern secession is, again, very difficult to determine.[50] But many Southern Democrats were eager to grasp some tangible benefit from their furious congressional efforts of 1854–8, to score some obvious victory for Southern rights, and to exploit the theoretical gains made in the Dred Scott decision.

Yet some Southern Democrats were less than enthusiastic about pressing for a slave code in 1858–9. One thought the discussion concerned 'imaginary issues'; both senators from South Carolina and the South Carolinian speaker of the House of Representatives in 1857–9 thought the demand for a slave code unwise; Senator Robert Toombs believed the effort to expose, isolate, and humiliate Douglas in such manner to be foolish and self-defeating.[51] Although the idea of a federal code to protect slavery in the territories flowed logically from the failure of slavery to expand into Kansas and from the Dred Scott decision, it

[50] *Ibid.*, pp. 507–13.
[51] *Ibid.*, pp. 508, 512–13.

failed to unite Southern Democrats in 1858–9. Only in the spring of 1860 did Southern Democrats generally embrace demands for a federal slave code. This shift followed John Brown's abolitionist raid into Virginia and the subsequent panic felt about Northerners' direct intervention against slavery itself. But it followed also a renewed outburst of Republican anti-Southernism in the new Congress of 1859–60; and it was part of a concerted drive to clutch the Democratic presidential nomination from Douglas's grasp.[52]

How worrying, then, was the Kansas dispute to the South? The Kansas–Nebraska act and the actions of Kansas's pro-slavery territorial legislature, by producing an anti-slavery extension party in the North, created grave problems for Southern politicians and great anxieties for many other Southerners. One historian has concluded that 'The political campaign and election of 1856 did more to reawaken Southern fears and develop Southern unity than any other event since the introduction of the Wilmot Proviso'. In various parts of the South, not just in the Deep South, considerable thought was given in 1856 to the possibility that secession would be the best answer to a Republican victory in the presidential election. In September 1856, for example, the governor of Virginia tried to summon a meeting of slave state governors to discuss that option. The fear of Republicanism was expressed in social and not simply in political terms. One newspaper in New Orleans warned in October 1856 of the Republican threat: 'If they should succeed in this contest . . . they would repeal the fugitive slave law . . . they would create insurrection and servile war in the South . . . they would put the torch to our dwellings and the knife to our throats'. Privately, Chief Justice Taney thought the South — unless it united and resisted — would be subordinated to a Republican North in a complete and humiliating way: as Ireland was to Britain and Poland was to Russia, so the South would become to the North.[53]

These fears were not greatly assuaged by the Democrats' narrow victory in the presidential election of 1856. They probably encouraged Chief Justice Taney to deliver his sweeping and radical judgement in the Dred Scott case in March 1857. By declaring that Congress had no power to exclude slavery from any federal territory, Taney brushed aside the precedents of the first two generations of congressional practice. By declaring that a black man could never become a US citizen, Taney dismissed a long history of state and federal action on the vexed question of blacks' civil rights. In his stern refusal to draw any significant legal distinctions between slaves and free blacks, he bluntly defied a long tradition of thought and writing on a complex and perplexing subject.[54] Taney was correct in believing that all blacks' civil rights could readily be

[52] Phillips (ed.), *Correspondence of Toombs, Stephens, Cobb*, pp. 448–50, 459–62.
[53] Craven, *Coming of Civil War*, pp. 377–9; Potter, *Impending Crisis*, p. 263; Fehrenbacher, *Dred Scott Case*, pp. 557–8.

sacrificed to Democratic party unity and the Southern cause, for Democrats generally accepted harsh racism, and the Republicans secured no material electoral advantage from a defence of free blacks' rights in the North. Yet Taney's judicial resolution of questions about the place of slavery in the territories became, within about 18 months, the starting-point for a new dispute over the need for a slave code. This demand for full federal protection of slavery in the territories – flowing from Taney's ruling – was as much a political response to Douglas's attack on the Lecompton Constitution as to his 'Freeport Doctrine' that territories retained power over slavery because they could refuse to protect slavery. But it clearly arose – as did Taney's judgement in the first place – from a deeper anxiety about the South's security in the Union. In July 1859 Jefferson Davis proclaimed, 'We need to be assured of the rightfulness of Slavery';[55] the doctrine of popular sovereignty had clearly failed to re-assure the South and remove slavery from the agenda of congressional debate.

Even so, many Democrats in 1858 believed they could hold their party and the Union together. They shared a firm conviction that any inter-ference with, or change in, the South's racial order would have disastrous social consequences. And they continued to argue, despite the evidence of 1844–8 and 1854–8, that the best course of national action would be to engage in a further round of territorial expansion. National pride and Southern wants – symbolic and real – might be satisfied at the expense of Cuba and Mexico. For many Southern Democrats, therefore, the national party and the nation itself were well worth preserving despite the 'loss' of Kansas. Yet in 1859 many Unionist Southern Democrats saw no future in the federal Union if it were to be headed by a Republican president.[56]

[54] Fehrenbacher, *Dred Scott Case*, chs. 15, 16.
[55] Eaton, *Jefferson Davis*, p. 97.
[56] For example: Phillips (ed.), *Correspondence of Toombs, Stephens, Cobb*, pp. 448–50.

8 The Republican Challenge, 1854–1860

No event in the 1850s did more to intensify sectional animosities than the formation of the Republican party between July 1854 and February 1856. In the summer of 1854 this new party began to be established in various states of the Midwest; in February 1856 it consolidated its organization by holding its first national meeting. Many Republican leaders hoped that they would acquire a Southern wing by exploiting conservative fears of disruption in the South, by securing the support of former Southern Whigs who would never stomach the Democrats, and by winning over non-slaveholding whites chafing at the humiliations imposed by the Slave Power's rule.[1] Despite these imaginings, the Republican party captured virtually no votes outside the free states, except in the border state of Missouri. The Republicans' very existence, unacceptable as it was to the South, was, therefore, a challenge to, and departure from, the notion of a national two-party system.

The form of the Republican challenge to the South was not precisely clear in the 1850s. In February 1861 Chief Justice Roger B. Taney – a Democrat and a Southerner – privately described Republicanism as 'at best abolitionism in disguise only waiting for an opportunity'.[2] This view was commonly held in the South, and prevented the Republicans from gaining a political foothold in the slave states. Fear of abolition by stealth was widely expressed in numerous Southern writings of the late 1850s: Republicans would either act directly to end slavery, conduct a legislative and political guerrilla warfare against the institution, or simply encourage and inspire slave rebellions by their own activities or by their presence in power. Such fears were intensely felt before the presidential election of 1856: Taney argued during the presidential campaign that

---

[1] All discussion of the Republican party must centre on Eric Foner, *Free Soil, Free Labor, Free Men: the Ideology of the Republican Party before the Civil War* (New York, 1970): for the Southern strategy, see pp. 119–23. It has been pointed out that the Republicans' position in the North was not secure until May – June 1856. Many conservative Northerners were outraged at Southern responses to the caning of Senator Sumner by a Southern congressman, and so finally accepted the Republicans' sectional attack on the Slave Power. William E. Gienapp, 'The Crime Against Sumner: the Caning of Charles Sumner and the Rise of the Republican Party', *Civil War History*, XXV (1979), pp. 218–45.

[2] Don. E. Fehrenbacher, *The Dred Scott Case. Its Significance in American Law and Politics* (New York, 1978), p. 555.

the South would be 'doomed' in the new political order if the Republicans gained the presidency.[3]

The charge of abolitionism was not entirely fanciful. Granted, very few Republicans were immediate abolitionists. Abraham Lincoln said of slavery in 1854: 'If all earthly power were given me, I should not know what to do, as to the existing institution'.[4] The Republicans insisted that slavery was morally wrong, and thereby aroused acute and active resentment in the South. Moreover, *radical* Republicans insisted that the federal government be entirely separated from slavery; the federal authorities should exclude slavery from the territories and the District of Columbia, forbid the entry of any further slave states, more strictly enforce the prohibition on the overseas slave trade, and abolish the inter-state slave trade.[5] Such a policy – even though stopping short of outright interference with slavery within the individual states – would have been intolerable to slaveholders.

Yet the Republicans as a party never endorsed the radical programme. Their one, clear, united demand was that the federal government should prevent any further extension of slavery into the territories. Territorial exclusion was usually pressed as a defence of ordinary Northerners' economic opportunities in the far west against unfair competition from slaveowners. As Senator Lyman Trumbull told a Republican convention in 1856: 'It is not so much in reference to the welfare of the Negro that we are here, but it is for the protection of the rights of the laboring whites, for the protection of ourselves and our liberties'. Why, then, were many Southerners terrified at the prospect that slavery would be excluded from the territories? As the leading Republican newspaper, the *New York Tribune*, explained in October 1856: 'To restrict Slavery within its present bounds is to secure its speedy decline and ultimate extinction'.[6] This belief – however erroneous – was widely shared in the 1850s; it made the Republican challenge to slavery's extension more than just a peripheral and symbolic threat.

Why that threat arose and how seriously it might be acted upon confused contemporaries and confuses historians. The Republican party was a complex hybrid: a response to political developments in the mid 1850s, an expression of progressive ideology, and an engine of con-stitutional conservatism.

First, political developments (narrowly conceived) encouraged the establishment of a new Northern party.[7] For various reasons, the national

[3] Avery O. Craven, *The Coming of the Civil War* (Chicago, 1957 edn), pp. 370–81, 423–5; Fehrenbacher, *Dred Scott Case*, pp. 557–8.

[4] James A. Rawley, *Race and Politics. 'Bleeding Kansas' and the Coming of the Civil War* (Philadelphia, 1969), p. 76.

[5] Foner, *Free Soil, Free Labor, Free Men*, ch. 4, esp. pp. 116–19.

[6] Rawley, *Race and Politics*, p. 150; Foner, *Free Soil, Free Labor, Free Men*, p. 116.

[7] For the following two paragraphs, see: Glyndon G. Van Deusen, *Life of Henry Clay* (Boston, 1937), pp. 367–8, 387–93; William R. Brock, *Parties and Political Conscience: American Dilemmas, 1840–1850* (Millwood, N.Y., 1979), pp. 184–9; Michael F. Holt,

two-party system, which constricted sectional antagonisms from the mid 1830s to the mid 1840s and contained them in 1846–52, became less viable in the North in the early 1850s. Many of the issues which divided Whigs from Democrats, in the North at least, had been economic ones. With the ebbing of economic recession and the new wave of economic expansion in the late 1840s and early 1850s, these issues receded in importance. Not only did economic prosperity soothe some of the earlier bitterness over banking, tariffs, and internal improvement, it also created widespread demands for more active government promotion of economic development. Whigs and Democrats moved to the centre on economic policy: in 1848 the Whigs dropped their most ambitious schemes for tariff protection and an American System; and in the early 1850s a large body of Democrats in the states dropped their most radical objections to state promotion of easy banking. During the early 1850s numerous western Democrats embraced bold development schemes: federal aid to railroads and federal free homesteads to western settlers were especially popular. This enthusiasm – matched by western Democrats' readiness to soften their hostility to banks – reduced the contrast between the main parties.

At the same time, new issues arose which eluded ready manipulation by the existing parties. Nativism and anti-Catholicism sprang up in the wake of heavy foreign immigration in the late 1840s and early 1850s. The Whigs failed to exploit this growing antagonism to immigrants and Roman Catholics. Indeed, despite the reputation they had for being more nativist than the Democrats, the Whigs appealed to immigrant voters in the presidential election of 1852. Just as the Whig party was becoming nationally polarized – with its free soil Northern wing increasingly uncomfortable with the Southern Whigs – so it was losing its sense of purpose in the North. New nativist movements emerged in various Northern cities in 1853, hastened the break-down of the old party system in 1853–5, and came together (secretly at first) in an anti-immigrant, anti-Catholic party, the Americans or Know-Nothings. But, although nativism helped disrupt the old party system, the Know-Nothings did not become the major opposition to the Democrats and the anti-slavery-extension Republicans did not become explicitly nativist. Why?

Conditions changed rapidly in the mid 1850s. By 1856, and more markedly by 1858–60, the number of foreign immigrants entering America each year fell appreciably. Even though the outward signs of Catholic activity were abundantly obvious – cathedrals were being built in, for example, New York City and Chicago in the late 1850s – the

The Political Crisis of the 1850s (New York, 1978), pp. 101–14, 120–38; Robert W. Johannsen (ed.), *The Letters of Stephen A. Douglas* (Urbana, Ill., 1961), pp. 187–8, 235; Ronald P. Formisano, *The Birth of Mass Political Parties: Michigan, 1827–1861* (Princeton, 1971), pp. 217–42, 248–53.

aggressive phase of Roman Catholic expansion seemed to have ended. Moreover, the immigrants' and Catholics' potential political leverage was weakened by the elections of 1854, for those groups were associated politically with the Northern Democrats, whose electoral triumphs of 1850 and 1852 were reversed in the mid-term congressional elections of 1854: the political threat posed by the immigrants — in the nativists' eyes — immediately declined. Given these developments, it is easy to see why the nativist movement lacked sufficient staying power to keep nativism at the top of the Northern political agenda, and to encourage nativist state legislators to undertake the very radical legal and constitutional state reforms necessary to regulate and restrict the foreign-born population.[8]

Even so, some 13 per cent of Northerners in 1856 voted for the Know-Nothing party, and only in 1858 did the Republicans gather many residual nativist voters into their fold. Republicans appealed to nativists by stressing that territories open only to free settlers would help siphon off the immigrant population packed into eastern cities. Secondly, the Republicans turned the economic recession of 1857–9 to their own advantage by advocating tariff protection for depressed industries in language designed to please nativists: for American workers needed protection against cheap foreign goods produced by ill-paid foreign labour.[9]

Yet the main effect of Republican activity in 1854–6 was to weaken the nativists' appeal by strenuously denouncing the Slave Power. The propaganda used against the Slave Power in 1856 — with its alleged responsibility for 'Bleeding Kansas' and, following a Southern congressman's assault upon the Republican senator, for 'bleeding Sumner' — was amongst the most powerful, pervasive, and effective in American history. But how far it was devised simply to gain the widest possible electoral support for a party formed in the chaos of events of 1854 is difficult to say. The Kansas–Nebraska act and the protest against it certainly created an anti-slavery *interest* where there had previously been an anti-slavery sentiment. One Whig senator privately described his

[8] The failure of the Know-Nothings in power is very well analysed in one state by Jean H. Baker, *Ambivalent Americans. The Know-Nothing Party in Maryland* (Baltimore, 1977). The party suffered from their legislators' need to acquaint themselves with legislative business, since 96 per cent of their representatives in the state's lower house served their first term in 1856 (pp. 81–2). Know-Nothings suffered also from the sheer burden of local, individual, or interest group legislation — 90 per cent of the bills passed in 1856 were of parochial or particularist character (pp. 93–4) — and from the brevity of biennial legislative sessions (p. 97). Know-Nothings ended up espousing constitutional changes to ease the path to legislative reform (pp. 97, 103). But even in their hey-day, the Know-Nothings rarely gained absolute control over individual states; for example, in 1855 they held 9 state governorships and controlled the lower houses of 12 state legislatures, but complete control — of legislative upper houses and state courts — eluded them (pp. 3, 87–90).

[9] Foner, *Free Soil, Free Labor, Free Men*, pp. 168–76, 236–7; William Dusinberre, *Civil War Issues in Philadelphia, 1856–1865* (Philadelphia, 1965), p. 78.

reaction to the Kansas–Nebraska bill in February 1854: 'The thing is a terrible outrage and the more I look at it the more enraged I become. It needs but little to make me an out and out abolitionist'. Once established, the Republicans naturally added to their anti-Southern arguments and claims until in 1857–8 serious Republican politicians asserted that the Slave Power threatened to extend slavery into *all states*.[10] But the Republicans did not simply fumble into being in 1854–5 during a period of intense Northern anti-Southern and anti-party sentiment; nor did they promise merely to provide new leadership and new unity to the North; nor did they regard their own victory in the presidential election of 1860 as a sufficient political achievement in itself, an act rescuing the free states from the Slave Power and redeeming the Republic.[11] The Republicans also embodied certain elements of a 'progressive' ideology.

Republican ideology is difficult to define exactly because Republicans were much divided into factions, because Republicans' pronouncements were often contradictory, designed to satisfy different audiences and interest-groups at different times, and because the moral dimension in Republican thought has been either exaggerated too eagerly or dismissed too cavalierly by historians. Too much should not be claimed for the ante-bellum Republicans. Their belief in the primacy of free labour, in republican government, in open opportunity – political and economic – for ordinary whites, and in general 'improvement' was widely shared in the North and indeed, for the most part, in the South.[12] The Republicans in power in Northern states were not notable social reformers, nor did their party discover after the Civil War any clear commitment to domestic reform.[13] Granted, Republicans appealed to the most intense moralism in their rhetoric; Lincoln in 1858 not untypically described his senatorial contest with Senator Douglas as 'the eternal struggle between these two principles – right and wrong – throughout the world . . . . The one is the common right of humanity and the other the divine right of kings'.[14] Moral invocation was, however, no Republican monopoly in the 1850s: Douglas defended political and cultural pluralism within the existing Union as a moral end in itself; and Southerners generally crowed about both the morality of slavery and their moral duty

[10] David M. Potter (completed and ed. by Don E. Fehrenbacher), *The Impending Crisis, 1848–1861* (New York, 1976), pp. 218–24; Fehrenbacher, *Dred Scott Case*, p. 192; Richard H. Sewell, *Ballots for Freedom: Antislavery Politics in the United States 1837–1860* (New York, 1976), p. 259; Don E. Fehrenbacher, *Prelude to Greatness. Lincoln in the 1850s* (Stanford, 1962), pp. 79–82.

[11] Holt, *Political Crisis of the 1850s*, pp. 216–17.

[12] Bruce Collins, 'The Ideology of the Ante-bellum Northern Democrats', *Journal of American Studies* XI (1977), pp. 103–21; J. Mills Thornton, III, *Politics and Power in a Slave Society: Alabama, 1800–1860* (Baton Rouge, 1978).

[13] The general argument in James G. Mohr (ed.), *Radical Republicans in the North: State Politics during Reconstruction* (Baltimore, 1976) seems to me to need qualification: Bruce Collins, 'Non-sectional Issues in American Politics, 1830–1875', *Historical Journal*, XXI (1978), 709–19, esp. 717–19.

[14] Robert W. Johannsen, *The Lincoln – Douglas Debates of 1858* (New York, 1965), p. 319.

to protect their constitutional rights. Despite these reservations, Republican thought contained notable 'progressive' features, concerning race, the distribution of power, and economic policy.

On race, the majority of Republicans probably agreed that America's blacks deserved a better deal, even if their party could not decide precisely what that better deal might be. Very few Republicans, as we have seen, were immediate abolitionists, but most leading Republicans insisted on saying what Southerners in the 1850s regarded as unspeakable: slavery should end in the future, even if that desirable future were a hundred years away. Northern Democrats in the late 1850s deprecated such talk as impolitic, unreasonable, and irrelevant, for, they held, it would merely serve to irritate the South, set up false standards of racial improvement, and give significance to black Americans – slave and free – totally unwarranted and undeserved. Northern Democrats boasted of their indifference to the question of slavery and warned of the dangerous practical consequences for Northern society of identifying the North in black Southerners' minds with the prospect of freedom and advancement. Republican pronouncements on slavery would, they maintained, simply encourage Southern blacks – slave and free – to flee northwards, with dire consequences of racial miscegenation and loss of jobs for whites.[15] Against this attack, Republicans proposed various alternatives.

Lincoln and a number of influential Midwestern Republicans felt that the freed slaves should be packed off to Central America or Liberia. One senator pointed out that three and a half million Europeans had sailed to America during the years 1847 to 1860: why should not the four million black slaves leave in the same way? This harsh suggestion at least recognized the extreme difficulties that would be raised by racial adjustment in the South if the slaves were to be freed. Another view – more essentially conservative – was put by Senator Sumner; freedom would leave most blacks in the South as 'a dependent and amiable peasantry'. No Republican wanted an exodus of blacks to the North or the western territories and many Republicans waged a veritable 'crusade for white men's freedom' to keep blacks – slave or free – from those territories. Clearly, the question of the slaves' future confused and divided the Republicans. But their party was not obliged to spell out a coherent policy, for Republicans did not argue that the federal government could or should end slavery in the states. Republicans, quite unlike Northern Democrats in 1854–60, wanted to stop the federal government from actively extending slavery, and to set the tone and pace of a debate on the 'ultimate extinction' of the South's cherished labour system. The

---

[15] Leon F. Litwack, *North of Slavery. The Negro in the Free States 1790–1860* (Chicago, 1961), pp. 263, 267–79; Fehrenbacher, *Dred Scott Case*, pp. 435–6; B.W. Collins, 'Economic Issues in Ohio's Politics During the Recession of 1857–1858', *Ohio History*, 89 (1980), p. 48 (note 11).

two leading Republicans in 1860 — Lincoln and Senator Seward — both insisted that blacks' basic natural rights be recognized and that Northern free blacks, even if not accorded full political or social equality, should nevertheless be raised from a condition of perpetual inferiority.

Republicans, far more than any other political group in the late 1850s, attempted to open up opportunities for blacks. And they fiercely denounced — without gaining any apparent electoral benefits — the Dred Scott decision and its implicit assumption that free blacks were hardly distinguishable from slaves in the federal courts. The radical or more tolerant Republicans' attitudes to free blacks resembled British liberals' attitudes to the working class: they should not be entirely denied civil rights, but instead should be given reasonable encouragement, allowed to demonstrate their individual worth and respectability, and, then, very gradually and as circumstances warranted, accorded a larger stake in politics.[16] And, just as mid-nineteenth-century Britain witnessed an increasing philanthropic, if paternalistic, political concern for the improvement of the working classes, so in the 1850s Republican concern about slavery grew from emotional and religious, as well as political, roots. Various individual fugitive slave trials, the overwhelming popular impact of Harriet Beecher Stowe's *Uncle Tom's Cabin*, and the marked Republican sympathies shown by Northern evangelical clergymen all reinforced this moral concern.[17]

Beyond 'progressive' morality, Republicans evinced 'progressive' attitudes in their social and economic analysis of sectional differences. Northern Democrats did not share the Republican belief that the Southern (white) class structure and Southern economy were irreconcilably and objectionably different from their own. How far Republicans emphasized these differences for their own political advantage within the North is unclear. There was certainly something ironic in Republican establishment figures urging Northern voters 'to encounter the *Oligarchs* of Slavery'; those Southern leaders were usually elected by open procedures and ordinary people, just as open procedures and ordinary people in the North provided affluent Republican lawyers with their ladders to high office. By following the time-honoured American procedure of pin-pointing an external enemy and denouncing it as conspiratorial, aristocratic, or oligarchical, the Republicans' attack on the Slave Power consolidated their Northern support and contained divisive

---

[16] Foner, *Free Soil, Free Labor, Free Men*, ch. 8, esp. pp. 267–80, 290–8 (p. 292 n. draws a comparison with the progress of the English working class); Rawley, *Race and Politics*, p. 125; Formisano, *Birth of Mass Political Parties*, pp. 277–9, 287–8. Fehrenbacher, *Dred Scott Case*, pp. 417–23, 429–37, 563–7.

[17] Stanley W. Campbell, *The Slave Catchers: Enforcement of the Fugitive Slave Law 1850–1860* (New York, 1972 edn), pp. 87–95, 116–47; W.L. Rose, *Race and Region in American Historical Fiction: Four Episodes in Popular Culture* (Oxford, 1979), pp. 9–16; Formisano, *Birth of Mass Political Parties*, pp. 269–70, 310–18, 323–4. (Formisano finds little active sympathy for blacks among Michigan's Republicans, but emphasizes their evangelical Protestantism.)

local conflicts and issues within the free states.[18]

But many Republican leaders sincerely believed that the Southern class structure was distinctive from that in the free states. Their observation was sharpened by a double resentment. For many Republicans, the overt manifestation of the Slave Power's narrow and concentrated interest in slavery extension in 1854 came as a powerful jolt and stimulus to political action.[19] And, secondly, when upper-middle-class Republican lawyer-politicians found Congress controlled, or at least checked, by Democrats strongly influenced by Southerners, they naturally resented, as men powerful, wealthy, and respected in their own section, the Southern minority section's disproportionately large blocking strength at Washington. If the House of Representatives − which reflected the free states' preponderance in population over the South − had been the sole chamber in the Congress, the attack on Southern oligarchs would have been unnecessary. But linking excessive Southern political weight in the Senate with an anachronistic and un-American social class was an integral part of the Republican cause and give it a further 'progressive' tinge.

An additional 'progressive' quality was displayed in Republican economic rhetoric. The Republicans took over the Whigs' arguments for tighter economic integration between farming and manufacturing sectors, for more widely dispersed industrialization, and for bolder federal government policies to promote economic advance. These arguments were transposed from party thought to sectional rhetoric. Some of the leading enthusiasts for the Whigs' American System − notably Horace Greeley and Henry C. Carey − became prominent Republican publicists. They described the North as a complex, dynamic, semi-industrial economy and they urged that federal policies recognize that fact. They described the South as a far more simple, relatively backward, entirely agricultural economy, and they deplored the anti-Northern economic policies foisted upon Congress by the powerful Southern Democratic lobby. They never tired of pointing to the South's relative economic failings, attributing them to slavery, and emphasizing that the North's superior free labour system only needed a little extra legislative help from its Republican friends to achieve a more nearly perfect harmony of economic interests.[20]

In these various ways, different groups of Republicans revealed their commitment to a 'progressive' ideology. Not all Republicans felt equally

[18] Donald, *Charles Sumner*, p. 267; William J. Cooper, Jr, *The South and the Politics of Slavery, 1828–1856* (Baton Rouge, 1978), ch. 2; B.W. Collins, 'Community and Consensus in Ante-bellum America', *Historical Journal*, XIX (1976), 635–63.

[19] Fehrenbacher, *Prelude to Greatness*, pp. 22–5, 34–43.

[20] Compare the arguments in Horace Greeley, 'Why I am a Whig', *Whig Almanac and Statistical Register for 1852* (n.p., n.d.), pp. 6–12 with those in the pamphlet, *The North and the South. Reprinted from the New York Tribune* (New York, 1854) and Henry C. Carey, *The Harmony of Interests, Agricultural, Manufacturing, and Commercial* (New York, 1852 edn), pp. 136–41, 145–50, 161–9, 191, 209–29.

strongly about each of these elements of 'progressive' thought; but the party as a whole hoped for a better deal for free blacks, was uncomfortable with, if not openly critical of, slavery, repudiated the Slave Power and its excessive influence in the federal Congress, and contrasted Northern economic prosperity and rapid development unfavourably with Southern economic backwardness. Yet, the question arises: if Republicanism was such a profound, wide-ranging ideological challenge to the South, why did the challenge, based on supposedly striking moral, social, and economic differences between North and South, emerge only in 1854 and fail to capture the support of a secure majority in the North until 1858?

One answer to this question is that the essential elements that made up the Republican party existed in the North long before 1854. The Liberty party and the Free Soilers of 1848 prepared the way. After 1850 many Northern Whigs, despite their continuing loyalty to their organization, were increasingly frustrated with the rigid Southern attitude to slavery, with the Slave Power in Washington, and with the lack of more promotional federal economic policies. These two elements thus logically came together in 1854–5. Although they differed sharply over practical details of policy, they could agree in 1854–6 upon a party platform opposed to slavery extension and to the Slave Power. Only in 1857–60 did the party broaden its platform and its appeal: greater emphasis was laid upon its Whiggish economic policies, especially in eastern industrial areas hit by the recession of 1857–9; much prominence was given to the Republicans' rôle as a respectable alternative government, ready to take over from the factious, tired, and corrupt Democratic federal administration; and, in the presidential election year of 1860, Republicans softened their image by promising repeatedly not to interfere with slavery where it already existed and by dismissing suggestions that their victory in the election would have much impact upon Southern opinion.[21] Yet this very marked tension in Republican thinking – with the moral sentiment against slavery counter-balanced by a reluctance to interfere with slavery in the states – suggests an emphasis upon a further Republican characteristic.

Republicans frequently depicted themselves as constitutional conservatives. Although their arguments against the South were often pitched in highly moralistic terms, moral emphasis was typical of much political rhetoric used by nineteenth-century liberals. It hardly differed from the grandiose moral claims made in the 1830s by Jacksonian Democrats in their 'war' upon the Bank of the United States. American

---

[21] Foner, *Free Soil, Free Labor, Free Men*, pp. 124–48, 168–76. For much information on this period, and a rather different interpretation, see Holt, *Political Crisis of the 1850s*, pp. 199–217; B.W. Collins, 'Economic Issues in Ohio's Politics During the Recession of 1857–1858' sees the Republicans' appeal in 1858 as increasingly conservative: cf. Jeter A. Isely, *Horace Greeley and the Republican Party, 1853–1861* (Princeton, 1947), pp. 196–254.

politicians are normally most effective when they can bring moral fervour — some historians call it a crusading style — to constitutional causes. But the heady froth of moral rhetoric should not be allowed to obscure the real underlying substance of a struggle over constitutional power.

While Republicans were not well qualified to engage in social engineering for the blacks' benefit, and were indeed confused, embarrassed, and divided as to what the federal government might do for free or enslaved blacks, they were very well qualified to perceive, and respond in unison to, a shift in the national balance of power. The Republicans were, after all, a league of diverse politicians joined together to resist the further extension of slavery. The Kansas–Nebraska act set them to work; the events in Kansas in 1854–6 broadened their alliance; the Dred Scott decision confirmed their worst fears; and the fiasco over Lecompton in 1857–8 consolidated their party. Their opposition to slavery's extension was based on conservative constitutional principles. They argued that the Declaration of Independence — asserting that all men are created equal — applied, at least with respect to basic natural rights, to blacks as well as whites, and was intended by the Founding Fathers to do so. This claim was rejected by Southerners and Northern Democrats alike; there were good grounds for stressing, as Senator Douglas did, that the American whites in the 1770s would not have taken blacks' rights very seriously. The Republicans could, however, make a safer claim.

They refused to accept that Congress lacked the power to *exclude* slavery from the territories. In 1787 the Confederation had banned slavery in the North-West Territory. As late as 1849 and 1853 territories had been created by Congress with slavery excluded from them. As early as 1798, a significant number of Northern congressmen had even tried to prevent *all* further extension of slavery in the territories. In 1820 that idea won greater congressional support, and in 1846–8 it repeatedly secured the endorsement of a majority in the House of Representatives. Yet in 1854 the Democratic Congress and president approved an act that effectively denied ultimate congressional authority over the territories, and in 1857 the Democratic judges on the Supreme Court explicitly denied that Congress had the power to exclude slavery from federal territories. During the presidential election campaign of 1856 Republicans constantly harped upon this fundamental defect in the Northern Democrats' doctrine of popular sovereignty; after all, they declared, Congress had exercised power over slavery in the territories for two generations. And so the argument remained in 1858–60. While Douglas and the Northern Democrats were trying desperately to quash Southern Democratic extremists' efforts to force a federal slave code upon the party, they were also peddling their national balm of popular sovereignty to the Northern voters. Republicans simply reiterated their earlier demands: whatever the bigoted judges of the Supreme Court proclaimed, Congress had traditionally enjoyed power over slavery in the territories and Congress should in future forbid any further extension of slavery into the territories.[22] As Lincoln said in February 1860:

> Wrong as we think slavery is, we can yet afford to let it alone where it is, because that much is due to the necessity arising from its actual presence in the nation; but can we, while our votes will prevent it, allow it to spread into the National Territories, and to overrun us here in these Free States?[23]

To say that all Republicans were determined to restore Congress's power over territorial policy is not to explain why their party won a majority of Northern votes in the mid-term elections of 1858 and then won a larger majority, and the presidency, in 1860. Many different factors affected Northerners' voting behaviour. Some Northerners had objected to the Democrats in the past and would vote for whoever opposed them. Some Northerners associated the Democrats with Catholicism and the immigrant Irish and voted accordingly. Some Northerners sought more positive federal government economic policies — in building a railway to the Pacific, in providing western settlers with free homesteads, and in giving firm tariff protection to eastern industries — than Democratic administrations condoned. Some Northerners disliked or despised slavery and the South and expressed that sentiment by supporting a purely Northern party.

But, for whatever reasons they became the North's majority party, Republican politicians in power were committed to constitutional conservatism. However much those politicians portrayed themselves as enemies to narrow class rule by the Slave Power, or as the purveyors of 'progressive' ideas, their central political purpose was to restore powers once exercised by Congress. This constitutional conservatism in the face of Southern Democrats' constitutional radicalism was a vital element in the Republicans' electoral appeal, the main reason why the party emerged in 1854, and the primary challenge to the Southern Democrats' need for a Union friendly to slavery. When the Republicans gained the presidency in November 1860, they did so as a party pledged to reversing the federal territorial policies of the previous decade. And in economic policy, they promised an expansion of federal activity and power. With good reason therefore and long before the election, many Southern Democrats decided to meet constitutional restoration with a constitutional revolution.

---

[22] Fehrenbacher, *Dred Scott Case*, pp. 79–82, 88, 104–7, 131, 192, 197, 367–84, 437–43, 450–5; for a typical Republican argument in 1856 see, e.g., Israel Washburn, Jr, *Appendix to the Congressional Globe* 34th Congress, 1st Session (Washington, D.C., 1856), p. 638.
[23] Sewell, *Ballots for Freedom*, p. 360.

9 Secession and War, 1860–61

The Election of 1860

The presidential election of November 1860 was one of the most confusing and fateful in American history. In the free states, the Republicans piled up hefty majorities and so easily captured the electoral college.[1] Yet they won only 39.8 per cent of the national popular vote: a proportion similar to those gained by such pronounced losers of twentieth-century elections as Herbert Hoover in 1932, Barry Goldwater in 1964, and George McGovern in 1972. The secret of Republican success was that their support was concentrated, not dispersed, for their party was virtually non-existent in the South. Although the Republicans may have been aided by divisions among their opponents, the only marginal free states they carried were Illinois (50. per cent Republican) and Indiana (51.1 per cent); a united opposition might conceivably have increased turn-out and so defeated Lincoln in these two states, but that possibility cannot be proven.

The Republicans' main opponents in the free states were the Northern Democrats under Douglas. Douglas's candidacy had split the Democratic party at its national convention – held in two bitterly contested sessions in May and June – but the Northern Democrats persisted in campaigning, hopelessly, to the end. Douglas, unlike Lincoln, campaigned in the South, but he won only 12.8 per cent of the slave states' votes. Even so, he much weakened the Southern Democrats' customary hegemony in the slave states. Objecting fiercely to Douglas and insisting upon a federal slave code for the territories, the Southern Democrats had established a separate party in 1860: they won 44.7 per cent of the South's popular vote, and captured 10 of the 15 slave states, although they secured majorities in only 6 of them, in the Deep South. Gathering up the rest of the Southern popular vote (38.1 per cent) was the ad hoc Constitutional Union party, a conservative Whig–Know-Nothing remnant, strong in the Upper South and with some support in parts of the North. Not the least of the ironies of the election of 1860 was the fact that the South, on the verge of independence, was far less dominated by one party than the North; in purely party terms, the South was the less solid section in 1860.

[1] The election is ably analysed in W. Dean Burnham, *Presidential Ballots, 1836–1892* (Baltimore, 1955), pp. 75–87.

If the election of 1860 had been a referendum on the parties' federal policies — which, of course, it was most assuredly not — then the victory would have gone to the two national parties — Douglas's Northern Democrats and the Constitutional Unionists — which between them captured only 5 of the 33 states.[2] A majority of American voters in 1860 acquiesced in the possible future extension of slavery: only the Republicans ruled this out entirely. Granted, Northern Democrats hedged slavery extension around with the restrictions that might arise from an energetic exercise of popular sovereignty. But they did not preclude further slavery extension, and they envisaged, as did the Southern Democrats, future expansion for slavery into Cuba. A rather different majority in 1860 also approved of the continued existence of the Union. Republicans insisted on Unionism, and the Douglasites and the Constitutional Unionists pressed very hard for the cause, even though Constitutional Unionists in the South put it second to Southern rights during the campaign. Only the Southern Democrats explicitly, openly, and frequently questioned the value of the Union in 1860. Yet the sectional victors in 1860 were not the Douglasites and the Constitutional Unionists, who both adhered to Union and allowed for slavery's further extension. In the North, the Republicans refused to accept any further spread of slavery and, while lauding Union, were a thoroughly sectional party. In the South, the Southern Democrats prated about the need for full guarantees of their constitutional rights within the Union, while conceding nothing to Northern distaste for a territorial slave code. So, if a national majority in 1860 probably endorsed Union and some further extension of slavery, neither sectional majority accepted this soothing mixture. There was no scope — in the distribution of electoral college votes and congressional seats — for a repeat of 1850.

The election of 1860 — and the campaign preceding it — have long been the subject of intense discussion.[3] Could different political formulae have worked in 1860? Could the Democratic party have stayed together? If the Democrats had united upon a moderate and generally acceptable candidate, would they have captured the presidency? Were the Republicans guilty of excessive complacency in dismissing Southern separatist rhetoric in 1860 as idle boasting heard often before? All these questions are interesting and worth consideration.

But the plain fact of the situation in 1860 is that Republican attitudes

---

[2] The party platforms are available in, e.g., Arthur M. Schlesinger, Jr and Fred L. Israel, *History of American Presidential Elections, 1789–1968* (New York, 1971), II, pp. 1123–7; there is no satisfactory book on the election of 1860, although many studies discuss the election in particular states or localities. Ollinger Crenshaw, *The Slave States in the Presidential Election of 1860* (Baltimore, 1945) is still useful. John V. Mering, 'The Slave-State Constitutional Unionists and the Politics of Consensus', *Journal of Southern History*, XLIII (1977), pp. 395–410, stresses the agreement among Southerners to preserve slavery and oppose the Republicans.

[3] See, for example, George H. Knoles (ed.), *The Crisis of the Union, 1860–1861* (Baton Rouge, 1965), pp. 3–59.

– and indeed some of Douglas's attitudes – and Southern needs were irreconcilable. In speech after speech, the Republicans had deplored the extension of slavery, demanded some future adjustment of slavery in America, and abused the Slave Power. Southerners in general, and Southern Democrats in particular, demanded an end to such disapprobation, a proper, full, and uniform enforcement of the Fugitive Slave Act, and a rejection of the Republican doctrine that there should be no further slave states. As Vice-President John C. Breckinridge (the Southern Democrats' presidential candidate in 1860) told Kentucky's state legislature in December 1859:

> It is the avowed purpose of the Republican party to agitate; to overturn the Constitution itself, until they succeed not only in drawing a *cordon* around you, and shutting you within your present limits but to put you in a position where you were about, for peace sake, to emancipate your slaves.

The only hope for the Union, according to the vice-president in December 1859, was for all 'conservative' men – all Democrats and the remaining Old Whigs, North and South – to unite against the dangerous and provocative Republican agitators.[4] By June 1860 at the latest, such unity had proved to be unattainable. The logic of events was then flowing swiftly in the Southern separatists' direction.

The First Wave of Secession

No single leader or coterie of leaders took the Deep South out of the Union in response to Lincoln's election to the presidency in November 1860. So pervasive and compelling was secessionist feeling that separatist politicians were able to force fresh elections – to state secession conventions – almost immediately after the presidential election had occurred. In these convention elections, party labels were discarded and secessionist candidates fought co-operationist candidates. But even co-operationists were not necessarily opposed to secession; they merely argued for co-operation among Southern states before individual states seceded, or for a delay to secession until Lincoln became president in March 1861 and committed an 'overt act' against the South.[5]

On 20 December South Carolina seceded, followed very quickly by six other cotton states. During 4–9 February 1861 a convention met at Montgomery, Alabama, drew up a constitution, established the Confederate States of America, and appointed a fully-fledged provisional government, headed by President Jefferson Davis and Vice-President Alexander H. Stephens. After the prolonged, often tedious,

---

[4] *A Political Text-Book for 1860* (New York, 1860), p. 152.
[5] Dwight L. Dumond, *The Secession Movement, 1860–1861* (New York, 1931), pp. 121–3.

constitutional and political wranglings of the previous decades, why did secession occur, and occur so swiftly?

In recent years, historians have studied secession in four of the seven states of the original Confederacy. One thing they agree upon is that secession was not simply a class rebellion by Southern planters against the North; but what precisely happened in the Deep South in 1860–1 is still a matter of intense controversy. Available interpretations include a social theory of secession, an economic expansion theory, a political theory, and a psychological theory.

Professor Johnson, for example, argues that Georgia's secession amounted to an *internal* class revolution.[6] The slaveholding class sought in separation a durable safeguard against any possible anti-Slave Power and pro-Republican movement among the state's non-slaveholding, poorer whites. This fear – that a Republican administration in Washington would succour anti-planter political support for itself in non-slaveholding regions of the Deep South – was certainly a factor influencing planter politicians. But Johnson's evidence fails to show that it was *the* critical factor. Very few specific instances of such class fears within Georgia itself are cited – and some examples provided, notably from the Charleston *Mercury*, come from wildly extremist writers. Johnson proceeds to argue that the secession convention, in revising the state's constitution, revealed a similar class interest at work. Again, however, the evidence is somewhat strained, for the work done by the state's secession convention was hardly reactionary in effect. Reducing the size of the state senate and making county formation more difficult simply brought Georgia into line with other states throughout the country; tightening up on bank chartering was a Democratic response to the rapid bank expansion of 1850–6 and the anti-bank feeling aroused by the financial crash of 1857; banning state aid to railways was a reaction to the fiscal difficulties created by state aid in the 1830s, 1840s, and 1850s, a response adopted, for example, by New York state over a decade earlier. These changes in the state constitution were relatively minor, related to events in the 1850s, and paralleled by constitutional revisions made or attempted elsewhere in states which had neither seceded nor flung themselves into an upper-class counter-revolution. There is some evidence of class power being defended in 1861; but the shift from election to appointment of superior court judges and the retention of an unequal distribution of state legislative seats hardly revealed a radical drive among planters to consolidate their control.

What stands out instead in Johnson's book is the considerable

[6] Michael P. Johnson, *Toward a Patriarchal Republic. The Secession of Georgia* (Baton Rouge, 1977), pp. xx–xxii, 43–5, 65–70, 88–94, 101, 124–82, 194–5, 198: the figures cited are drawn from the last of these pages, which are part of a very valuable statistical appendix. Johnson's book contains much useful material and tries to connect developments often left unrelated; but I find – although others may not – the overall interpretation strained and unproven.

complexity of factors at work. No statistical correlation made between the vote for secessionist candidates to the secession convention and a range of political, economic, and social variables yields any very convincing explanation of why secession occurred. Only at the very extremes did clear divisions of voting behaviour emerge in Georgia. In counties with under 15 per cent of their populations as slaves, only 41 per cent of the voters favoured secession; yet only 20 out of 132 counties had so few slaves. Again, in counties with under 15 per cent of their voters as slaveholders, only 34 per cent of the voters favoured secession; yet only 13 of 132 counties had so few slaveholders, and in all other groups of counties by proportion of slaveholders there were majorities for secession. Finally, in counties where under 40 per cent of the voters in 1860 had supported Breckinridge, the Southern Democratic presidential candidate, backing for secession came from 42 per cent or less of the convention voters; yet only 33 of the 132 counties had been strongly anti-Breckinridge in 1860. And so on: the difficulties of formulating a clear relationship between 'objective' economic, social, and political variables (*if* they are indeed objective, which is open to statistical and conceptual doubt) and support for secession are enormous.

One problem Johnson raises is that the Georgian secessionists did not press for territorial *expansion* as a key reason for revolution. In Mississippi and Alabama, according to Professor Barney, the most important socio-economic division was not the general one between slaveholders and non-slaveholders.[7] Instead a more subtle division existed. Groups eager to rise to planter or slaveholder status pressed for secession against those who were already firmly established in the planter class, or were completely cut off from the plantation system and its values, and were consequently less anxious about the prospects for future mobility. Barney's interpretation has the virtue of relating the 'secessionist impulse' for slavery's further territorial extension to the central issue in antebellum federal politics. It may well be that Mississippi and Alabama — more westerly than Georgia and established as states only in 1817 and 1819 respectively, as opposed to Georgia's colonial foundation in 1732 — were simply more anxious about future expansion than the Atlantic seaboard states. But a number of Barney's more precise arguments — especially his contention that the economically faster growing counties with less stable agriculture tended to be secessionist, while the counties' with more stable agriculture tended to be cooperationist — have been questioned.

In studying Alabama's secession and the long-term background to it, Professor Thornton argues against any socio-economic explanation of the Southern revolt in 1860–1.[8] On very general grounds, he stresses that

[7] William L. Barney, *The Secessionist Impulse. Alabama and Mississippi in 1860* (Princeton, 1974), pp. 270–89, 296.
[8] J. Mills Thornton, III, *Politics and Power in a Slave Society. Alabama 1800–1860* (Baton Rouge, 1978), pp. 12, 343–7, 368–9, 372, 375–6, 418–26.

slavery depended not on planter rule but on mass consent, and that Alabama was a highly democratic state. On specific grounds, he finds no persuasive connection between particular social or economic interests and the rush to secession. Support for secession was a personal response to perceived Republican challenges in the future and a product of complex political calculations. Secessionists won control of Alabama, according to Thornton, by uniting three groups. Separatist fire-eaters of long standing, led by William L. Yancey, provided the energy and the vision, for they harped upon the failure of Southern expansion dreamt of in 1856, into Kansas, Cuba, or Latin America; many Democrats, disillusioned with state policies adopted by the party establishment in the 1850s, condoned a party putsch; and Old Whig or opposition leaders, lacking a real organization of their own after 1856 and unwilling to remain forever excluded from office and power, provided the necessary extra support in southern Alabama. These groups were joined together by the separatists' distinctive appeal; secession became a broad, anti-party movement aimed as much against the Democratic establishment within Alabama as against the Republican threat in Washington. So in this view the mechanics of secession depended upon politics, not social rivalries or economic imperatives. But what of the logic behind secession?

Although secession was engineered mainly by South Carolina and by fire-eaters across the Deep South, the psychological reasons behind the rebellion emerged from political assumptions shared throughout the Deep South during the previous 30 or 40 years. Secession was a moralistic crusade for the defence of white men's liberties against Northern encroachment or restriction; Southerners resented infringements on their right to take slaves into federal territories, just as they resented Northern states' interference with the Fugitive Slave Act. These resentments were reinforced by a general resentment at the relative loss of Southern political weight in the Union. Challenges to sectional rights and individual liberties were so enmeshed together that all three parties in Alabama in 1860 – Southern Democrats, Douglas Democrats, and Constitutional Unionists – regarded the extension of slavery as essential to the proper recognition of Southerners' rights; and all three agreed that at some point, immediately or later in the Administration's existence, Lincoln's accession to power would create a genuine crisis for the Deep South.[9]

That crisis was one of fear.[10] As early as the 1830s and 1840s Calhoun had asserted that the South needed to find long-term security against Northern anti-slavery sentiment. In March 1850 James H. Hammond, a prominent South Carolinian politician and occasional office-holder, warned darkly: 'If we do not act now, we deliberately consign our

[9] *Ibid.*, pp. 442–61, 401–3.
[10] Steven A. Channing, *Crisis of Fear. Secession in South Carolina* (New York, 1970), chs. 1, 2, 9, pp. 94–112, 235–6.

children, not our posterity, but *our children* to the flames'. In September 1857 the separatist *De Bow's Review* urged unity and steadfastness upon the South:

> There is room now for but one party at the South, a 'hearth and home party', a 'wife and children party', a party which shall interpose hereafter its united breasts against the sure strides of the power which threatens and promotes servile insurrection, the laying waste of fields . . . the recession of civilization

and sundry other indignities to the whites. Adopting similar imagery in December 1859 Senator Robert Toombs of Georgia, a firm Unionist in the early 1850s, viewed the possibility of a Republican presidential victory with dismay: 'If they beat us I see no safety for us, our property and our firesides, except in breaking up the concern . . . if such a calamity should come, we should prefer to defend ourselves at the doorsill rather than await the attack at our hearthstone'.[11] This fear was intensified by John Brown's raid at Harper's Ferry in October 1859, when the abolitionist Brown sought to ferment slave rebellions in Virginia and elsewhere in the South. But Southern white fears of slave risings had long existed: since the 1790s and the slave rebellion in St Domingue, such anxieties had never been entirely absent from Southern thought. The prospect of Republican victory in the presidential election merely gave them concrete, immediate, and significant form. After July 1860 most politicians in South Carolina believed that Lincoln would win the presidency and that secession was the only alternative to eventual emancipation.

A Republican federal administration was objectionable to the South on several counts. For one thing, it might build up a following within the South itself consisting of malcontents and non-slaveholders lured by the prospect of place, patronage, contracts, and favour. Although non-slaveholders generally supported slavery as a means of repressing and restricting the slaves and preventing blacks from competing with them for jobs,[12] they might still fall victim to the political and material blandishments of Republican demagogues. Yet anxiety on this score was probably subordinate to a general social fear that the Republicans would seek to undermine slavery by hedging it in, by failing to enforce the Fugitive Slave Act, and by spreading abolitionist propaganda in the South. After the presidential election, with an administration composed of men who held slavery to be morally wrong coming into power at Washington, that fear become rampant. As Senator Hammond wrote in February 1861:

Here we have in charge the solution of the greatest problem of the

---

[11] Major L. Wilson, *Space, Time and Freedom. The Quest for Nationality and the Irrepressible Conflict, 1815–1861* (Westport, Conn., 1974), pp. 148–9; *De Bow's Review*, XXIII (1857), p. 231; Ulrich B. Phillips (ed), *The Correspondence of Robert Toombs, Alexander H. Stephens and Howell Cobb* (Washington, D.C.; 1911), II, p. 450.

[12] Frederick Law Olmsted, *The Cotton Kingdom. A Selection*, ed. by David F. Hawke (Indianapolis, 1971), pp. 191–2, 203–4.

ages. We are here two races — white and black — now both equally American, holding each other in the closest embrace and utterly unable to extricate ourselves from it. A problem so difficult, so complicated, and so momentous never was placed in charge of any portion of Mankind. And on its solution rests our all.[13]

The solution to this problem of racial co-existence was seen not in an orderly programme of improvement and emancipation, but in the more secure and permanent maintenance of slavery. Upon this point, folk wisdom, social and economic theory and political rhetoric throughout the Deep South and in most of the Upper South was in full agreement.

Not only did slavery provide the sole framework for a bi-racial society acceptable to whites; it was also a major source of wealth and status. The acquisition of slaves, to Southerners, was as important as buying a house to modern 'Western' people. Any active interference with, or threat to, slavery would have calamitous economic as well as social consequences for the South. Slaveholders, irrespective of rank and fortune, and those who aspired to slaveownership, supported secession because they feared that new political conditions might undermine confidence in a highly profitable economic system in which large numbers of Southern whites had invested. Confidence undermined, after all, was usually reflected in falling prices.[14] As a rich senator from the most borderline of slave states, Delaware, privately wrote in December 1860: 'The sole cause of the existing disunion excitement which is about to break up the government is the war which has been carried on for years past by all manner of devices by the antislavery fanatical sentiment upon more than $2,000,000,000 of property'.[15]

These social and economic fears were especially pressing in the Deep South, where nearly half the total population was enslaved and where, despite stereotypes of the class-ridden plantation order, slaveownership was widely diffused. In 1860, 31 per cent of white families owned slaves in those 11 states that eventually joined the Confederacy; in South Carolina and Mississippi, the proportions rose to 48.7 per cent and 48 per cent respectively.[16] The extent of slaveowning was even more impressive when one considers the age-profile of the population. In 1860 there were 181,521 slaveowners in the Deep South; yet there were only 380,067 white males over the age of 30 years.[17] While slaveowners were not all aged over

---

[13] Channing, *Crisis of Fear*, p. 293; Allan Nevins, *The Emergence of Lincoln* (New York, 1950), II, p. 468.

[14] Gavin Wright, *The Political Economy of the Cotton South. Households, Markets, and Wealth in the Nineteenth Century* (New York, 1978), pp. 140–156.

[15] Nevins, *Emergence of Lincoln*, II, p. 331.

[16] Otto H. Olsen, 'Historians and the Extent of Slave Ownership in the Southern United States' *Civil War History*, XVIII (1972), pp. 101–16.

[17] J.G. Randall and David Donald, *The Civil War and Reconstruction* (Boston, 1969 edn), p. 68; figures of population by age and sex are available in: *Population of the United States in 1860; Compiled from the Original Returns of the Eighth Census* (Washington, D.C., 1864), pp. 592–3.

30 (or indeed entirely male), the sheer youthfulness of the population presumably heightened hopes of future gain. Age had not yet withered an infinite variety of economic aspirations.

Moreover, the youthfulness of the population explains both the domestic emphasis in much separatist rhetoric – the concern for hearth, home, and children – and the prolonged quest for territorial expansion. In all states of the Deep South in 1860 (except Louisiana), 52–6 per cent of the white males were *under* the age of 20.[18] Not surprisingly, therefore, fears for the future of race relations in this young society, and for the future viability of a leading source of wealth and status, gripped the Deep South in 1860.

Within the framework of their own racial and racist assumptions, and given the broad consensus among whites that slavery should be maintained, the separatists acted in statesmanlike fashion in 1860–1. They believed sincerely, if misguidedly, that peaceful secession would be possible because Britain, dependent upon the Cotton South for a vital raw material, would not permit the North to attack on autonomous South.[19] And secessionists further argued that, even if such an attack occurred, the North's military capacity would be derisory. Expecting no insuperable military difficulties ahead, the separatists instead spoke repeatedly of the direct threat which a Republican administration would pose to slavery, and the loss of sectional equality within the Union which Republican policies would accentuate. Hence the symbolic importance attached to slaveowners' rights in the territories. For if those rights were not respected and fully protected, then the basic principle of slaveownership was indirectly questioned; and Republicans indeed regarded the prevention of slavery's extension as the very least they could do to undermine a morally repugnant institution. This passionate concern to have rights respected was intensified – and given practical relevance – in the 1840s and 1850s by material pressures among slaveowners to go westwards – into Texas and Arkansas, if not into Kansas – with their property.

Secession emerged, therefore, from the territorial question of the 1840s and 1850s. It did so because westward expansion had guaranteed economic opportunities for generations of Southerners as well as Northerners, and because the federal government was responsible for territorial affairs; the Republicans were pledged to stop the westward extension of slavery and had captured the most conspicuous branch of the federal government. Their policy was regarded in the Deep South and in much of the Upper South as the first step to the 'ultimate extinction' of slavery envisaged by Seward in 1850 and Lincoln in 1858. Their practice might be overtly conciliatory but, according to the separatists, was bound to be covertly abolitionist. A majority in the Deep South appear to have accepted that contention.

[18] Percentages based on figures in *idem*.
[19] Wright, *Political Economy of the Cotton South*, pp. 146–7.

But if the threat to slavery became so great and so obvious, why did *only* the Deep South break away from the Union following Lincoln's election?[20]

At first glance, the Upper South and border slave states' refusal to secede seems odd. If the main reason for secession was to avoid the creeping abolitionism encouraged by the Republicans, surely that threat would have been greater in states nearer to the free states than in the Deep South? In the first place, however, the stake in slavery was less in the Upper South, and far less in the border states, than it was in the original Confederacy. Moreover, in those states the number of slaves increased only slightly, or actually fell, from 1850 to 1860. Added to this, the proportion of slave holders to the total number of slave families was *somewhat* lower in the Upper than in the Deep South.

But perhaps a more compelling reason for reluctance to secede immediately was the existence of different political traditions outside the Deep South. Of the eight slave states of the Upper South and border region, only one gave a majority of its presidential votes in 1860 to the Southern Democratic candidate. Although Southern Democrats were not all immediate secessionists, they provided the driving force and popular support for secession. Among a range of factors correlated statistically with votes for immediatists to the state secession conventions, electoral backing for Breckinridge provided the best, though by no means a complete, guide to immediatist strength.[21] It was in the Deep South that the Democrats were extremely powerful: being so strong, they were more prone there to radical influence; and they were more likely to be enraged there by the failure of slavery to establish firm roots in Kansas in 1857–8, and by the failure of 15 years of Democratic national expansionism to yield richer rewards for the South. If Democratic rule in the Deep South was based on the party's claim to be an effective agent for Southern interests – to protect and extend slavery in the nation and push it into the Caribbean as well – then clearly Democrats in the Deep South were trapped in 1858–60 by their own rhetoric. Despite constant promises to extend slavery, and despite the unprecedented power they enjoyed in the federal government,[22] Southern Democrats had not advanced the peculiar institution westwards or southwards in the Caribbean during the previous decade. For this reason, Southern Democrats in 1858–60 undoubtedly felt betrayed – even if with little good reason – by Senator Douglas and the Northern party.

Outside the Deep South, however, the Southern Democrats were

[20] A fresh and stimulating discussion of the problem is in Michael F. Holt, *The Political Crisis of the 1850s* (New York, 1978), ch. 8; other good, brief discussions are Nevins, *Emergence of Lincoln*, II, pp. 328–35; Avery Craven in Knoles (ed.), *Crisis of the Union*, esp. pp. 60–8.

[21] Johnson, *Toward a Patriarchal Republic*, pp. 195; Peyton McCrary, Clark Miller, and Dale Baum, 'Class and Party in the Secession Crisis: Voting Behavior in the Deep South, 1856–1861', *Journal of Interdisciplinary History*, VIII (1978), pp. 429–57.

[22] This point is made by Charles G. Sellers in Knoles (ed.), *Crisis of the Union*, p. 86.

neither so prone to radical pressure nor so frustrated by recent failures to translate their own promises and plans into tangible achievements. Because the Upper South and border states experienced genuine two-party conflict in the 1850s, the Democrats there were less easily manipulated by radicals, and could readily blame faint-hearts within their own states for failures to impress the Southern cause upon Congress. Those states were also less likely than the Deep South to be frightened at the Republicans' victory in the presidential election, for they were accustomed to the ebb and flow of party fortunes and to the contrast between party politicians' exaggerated rhetoric and their modest legislative enactments. In the Upper South and the border states there was a circumspect yet firm desire for evidence of an 'overt act' from the Republicans before the bold course of secession would be adopted.

Reinforcing this cautious approach to revolutionary action was a clear understanding that secession was indeed a revolutionary act fraught with danger. If secession led to war — so it was argued in the Upper South and in the border states — then the bloodiest battlefields would be in those regions and not in the distant Deep South. An ambivalent attitude thus prevailed outside the Deep South. There was less alarm at the possible consequences of Lincoln's election; party rule was not absolute and the Republican party was seen as a diverse coalition open to internecine disagreements; the prospect of mass secession and power being placed in the hands of the separatist fire-eaters was considerably more frightening.

At the same time, however, one should not over-emphasize the division between immediatists and co-operationists either in the Deep South or elsewhere in the slave states. There are considerable dangers in erecting complex ideological or socio-economic explanatory models upon the flimsy and fleeting base of voting in the elections for secession conventions. In some cases, the precise labels adopted by candidates for those elections were vague or misleading. In many cases, the statistical evidence leaves one to conclude that a vote for immediate secession or co-operation was a personal and temperamental preference rather than a momentous choice.[23]

But, most importantly, the very term co-operationist is imprecise and confusing.[24] Some co-operationists simply opposed individual state secessions, arguing instead that Southern states should join together before leaving the Union. Other co-operationists wanted the Southern states to hammer out an agreed set of negotiating demands which would provide the framework for a peaceful reconstruction of the Union. Yet other co-operationists insisted that secession could be justified only if there were an 'overt act' against slavery by Lincoln's Administration. And some co-operationists — but probably very few outside the border states in 1861 — were fervent Unionists and hostile to any revolutionary action.

[23] Thornton, *Politics and Power in a Slave Society*, p. 343–7; see also pp. 398–426.
[24] Dumond, *The Secession Movement*, ch. 7.

In the Upper South, co-operationists objected to the timing and rationale of the Cotton South's secession. They were not much moved by the expansionist case, and they were not impressed by the contention that Northern failure to implement the Fugitive Slave Act was a major reason for separation. How, they asked, would fugitives be recaptured more readily when the North was a foreign country? But, despite these grave reservations, co-operationists even in the Upper South would not accept any interference with slavery, nor would they accept the Northern view that secession of its very nature was unconstitutional.[25] A sense of Southern consciousness had developed so far by 1860–1 that separation itself was not widely condemned in the slave states, and even the Upper South conceded that the Union was fairly and properly on trial.

A curious peace – a temporary, tense, and artificial lull – therefore followed the revolutionary events of 4–9 February at Montgomery, Alabama. President Buchanan, weary, reviled, and deeply troubled, condemned secession, but haplessly proclaimed that the federal government, the agent of the sovereign states, could not coerce a seceded state. So, everything depended on the actions taken by the new Republican administration when Lincoln entered office in March. The states of the Upper South and the border region anxiously awaited an 'overt act' against slavery or against the new Confederate republic.

The Republican Response

Secession raised very acute problems of constitutional theory. Southerners almost unanimously believed by 1860 that the federal Union was a compact between sovereign states. Primary sovereignty had been with the states before 1787 and it remained ultimately with them, with the result that, as Jefferson Davis described it in 1851, the federal government became merely 'the agent of the States in their foreign relations' and 'an umpire between the States in their relations one to another'.[26] Northerners were less clear on this point. President Buchanan, naturally influenced by his Democratic commitment to state rights, did not believe that individual states possessed so much sovereignty that they could secede; yet he also believed that the federal government lacked the moral or constitutional power to force states to return to the Union. Republicans, in contrast, held that the Union was created by the sovereign people of the United States; states, having surrendered their independence in ratifying the Constitution, held no residual sovereignty that would allow them to secede. Moreover, as a practical measure, secession could not be tolerated, since it would lead to complete anarchy, with states threatening to leave or leaving the Union whenever their

---

[25] I am indebted to Mr David Scarboro's work on North Carolina for these points.
[26] Dunbar Rowland (ed.), *Jefferson Davis, Constitutionalist: His Letters, Papers, and Speeches* (Jackson, Miss., 1923), II, p. 18.

interests were not catered for by the federal government. Finally, in Republicans' eyes, the anarchy and disruption caused by secession would reduce the unique American experiment in republican government to a mockery before the world. The Union, therefore, had to be preserved.

Between the presidential election in November 1860 and the change of administration on 4 March 1861 the old administration remained in office and the old Congress remained in session. What could be done to meet the crisis?

Initially, the Republicans were thrown off balance by the speed of the Deep South's rush to secession.[27] Many highly intelligent, politically perceptive Republican leaders believed that Southerners' threats to secede if Lincoln were elected flowed from the time-honoured Southern tactic of political bluff; many such threats had been made since the late 1840s. Having no organization of their own in the slave states, Republicans were not closely in touch with the real condition of Southern opinion. Lincoln for one wrote in August 1860: 'The people of the South have too much of good sense and good temper to attempt the ruin of the government rather than see it administered as it was administered by the men who made it. At least, so I hope and believe'.[28] But once they understood the gravity of the secession movement − by early December this had become clear − the Republicans were further handicapped by factional differences. One wing of the party wanted no truck with the slavocracy, was prepared to accept war, and insisted on condemning the gross immorality of the slave system. Many leading Republicans, however, were conservative, cautious, and conciliatory, although deeply Unionist. A tough internecine party struggle raged throughout the winter. But within the congressional party a clear, general Republican negotiating position soon emerged: this was shaped by Senator Seward, but decisively influenced by Lincoln's views.

Lincoln refused to bow to secession by offering to surrender the Republicans' election programme as an inducement for the seceded states to return to the Union. He and his party were prepared to guarantee the effective operation of the Fugitive Slave Act and to neutralize the personal liberty laws passed by various free states; and they repeated their commitment not to interfere with slavery in the several states. But they refused to budge on their key election promise: there must be no further extension of slavery westwards into the federal territories. On that Lincoln personally insisted in order to scotch any plans for reviving the Missouri Compromise line. Thus at the moment of

---

[27] I rely heavily in this section on: David M. Potter, *Lincoln and His Party in the Secession Crisis* (New Haven, 1962 edn). See also: Kenneth M. Stampp, *And the War Came. The North and the Secession Crisis, 1860–1861* (Baton Rouge, 1970 edn); Knoles (ed.), *Crisis of the Union*, pp. 90–113. The later editions of Potter's and Stampp's monographs contain interesting new prefaces, discussing some of their disagreements in explaining Republican policies in the period leading to war.

[28] Knoles, *Crisis of the Union*, p. 99.

crisis, the Republicans stood firm on the principle enunciated in the Wilmot Proviso of 1846, fought for by Free Soilers and many Northern Whigs in 1850, taken as the rallying-cry for the foundation of their new party in 1854, and invoked to condemn both the Dred Scott decision and the Lecompton constitution in 1857. Even so, many of them in December 1860 had considered seriously, if only fleetingly, the possibility of conceding that principle in order to save the Union.

The Republicans' position offered no chance for a speedy reconstruction of the Union; nor was it intended to do so. Instead, it provided a real hope of dividing the slave states by keeping the eight states of the Upper South and the border loyal to the Union. There was to be no 'overt act' against slavery.

From December to March Congress busied itself in trying to reach a settlement through various committees and conferences. These were sincere and worthy in intension, but futile. Numerous politicians believed that some formula of new constitutional amendments or reassuring guarantees for the future of slavery would smooth the way for the re-entry of the Confederate states into the Union. Senator R.M.T. Hunter of Virginia, for example, proposed an elaborate re-structuring of the federal constitution with massive entrenched powers for the South as a minority section; Hunter's scheme was drawn from Calhoun's writings, and revealed a vision of the Union as a virtual alliance between a distinctive North and South which had no place in Republican thinking.[29] The central point, as Lincoln saw it, was that the Union should not be reconstructed in order to create a permanent minority section with equal power and weight to that of the majority in the North and West.

In two ways the Deep South's secession and the Calhounite arguments for a bi-sectional constitution – produced by leading so-called Southern moderates such as Hunter – strengthened the Republicans' moral authority in the North. After all, in November only 40 per cent of all Americans had voted for the party utterly opposed to any further extension of slavery; the overwhelming majority of Americans in 1860 supported candidates prepared in some form, however reluctantly, to tolerate the further extension of slavery. Yet, in seceding, the Deep South had raised the new spectre of anarchy in government and had refused to abide by the legal process by which Lincoln attained the presidency. Republicanism thereby became a conservative force opposed by those who disregarded the Constitution and the normal procedures of self-government.[30] Secondly, Southerners, in offering supposedly moderate proposals for constitutional reconstruction, raised a new issue of majority rights; for they demanded equal power in the Union for the Southern

[29] William S. Hitchcock, 'Southern Moderates and Secession: Senator R.M.T. Hunter's Call for Union', *Journal of American History*, LIX (1973), 871–4.

[30] This theme is expanded upon in Phillip S. Paludan, 'The American Civil War Considered as a Crisis in Law and Order', *American Historical Review*, LXXVII (1972), pp. 1013–34.

minority which Northerners, through the Republicans, would never stomach. So, instead of merely representing a policy supported by a minority of Americans, the Republicans by March 1861 stood for the defence of the Union and majority rights. This had become a very powerful position.

Lincoln's plans for dealing with the crisis when he entered office are far from clear. Perhaps he realized as soon as secession began that federal authority in the seceded states would have to be maintained to some extent and that force might be required. Envisaging no compromise on the central issue of Republican hostility to secession and slavery extension, Lincoln worked to confine secession to the seven states of the Deep South and to ensure that, if force had to be used, it would be invoked for limited objectives and only in response to Confederate intransigence.

Another interpretation is that Lincoln and Seward sought peaceful reunion. They were not excessively perturbed by the establishment of the Confederacy, as long as it was confined to the Deep South. By making no hostile gestures, by avoiding confrontation and by taking no military precautions, they hoped to hasten the collapse of the secessionist movement in the Confederacy. Negotiations would then be initiated by the rebel leaders once popular enthusiasm for separation had waned and harsh economic and political realities began to intrude. One influential Republican newspaper explained the situation on 21 March 1861:

> The true policy of the government is unquestionably that of *masterly inactivity*. The object to be aimed at is, the conversion of the Southern people from their Secessionism. The appeal of the Government must be to the minds of the people – to their judgement, their political sagacity, their common sense. Force, as a means of restoring the Union, or of permanently preserving it, is out of the question.[31]

While waiting for the Confederacy to crack, however, Lincoln had to maintain the pretence of his authority over the seceded states, for he insisted they remained part of the country over which his administration presided. On becoming president, he declined to appoint federal officials or to collect federal customs or to press for the delivery of mails in areas where such acts would be unfavourably received: here was a substantial renunciation of federal authority over the Deep South. To compensate for this retreat from the full use of his power, the president attached great symbolic importance to the retention of two federal forts in the Confederacy, Pickens and Sumter. These would provide the full test of the Union's continuing legitimacy.

In declaring that his administration would maintain federal control of Pickens and Sumter, Lincoln initially believed that these forts could be

---

[31] Potter, *Lincoln and His Party*, pp. 329–30.

readily held for a lengthy period.[32] He learnt on assuming office, however, that Sumter would need replenishing within six weeks. The Confederate government would not allow the fort to be replenished, for, lying in Charleston harbour, it was in their territorial waters. So Lincoln, whether he had hoped for a drift back to Unionism in the Deep South or knew that the use of federal force would eventually be inevitable, soon faced the issue that would bring war. Hectic manoeuvrings ensued; some suggested that Fort Sumter might be held without a military show-down. But the crucial decision was whether to replenish or evacuate Fort Sumter, suddenly shrouded with symbolic meaning as an isolated, vulnerable outpost of federal authority in rebel territory. Seward, who had become Lincoln's secretary of state, sought evacuation, on the understanding that negotiations with the Confederacy would start once Sumter was evacuated and while Fort Pickens was reinforced. Seward further proposed that the Confederates' Unionism and patriotism might be heightened if the administration involved America in a war with Britain over Canada; America, however, was far too isolated in world diplomacy by the 1850s to find domestic unity in response to foreign threats.[33] On both points, Lincoln overruled Seward and, after much vacillation, dispatched federal ships with provisions to Fort Sumter. Informed of Lincoln's decision and blind to the political repercussions their action would have in the North, the Confederate government ordered the seizure of the fort. The Confederate bombardment began on 12 April and, after 33 hours of it, the garrison surrendered. Lincoln now called upon the states of the Union for a mere 75,000 troops to serve for only three months to suppress the insurgency. With such optimism, war began on 15 April, only six weeks after Lincoln's inauguration.

The Second Wave of Secession

Fort Sumter was attacked because the Confederate government hoped to face down the North, scotch Southern Unionism, and pull the rest of the South into its fold.[34] War itself cemented the Confederacy and created a folklore upon which Confederate patriotism – even after, and long after, defeat – flourished. While prospects for success seemed good in 1861, support for separation seems to have increased in the Deep South after fighting began. More concretely, war extended the Confederacy beyond the narrow realm of the Cotton Kingdom, and this expansion offered the Confederacy a genuine chance of survival. As soon as Lincoln called for troops, Virginia's secession convention, which had earlier

---

[32] David M. Potter (completed and edited by Don. E. Fehrenbacher), *The Impending Crisis, 1848–1861* (New York, 1976), ch. 20.

[33] A.E. Campbell, 'An Excess of Isolation: Isolation and the American Civil War', *Journal of Southern History*, xxix (1963), pp. 161–74.

[34] Allan Nevins, *The War for the Union* (New York, 1959), i, pp. 68–9; see also Grady McWhiney, 'The Confederacy's First Shot', *Civil War History*. xiv (1968), pp. 5–14.

rejected secession but decided to watch events, voted by 88 to 55 to join the C.S.A.[35] Virginia, as the most populous slave state, and one lying just across the Potomac river from Washington, provided enormous additional strength to the Confederacy. North Carolina, wedged between the seceded states of Virginia and South Carolina, promptly followed suit, as did Tennessee and Arkansas somewhat later. Four border slave states remained in no-man's land.

These accesssions to the Confederacy were invaluable. In military terms, the fighting frontier was thrust northwards and extended. Looking ahead, if the C.S.A. had warded off the Union armies and won independence, then Virginia, North Carolina and Tennessee would have provided it with a sufficiently diversified economy, plentiful population, and developed economic infrastructure to make separate nationhood feasible if not assured.

Yet these vital components of a viable Confederacy were acquired only when the federal government set out to crush the rebellion. The second wave of secession occurred because a majority in the Upper South realised that a federal victory over South Carolina would be inevitable without their intervention and that such a victory would certainly end slavery expansion in America and would probably destroy or very seriously undermine slavery in much of the Deep South. The prospect that social control over the Deep South's slaves would be impaired or removed – with all the fearsome possibilities that such a step conjured up in white minds – was intolerable to a large segment of the Upper South's leaders. Thus the use of federal force in mid April created the Confederacy we now remember. And federal force took four years to smash it.

[35] Ralph A. Wooster, *The Secession Conventions of the South* (Princeton, 1962), p. 149. A good, recent account of events in the Upper South in 1861 stresses that Unionist activity and strength depended very much on peace: hopes of building up a Union party in the Upper South fell off markedly once fighting began. Daniel W. Crofts, 'The Union Party of 1861 and the Secession Crisis', *Perspectives in American History*, XI (1977–8), pp. 327–76.

10 Conclusion

In the fourth century B.C., Aristotle offered the following explanation for domestic revolutions:

> inequality is generally at the bottom of internal warfare in states, for it is in their striving for what is fair and equal that men become divided. There are two kinds of equality, the one dependent on numerical equivalence, the other on equivalence in value.[1]

By 1860 the Southern whites had lost forever their 'numerical equivalence' in the nation. But their leaders insisted in 1861 that some plain and strong recognition be given to their section's 'equivalence in value'. Even the most Union-minded politicians from the slave states demanded permanent guarantees for the future existence of slavery in their midst; and most other Southern public men expected rather more than that − usually allowance for slavery's further expansion westwards − as an outward and visible sign of the national equality of esteem accorded the South. Some 20 years later, Jefferson Davis asserted:

> It was not the passage of the 'personal liberty laws', it was not the circulation of incendiary documents, it was not the raid of John Brown, it was not the operation of unjust and unequal tariff laws, nor all combined, that constituted the intolerable grievance, but it was the systematic and persistent struggle to deprive the Southern States of equality in the Union − generally to discriminate in legislation against the interests of their people; culminating in their exclusion from the Territories, the common property of the States, as well as by the infraction of their compact to promote domestic tranquillity.[2]

The quest for security from 'injury and strife in the Union',[3] flowing from Northern criticisms of slavery, from Republican policies directed against slavery and slaveowners, and from the possible social effects within the South of such criticisms and policies, explained the common drive to

---

[1] Aristotle, *The Politics*, trans. with an introduction by T.A. Sinclair (London, 1962), p. 191.
[2] Jefferson Davis, *The Rise and Fall of the Confederate Government* (New York, 1958 edn), I, p. 83. ·
[3] *Idem*, p. 85.

secession. And the defence of Southern rights during the two decades before 1860 had been motivated by a similar desire to ensure the South's 'equivalence in value' at a time when the very contrary tendency − to denounce, deplore, or degrade the South − powerfully influenced many Northerners.

But, if relations between North and South by 1860 were so acrimonious and full of distrust, and if the two sections' social systems were so sharply differentiated by the stubborn Southern attachment to slavery, why did Republicans not promote and applaud the severance of so troublesome and, for many Americans, so odious a connection?

An outsider might suggest with hindsight that America would have been better off shorn of the Deep South. After the Civil War and until the 1950s, if not later, the Deep South has been an unhappy, truculent, generally conservative, and fiercely racist region. American politics without the Deep South, or even the entire South, might have been more successfully 'progressive' and reformist in the late nineteenth and early twentieth centuries; and America probably would not have inherited its mid-twentieth-century race problems. Moreover, it is possible to imagine, as many Northerners did regularly in the nineteenth century, and as British ministers did in 1861, that the free states might have looked more keenly northwards, to the British colonies that became Canada, for additional territories, and so founded a quite new Union. Such notions, however, were inappropriate in 1860−1, for practical and emotional reasons.

Peaceful secession would have left unresolved a host of contentious matters. Where would the Confederacy's boundaries lie? Would the Upper South or parts of the border states try to join the new country? What would be done about slaves fleeing from the Confederacy? Moreover, the seceded states would claim portions − perhaps large portions − of the federal territories, and would be enmeshed in complex financial negotiations over government and private debts incurred within the former Union. Overriding all these considerations of major disputes connected with peaceful separation was the chronic Northern fear that the doctrine of dissolution might spread and leave the federal system prone to constant threats of disruption.

But, apart from raising practical questions of sovereignty and government, secession created an emotional upsurge of Unionism. For secession threw into question the Americans' past, present, and future. The Union meant to most Northerners in the 1850s much more than a mere constitutional convenience. It summed up their past: the Revolution, the war of 1812 against imperial Britain, the incessant struggles of pioneer farmers and settlers against the Indians, the breath-taking territorial expansion achieved between 1803 and 1853, and the even more impressive transformation of wilderness into well-peopled and profitably exploited countryside. It symbolized their present: a self-governing people had established their own system of institutions and laws and proceeded to co-operate energetically to maximize their individual political and economic benefits. It illuminated their future: united, America offered to Europe an inspiration for the betterment of the common (albeit white) man's material opportunities and moral and political self-respect. However grandiloquently expressed, however vague, however conceited such claims were, they provided Northerners with a vivid, satisfying, and pervasive secular religion. Unionism was the central article of that faith.

Hence the crisis in 1860–1. Secession did not merely entail a technical readjustment of boundaries about which rational men might disagree but upon which they could come to a negotiated solution. It challenged a whole range of beliefs, myths, and proud assertions in such a way that it inevitably had to be denied. A peaceful reconstruction of the Union was sought and worked for by some Republican leaders, but would have been extremely difficult, if not impossible, to achieve, given the majority of Republicans' opposition to any further extension of slavery. Coercion, therefore, became more politically acceptable as very tentative soundings made of Confederate attitudes proved to be time-consuming, hazardous, and unfruitful. It became politically necessary once the Confederates fired on Fort Sumter, the most prominent symbol of the Union's authority left in the Deep South.

Recourse to force marks a supreme defeat for any democrat or reasoning man. The American Civil War thus raises intractable, perennial questions of when, and for what cause, reasoning men should coerce their compatriots when they can no longer persuade them. This is why people have studied and should study the coming of the Civil War. To examine this problem because the 1850s supposedly witnessed a struggle between a cultured, landowning, chivalrous élite in the South and a thrusting, hard-headed, entrepreneurial democracy in the North, would be to romanticize and trivialize the past. Nor do subtler variants of such an interpretation satisfy. No peculiarly quasi-feudal, non-capitalist, aristocratic ideology dominated Southern society in the 1850s bringing that society into inevitable confrontation with a dynamic, *modernizing*, free society whose ideology was egalitarian. The economically modernizing élite of the North, the great merchants, bankers, and industrialists of New York, Philadelphia, and Boston, leaned towards compromise. The wealthy planters of the Deep South were much divided over secession. Although there was an economic depression in the late 1850s, no major economic dislocation had spawned a discontented or angry group of middle-class dissidents. The Confederacy was led by members of the established political leadership who, on the whole, embraced secession with sobriety rather than abandon. So, too, Lincoln's cabinet consisted of men who had been active in politics, and at various times elected to office, since the 1830s. Theories of rising or declining political élites, of alienated or frustrated middle classes, and of deep, underlying modernizing forces provide but partial explanations for the coming of war.

The enduring interest of the crisis of the 1850s lies in its posing *the* central dilemmas of a democratic political system. Here were people worshipping the same God, united by common language, common legal and political assumptions and practices, and similar economic aspirations and opportunities, and sharing a successful, if brief, history. Here were people confident of their place in the world, economically prosperous, optimistic about their future destiny. Yet they disagreed on the vital issue of sectional rights intertwined with the future of slavery. How could those Republicans who believed slavery to be morally wrong set that institution, in Lincoln's apt phrase, on 'the course of ultimate extinction'? How could they persuade Southern politicians or ordinary Southerners that slavery increasingly affronted, in various ways, the consciences, or economic interests, or natural rights ideas of a growing body of influential Northerners, and possibly of the majority of the inhabitants in the free states? And how could Southern whites, who almost to a man believed in some fashion or to some degree that slavery was morally right, or spiritually and materially beneficial to the blacks, or essential to their own economic well-being, or necessary for racial 'harmony', persuade the Republicans to desist from any action which might immediately or eventually interfere with slavery or slavery's extension? The political dilemma was how to resolve such a profound disagreement between people who shared so much in common without resorting to force. Americans failed in 1861. But the fundamental dilemma remains acute to this day.

Select Bibliography

The best single-volume analysis is David M. Potter (completed and edited by Don. E. Fehrenbacher), *The Impending Crisis, 1848–1861* (New York, 1976); it includes an excellent bibliography. A much longer, more discursive, but still rewarding account of the same period is Allan Nevins, *Ordeal of the Union* (New York, 1947), 2 vols; and *The Emergence of Lincoln* (New York, 1950), 2 vols. Avery Craven's *The Coming of the Civil War* (Chicago, 1957 edn) is stimulating and retains its place in the literature; but its portrait of the South as victim is unconvincing. Of shorter books, the best is Michael F. Holt's *The Political Crisis of the 1850s* (New York, 1978), which is strikingly original in its treatment of party politics, though not entirely satisfying as a discussion of the war's origins. A number of books covering longer periods are worth consulting on the origins of the war: James G. Randall and David Donald, *The Civil War and Reconstruction* (Boston, 1969 edn), which includes an exhaustive bibliography; Peter J. Parish, *The American Civil War* (London, 1975); William R. Brock, *Conflict and Transformation: the United States, 1844–1877* (London, 1973). A good guide to the historiographical debate is Thomas J. Pressly, *Americans Interpret Their Civil War* (Princeton, 1954).

There is no really satisfactory comparison of the social and economic differences between North and South. A general, thematic discussion is in Barrington Moore, Jr, *Social Origins of Dictatorship and Democracy* (London, 1966); it is too schematic for many historians' taste. Eugene D. Genovese, *The Political Economy of Slavery* (New York, 1965) has been very influential, but should be read against, for example, David M. Potter, *The South and the Sectional Conflict* (Baton Rouge, 1968) and Carl N. Degler, *The Other South. Southern Dissenters in the Nineteenth Century* (New York, 1974). Lee Soltow's *Men and Wealth in the United States 1850–1870* (New Haven, 1975) is a necessary corrective to easy generalizations about sectional differences in the distribution of wealth, but most readers will find it heavy going. Some very provocative thoughts on Southern economic performance are contained in Robert W. Fogel and Stanley L. Engerman, *Time on the Cross* (London, 1974); but Douglass C. North, *The Economic Growth of the United States, 1790–1860* (New York, 1966) and Gavin Wright, *The Political Economy of the Cotton South. Households, Markets, and Wealth in the Nineteenth*

Century (New York, 1978) are more reliable guides. Much has been published in recent years on social mobility and local life in Northern communities. The best case-studies are: Stephan Thernstrom, *Poverty and Progress: Social Mobility in a Nineteenth-Century City* (Cambridge, Mass., 1963); *The Other Bostonians, Poverty and Progress in the American Metropolis, 1880–1970* (Cambridge, Mass., 1973); Stuart M. Blumin, *The Urban Threshold: Growth and Change in a Nineteenth-Century American Community* (Chicago, 1976); Kathleen N. Conzen, *Immigrant Milwaukee, 1836–1860: Accommodation and Community in a Frontier City* (Cambridge, Mass., 1976); Clyde and Sally Griffen, *Natives and Newcomers: the Ordering of Opportunity in Mid-Nineteenth-Century Poughkeepsie* (Cambridge, Mass., 1978). Further work on Northern rural communities is needed, but Allan G. Bogue, *From Prairie to Cornbelt. Farming on the Illinois and Iowa Prairies in the Nineteenth Century* (Chicago, 1963) is important and valuable. We still await publication of comparable studies of Southern communities. Various detailed studies of Southern society were published in the 1930s and 1940s; the most influential and wide-ranging of these is Frank L. Owsley, *Plain Folk of the Old South* (Baton Rouge, 1949), but the whole subject needs fresh appraisal. An important preliminary study is Otto H. Olsen, 'Historians and the Extent of Slave Ownership in the Southern United States', *Civil War History*, XVIII (1972), pp. 101–16. The best introduction to the social history of the South is Clement Eaton, *The Growth of Southern Civilization, 1790–1860* (New York, 1961).

Professor Genovese, and Eric Foner in *Free Soil, Free Labor, Free Men. The Ideology of the Republican Party before the Civil War* (New York, 1970) and 'Politics, Ideology and the Origins of the American Civil War' in George M. Frederickson (ed.), *A Nation Divided: Problems and Issues in the Civil War and Reconstruction* (Minneapolis, 1975), pp. 15–34, see North and South in politically, as well as socially, contrasting terms. This view is not fully shared by Potter, in *The Impending Crisis* or Holt in *The Political Crisis of the 1850s.* Planter domination of Southern politics is questioned in Ralph A. Wooster, *The Secession Conventions of the South* (Princeton, 1962); *The People in Power. Courthouse and Statehouse in the Lower South, 1850–1860* (Knoxville, Tenn., 1969); *Politicians, Planters and Plain Folk. Courthouse and Statehouse in the Upper South, 1850–1860* (Knoxville, Tenn., 1975). These books contain a wealth of basic information. A more powerful re-interpretation of Southern politics and the origins of secession, following up some of Wooster's leads, is J. Mills Thornton, III, *Politics and Power in a Slave Society. Alabama, 1800–1860* (Baton Rouge, 1978). The only up-to-date, general account of Southern politics takes something of a middle course between Genovese and Thornton: William J. Cooper, Jr, *The South and the Politics of Slavery, 1828–1856* (Baton Rouge, 1978) is important and very readable.

For the debate over slavery and the development of sectional tension over slavery, I have relied heavily on: David B. Davis, *The Problem of Slavery in the Age of Revolution, 1770–1823* (Ithaca, 1975); Duncan J. MacLeod, *Slavery, Race and the American Revolution* (Cambridge, 1974); William S. Jenkins, *Pro-Slavery Thought in the Old South* (Gloucester, Mass., 1960 reprint of 1935 edn); Drew Gilpin Faust, *A Sacred Circle. The Dilemma of the Intellectual in the Old South, 1840–1860* (Baltimore, 1977); Louis Filler, *The Crusade Against Slavery, 1830–1860* (New York, 1963 edn); Ronald G. Walters, *The Antislavery Appeal. American Abolitionism after 1830* (Baltimore, 1976); Richard H. Sewell, *Ballots for Freedom. Antislavery Politics in the United States, 1837–1860* (New York, 1976); William W. Wiecek, *The Sources of Antislavery Constitutionalism in America, 1760–1848* (Ithaca, 1977).

The best single work on the constitutional problems created by slavery and slavery extension is Don E. Fehrenbacher, *The Dred Scott Case. Its Significance in American Law and Politics* (New York, 1978), a book of far wider scope than its title suggests.

For the politics of the 1840s, a reliable introduction is Glyndon G. Van Deusen, *The Jacksonian Era 1828–1848* (New York, 1959). The best single book for an understanding of sectional problems is William R. Brock, *Parties and Political Conscience. American Dilemmas, 1840–1850* (Millwood, New York, 1979), though its argument for disillusionment with party by 1850 is perhaps exaggerated. A very lively discussion of sectional issues in the mid 1840s is James C.N. Paul, *Rift in the Democracy* (Philadelphia, 1951); but Charles G. Sellers, *James K. Polk: Continentalist, 1843–1846* (Princeton, 1966) is fuller and more satisfying. For expansionism, see Frederick Merk, *The Monroe Doctrine and American Expansionism, 1843–1849* (New York, 1966). The following are also important for the 1840s: Holt, *The Political Crisis of the 1850s*, Lee Benson, *The Concept of Jacksonian Democracy. New York as a Test Case* (Princeton, 1961); Ronald P. Formisano, *The Birth of Mass Political Parties. Michigan, 1827–1861* (Princeton, 1971); Robert W. Johannsen, *Stephen A. Douglas* (New York, 1973); Eric Foner, 'The Wilmot Proviso Revisited', *Journal of American History*, LVI (1969), pp 262–79. There is no single work that deals fully with the complex relations between America, Mexico, Texas, and Britain in the early and mid 1840s. I have relied on portions of various works cited in chapter 5. Those that guided me most are: Kenneth Bourne, *Britain and the Balance of Power in North America 1815–1908* (London, 1967); Charles A. Hale, *Mexican Liberalism in the Age of Mora, 1821–1853* (New Haven, 1968); Jan Bazant, *A Concise History of Mexico from Hidalgo to Cárdenas, 1805–1940* (Cambridge, 1977).

The Compromise of 1850 is examined in Holman Hamilton, *Prologue to Conflict. The Crisis and Compromise of 1850* (New York, 1966 edn). Further discussions are in Johannsen, *Stephen A. Douglas*, Potter, *The Impending Crisis*, Holt, *The Political Crisis of the 1850s*, and Brock,

Parties and Political Conscience. See also: Robert F. Dalzell, Jr, *Daniel Webster and the Trial of American Nationalism, 1843–1852* (Boston, 1972); David Donald, *Charles Sumner and the Coming of the Civil War* (New York, 1961); Arthur C. Cole, *The Whig Party in the South* (Washington, D.C., 1914).

The political history of the period 1854–61 has been very extensively analysed. The best guide is Potter, *The Impending Crisis*, though Holt's *The Political Crisis of the 1850s* has many fresh ideas. Unfortunately, Cooper's *The South and the Politics of Slavery*, which is excellent on 1848–56, ends in 1856: there is no fully satisfactory general account of Southern politics in the late 1850s. James A. Rawley, *Race and Politics. 'Bleeding Kansas' and the Coming of the Civil War* (Philadelphia, 1969) is a useful account of a central issue.

Much can be learnt about the Democratic party from Johannsen's *Stephen A. Douglas*, and, for the years 1857–61, Roy F. Nichols, *The Disruption of American Democracy* (New York, 1948). The reasons for continued Democratic support in the North in the late 1850s are analysed in Bruce Collins, 'The Ideology of the Ante-bellum Northern Democrats', *Journal of American Studies*, XI (1977), pp. 103–21; 'The Democrats' Electoral Fortunes during the Lecompton Crisis', *Civil War History*, XXIV (1978), pp. 314–31; 'Economic Issues in Ohio's Politics During the Recession of 1857–1858', *Ohio History*, 89 (1980), pp. 46–64; and in the first chapter of Joel H. Silbey, *A Respectable Minority: The Democratic Party in the Civil War Era, 1860–1868* (New York, 1977).

The Republican party has been well served in the recent literature. Foner's *Free Soil, Free Labor, Free Men* is very important. Other distinguished works are: Donald, *Charles Sumner*; Don E. Fehrenbacher, *Prelude to Greatness. Lincoln in the 1850s* (Stanford, 1962); Glyndon G. Van Deusen, *William Henry Seward* (New York, 1967); Michael F. Holt, *Forging a Majority: The Formation of the Republican Party in Pittsburgh, 1848–1860* (New Haven, 1969); Formisano, *The Birth of Mass Political Parties*. See also, Dale Baum, 'Know-Nothingism and the Republican Majority in Massachusetts: The Political Realignment of the 1850s', *Journal of American History*, LXII (1978), pp. 959–86.

For the Southern Democrats in the late 1850s, there is some information in Clement Eaton's *Jefferson Davis* (New York, 1977); Nichols, *The Disruption of American Democracy*, and Craven, *The Coming of the Civil War* leave much unexplored in Southern politics. Two valuable studies of specific issues in late ante-bellum Southern politics are: Ronald T. Takaki, *A Pro-Slavery Crusade. The Agitation to Reopen the African Slave Trade* (New York, 1971); Robert E. May, *The Southern Dream of a Caribbean Empire, 1854–1861* (Baton Rouge, 1973). See also William L. Barney, *The Road to Secession* (New York, 1972). The events of 1860–1 are far better treated. Dwight L. Dumond, *The Secession Movement, 1860–1861* (New York, 1931) is a lucid, basic account, to be supplemented by Ollinger Crenshaw, *The Slave States in the Presidential Election of 1860* (Baltimore, 1945) and Wooster, *The Secession Conventions of the South*. Steven A. Channing, *Crisis of Fear. Secession in South Carolina* (New York, 1970); William L. Barney, *The Secessionist Impulse: Alabama and Mississippi in 1860* (Princeton, 1974); Michael P. Johnson, *Toward A Patriarchal Republic: The Secession of Georgia* (Baton Rouge, 1977); Thornton, *Politics and Power in a Slave Society* are essential to understanding secession in the Deep South. See also, Peyton McCrary, Clark Miller, and Dale Baum, 'Class and Party in the Secession Crisis: Voting Behavior in the Deep South, 1856–1861', *Journal of Interdisciplinary History*, VIII (1978), pp. 429–57. On the different behaviour of the Upper South in 1860–1 see Holt, *The Political Crisis of the 1850s* and William J. Evitts, *A Matter of Allegiances: Maryland 1850–1861* (Baltimore, 1974). For Southern Unionism, see John V. Mering, 'The Slave-State Constitutional Unionists and the Politics of Consensus', *Journal of Southern History*, XLIII (1977), pp. 395–410; Daniel W. Crofts, 'The Union Party of 1861 and the Secession Crisis', *Perspectives in American History*, XI (1977–8), pp. 327–76. The indispensable works on the Republican response to secession are: David M. Potter, *Lincoln and His Party in the Secession Crisis* (New Haven, 1962 edn); Kenneth M. Stampp, *And the War Came. The North and the Secession Crisis, 1860–1861* (Baton Rouge, 1970 edn).

Many collections of primary material are available. The most general, and yet very useful, is Henry Steele Commager (ed.), *Documents of American History*, I (New York, 1963). For vivid and critical impressions of the South in the 1850s see Frederick L. Olmsted, *The Cotton Kingdom. A Selection*, ed. by David F. Hawke (Indianapolis, 1971). For politics, see: Roy P. Basler (ed.), *The Collected Works of Abraham Lincoln* (8 vols.; New Brunswick, N.J., 1953); Robert W. Johannsen (ed.), *The Letters of Stephen A. Douglas* (Urbana, Ill., 1961); Ulrich B. Phillips (ed.), *The Correspondence of Robert Toombs, Alexander H. Stephens, and Howell Cobb*. A.H.A. *Annual Report* (Washington, D.C., 1911), II; Dunbar Rowland (ed.), *Jefferson Davis, Constitutionalist: His letters, Papers and Speeches* (10 vols.; Jackson, Miss., 1923); *A Political Text-Book for 1860* (New York, 1860; reprinted New York, 1969). Numerous other documentary collections might be consulted, but these are probably the most useful ones.

For election results, consult W. Dean Burnham, *Presidential Ballots, 1836–1892* (Baltimore, 1955) and *Congressional Quarterly's Guide to U.S. Elections* (Washington, D.C., 1975).

A final caveat is in order. The subject treated in this brief book is enormous and controversial. Many debates among scholars, and numerous topics relevant to the discussion of the war's origins, have been ignored or mentioned cursorily because of limitations of space. Moreover, much of what has been written here will need revision in the light of further research in this field. In order to keep abreast of that research, it is worth consulting the leading academic journals, of which the *Journal of American History*, *Civil War History*, and the *Journal of Southern History* are perhaps most relevant to this subject; *Reviews in American History* is also valuable for substantial essays on the latest books published on American history.

Index